AMERICA'S BUSINESS LEADERS AND THE PRESS PRAISE

Re-inventing the Corporation

* * * * *

"Remarkable changes are already under way which will reshape America's corporations. This book offers a vivid and insightful description of what's ahead for the most successful companies in the 1990's."
—**John Sculley, Chairman and CEO, Apple Computer, Inc.**

* * * * *

"The writing is excellent, the reasoning seamless."
—**Elwood Wardlow, Associate Director, American Press Institute**

more...

* * * * *

"They have fastened on a key notion with this work. Corporations, like other institutions, must adapt to survive and prosper. The important themes they sound read like a Baedeker for today's senior managers. . . . Does a service to all of us by gathering and blending information from so many diverse sources. Clearly, these conclusions signal important messages to America's managers."

—**Edward M. Ney, Chairman, Young & Rubicam, Inc.**

* * * * *

"An exciting reading experience. This book is a natural follow-up to *Megatrends.* As I read the book, I began to thrill with the realization that we are not only re-inventing the corporation, but with wisdom we are rebuilding America for the generations to come."

—**Philip Klutznick, Former Secretary, U.S. Department of Commerce**

* * * * *

"I not only enjoyed it, but found
it quite inciteful. I have
ordered several for my managers
and colleagues."
—**Max Hopper, Executive Vice-President,
Bank of America**

* * * * *

"Blueprints a new world for life
and livelihood in the late
1980's and beyond."
—*Publishers Weekly*

* * * * *

"Amazing.... It turns out that
corporations are consciously
creating exactly the sort of
environment we sought: a
framework within which we
could pursue our own goals and
be rewarded handsomely for
it... everyone should read this
book.... You'll learn some
surprising facts.... And, best of
all, you'll begin to understand
how our world is changing."
—*Milwaukee Journal*

* * * * *

Also by John Naisbitt

Megatrends
The Year Ahead 1986

Published by
WARNER BOOKS

Re-inventing the Corporation

Transforming your job and your company for the new information society

John Naisbitt and Patricia Aburdene

WARNER BOOKS

A Warner Communications Company

To the people in today's corporations, the entrepreneurs and intrapreneurs, the visionaries, the working mothers, the job sharers, the older people, the two-career couples, the nurturing managers, and all the others, especially the baby boomers, who are re-inventing the corporation from the bottom up.

Contents

Acknowledgments

We began the project that became this book with a not very modest goal. Our aim was to write a book about re-inventing the world we live in. We would do chapters on business, the family, the workplace, the arts, politics, education, and on and on. It was a great book idea, we thought, but as the proposed chapters began approaching one hundred pages each, we decided it was time to re-invent our book plan.

Re-inventing the Corporation was a natural solution. If we, as a society, are to succeed in re-inventing ourselves— from our families to our communities—we must begin with a solid economic grounding. By inventing the corporation into a place that is equally pro-profits and pro-people, we will achieve that solid ground.

Between the original plan and final book, we received assistance from many quarters. Win Morgan, our primary researcher, plowed through piles of articles, squinted through thousands of microfiche from The Naisbitt Group's data base, found key resource people, challenged our hypotheses, and distilled tons of information into readable form. His contribution to the health and work chapters was particularly strong.

When Win left to join the Peace Corps, we needed a savvy researcher to take over and wrap the project up. Free-lance reporter Sharon Geltner came to us with the help of Washington Independent Writers. With the persistence and passion for accuracy of a crack reporter, she tracked down final figures, located the dates of the lost articles, drafted stray footnotes, and verified quotations.

Henry Morgan and Elsa Porter read the manuscript and provided a depth of perspective and many excellent suggestions. Jim Autry read the manuscript and offered many a candid and humorous comment. A copy editor from way back, Jim couldn't resist applying pencil to page, and this book is better for it. Jerry Kline went through the manuscript at two different stages, improving it with his concerned comments and picking up many details that less careful eyes had missed. Thanks also to Hiroshi Peter Kamura and Tadashi Yamamoto, old friends who read and advised us on Chapter 8, "Re-inventing the Corporation in Japan."

Daniel Levinas, the president of The Naisbitt Group, not only ran the company but began the process of re-inventing it, while we worked on this book. And Hazel Branch, who manages our house, kept the home fires burning beautifully.

We are privileged to work with three extraordinarily dedicated professionals who are intimately connected with our writing and lecturing work. Rafe Sagalyn, our superb literary agent, is always ready to discuss a new idea, plan a better strategy, and help us out of a jam. Nansey Neiman, our editor, and now publisher of Warner Books, seems to know when to leave us alone, when to turn on the heat, and how to combine that role with a bigger one—being a dear friend. Bill Leigh, our lecture agent, supplies a special understanding of how lecturing and authoring fit together.

Writing a book is a stressful process, even more so when you have to re-invent it midway through. Special thanks must go to those loving friends, relatives, and trusted associates who supportively kept body and soul together during the long, sometimes painful creative process. They are Lexie Brockway, Barbara Carpenter, Donna Coombs, Linda Harned, Barbara Jones, Bertha Kazanjian, Peter Kolker, Mel Leshinsky, Carolyn Long, Michelle Lusson Sycalik, Claire Naisbitt, Bonnie Pendleton, Emily Marie Smith, Michel Sweeney, and Lilyan Wilder.

Finally, we want to thank the audiences with whom we have shared this book as a work in progress. We are grateful for the support and enthusiasm offered. But perhaps most important, we are thankful for those difficult questions that were uncomfortable at the time, stayed in our minds for days, and eventually produced the conceptual breakthroughs that we think hold this book together.

Introduction

Sometimes a book reveals itself only *after* it is written.
That was the case with *Re-inventing the Corporation*. The more we talked about it—in speeches and interviews and on television and radio—the more we understood it.

This introduction to the paperback edition permits us to share that deeper understanding as well as update readers on the still unfolding process of corporate evolution.

The main purpose of this book, as we see it now, is to help people evaluate the extent to which a company is changing to fit the demands of *today's* business environment and anticipating the new trends and changing workforce of the *immediate future*—the late 1980s and into the 1990s.

If you are a manager, entrepreneur or CEO, you must look to the future. It is part of your job.

But even if you simply "work for a living," you had better know what kind of company you are working for. *Megatrends* described the basic ways in which the world is changing. If the company where you work—are considering working—is not keeping pace with change, it might be out of business in five or ten years. By thoughtfully choosing your company, you can avoid that personal and professional loss.

But beyond preventing a career setback, there is a more profound reason to be selective about where you work: you owe it to yourself to work for a company that will bring out the very best in you.

Most of us do not possess great wealth. The capital we possess is our *human* capital—our talent, knowledge, experience and ability. It is up to each of us to invest that human capital into a corporation that will give us a good return on our investment.

How do you choose such a company? This book will guide and instruct your decision-making process.

The key themes in *Re-inventing the Corporation* can be distilled into a checklist of questions to help you measure the company where you work, or are considering working:

Is this a company where I will experience personal growth?

Will I get to take on challenging tasks—yet also get the support needed to succeed?

Will I work with senior people who can really teach me something? Once you get a good return on your investment of human capital, you can choose to reinvest it in the same company or find a new one.

Does this company reward performance and initiative or is everyone treated the same?

Do the people here have a stake in the company's success?

What is the policy on bonuses, profit sharing, employee stock ownership?

Are intrapreneurs rewarded here? How many people have left to start their own firms?

What is the vision of this company?
What are its values and ideals?
Where is it headed in the next five to ten years? Companies that do not know where they are headed often find themselves out of business, their employees out of a job.

How is this company structured?
Are divisions free to run their own show or is the company still basically a bureaucracy? Do the people in marketing, accounting and engineering work together in cross-disciplinary teams—or rarely speak to each other?

Where does the company stand on health and fitness?
Are people who work out on their lunch hour considered freaks here?
Does the cafeteria serve junk food?
What is the company smoking policy?
What has this company done about cutting health care costs?

Is this company flexible about job arrangements or is it strictly a 9-to-5 operation?
Has it experimented with flextime, job sharing, a flexible benefits plan?
Are there any professionals working part time here?
How many older people work here?

How successful have women been in this company?
What is the company policy toward day care?
Two-career couples? Will I be expected to move even though I have a working spouse? Will the company help him or her find a new job?
Are women being paid fairly here?

Is this company involved in any programs with local schools?
Companies that invest in the local schools build a com-

munity that can recruit the top people—which are increasingly a company's competitive edge.

Is this company thinking about lifelong training and education?

Do managers here see themselves as teachers or order givers? The most innovative corporations have become more like universities and have begun teaching the new basic skills of the information society—thinking, learning and creating.

Is this a company where people are having fun?

Where the personal relationships formed on the company softball team, aerobics class, or the Friday afternoon beer blast enhance the day-to-day experience of work?

These are guidelines, not absolutes. Only a handful of corporations would meet all these criteria.

Which are most important?

That depends on your personal priorities and work objectives, but corporations where you can experience personal growth and be rewarded financially for taking initiative are doing a lot of things right. How many of us can say that about our companies? Any organization that meets half these criteria is making a serious attempt to re-invent the corporation.

New Graduates and the Seller's Market

That checklist is especially useful if you are a new graduate. The seller's market described in chapter one puts you, the job seeker, in the cat bird seat for the first time in decades.

The employer's market of the 1970s has become the employee's market of the mid to late 1980s and 1990s. Since the publication of *Re-inventing the Corporation*,

America's job creation machine has continued to run at record levels.

In January 1986, 556,000 new jobs were created. An astonishing figure. Though the pace slowed somewhat in February, it picked up again in March. In total some one million jobs were created in the first three months of 1986. That is equal to the record level of 4 million jobs annually. (Compare that with an average of 2 million new jobs a year in the 1970s—at the time considered a phenomenal rate that could not be sustained.)

The formation of a seller's market continues along with a number of other benchmarks in the business news that impact on the process of re-inventing the corporation.

What About People Express and Apple Computer?

Some observers point to People Express's takeover of Frontier and Britt Airlines and Steve Jobs's departure from Apple Computer as evidence that People Express and Apple are somehow less successful and have moved away from the re-invention process.

Quite the contrary.

People Express will undoubtedly face challenging times attempting to "sell" nonunion management to Frontier staffers who are used to a traditional, union setting. But the bottom line is this: People Express's innovative management style, which has been ridiculed since the company went into business, possesses the kind of lean and energized structure that insures success in today's deregulated market and will continue to flourish into the next century. Unionized rivals like TWA, Eastern, and Pan Am are the companies people should worry about.

The difficult transition at Apple is over. Steve Jobs has gone on to do what he does best—innovate and lead the innovative process. Under CEO John Sculley, Apple's new vision of its work environment is that of a university—which makes and sells computers.

At Apple today, computers are being used the way the rest of us will use them in the corporation of tomorrow:

"We'll spend around $60 million over the next two years just taking the information systems inside Apple well beyond anything that's being done anywhere in business today," says John Sculley. "We figure if we can't learn to use our own products, how can we expect anyone else to?"

Business Week Gets Some TLC

The need for TLC, the new basic skills of thinking, learning and creativity discussed in chapter four, is growing increasingly apparent in corporate America. Even *Business Week*, which traditionally plays to big business and focuses exclusively on what can be measured, i.e., profit and loss, is getting into TLC.

In its September 30, 1985, issue *Business Week* ran a cover story entitled "Are you creative?" The well-researched story profiled the most important creativity consultants— William Herrmann, Roger von Oech and learning how to think consultant Edward de Bono—and described the results they and others have achieved for corporate clients.

The Wellness Dividend

While writing *Re-inventing the Corporation*, we were unable to find many examples of the cost effectiveness of wellness and fitness programs. Now the evidence is pouring in. A two-year AT&T study of facilities in Bedminister, New Jersey, and Kansas City, Missouri, by wellness program co-ordinator Molly McCauley showed AT&T could save as much as $160 million over a decade if everyone in the company participated in the program. A Health Research Institute Study of 1,500 employers showed corporations that enact wellness programs can expect to save $557 per employee annually in health care costs.

Boston Compact Update

Audiences and interviewers are surprised to hear about the Boston Compact, the deal between Boston's schools and corporations that virtually guarantees a job to every high school graduate (see chapter five). More remarkable, the Compact continues to meet its goals. Among nearly 3,000 1985 graduates, only 4 percent are unemployed and the average hourly wage for students placed in jobs by the Boston Compact is $5.25, substantially higher than minimum wage. Now schools and corporations will throw their attention to the program's one disappointment: the continued high, even increasing, high school drop-out rate.

Women and the New Leadership Style

Corporations as we have known them were created by men for men. And they were greatly influenced by the military model: after World War II, America's fighting men traded their military uniforms for pinstriped suits. Enlisted men joined the assembly line. The hierarchical structure built on authority remained the same.

Forty years later, most of the new jobs created are being taken by women (see p. 237). And women are the driving force behind corporate innovations such as flextime, cafeteria benefits plans, and, of course, day care. So long as men worked and women cared for children, the corporation could afford to act as though the people in it existed in a vacuum. They could be moved around the country at will, could be expected to work a rigid 9-to-5 schedule and could be treated interchangeably. But the reality of working women has forced the humanization of the workplace. Corporations must acknowledge that the people within them belong to another entity, pledge allegiance to another organization called the family.

Millions of new jobs are being created each year in young companies that aspire—at least partially—to fit the blueprint of the corporation of the future, rather than replicate the industrial companies of the past.

That means you have an excellent opportunity to find a company whose vision and goals are in sync with your personal values and career objectives.

"Many companies you write about are new," a frequent question begins. "What about re-inventing an older, more established company?" Clearly it is an awesome task to alter the culture, environment and vision of a large institution. As a senior manager of one such company told us, "Birth, after all, is infinitely easier than resurrection."

Nevertheless, America's large corporations are working harder at re-inventing themselves than their critics suspect. Even the most conservative people in the sunset industries know the old ways don't work anymore—in fact, they know it better than the rest of us.

And a tidal wave of change is headed toward even the most rigid bureaucracy: the baby boom is turning forty; older, more experienced, powerful enough to enact corporate change. Furthermore, many top managers already in their forties, a Don Burr or a John Sculley, for example, are taking the helm with new values and visions.

Millions of us work with successful managers who haven't made it to the top (yet) but have earned enough respect (and freedom) to run their divisions according to the new standards and values they espouse personally.

What if the people who run your company stubbornly refuse to face change? Should you stay and try to re-invent the place on your own, waiting for the seller's market to hit full force in the next few years? If that is your choice, this book will help you make the economic arguments of why being pro-people is ultimately profitable.

If you want to start looking for a company where

you will grow and develop, this book will help you find it.

Sometimes the most powerful statement you can make about re-inventing your company is to work somewhere else.

1

Re-inventing the Corporation

As a young man, Jan Carlzon made a name for himself by turning the domestic Swedish airline, Linejeflyg, into a very profitable operation. In 1981 Carlzon became president of Scandinavian Airline Systems, SAS, which, at the time, was losing $17 million per year. After a single year of Carlzon's leadership, SAS was earning $54 million. He did it by turning the organization chart upside down. Truly believing that SAS should be customer-driven, he put those who dealt directly with the customer in charge of the company. The rest of the company on the upside-down organization chart worked for those who dealt with the customers.

Delaware-based W. L. Gore & Associates, Inc., the maker of Gore-tex fabric, the sports and military material that keeps out rain but allows the body to breathe, is a well-publicized example of the new corporation. The company has no titles, no bosses, no map of managerial authority, and only two objectives: to make money and to have fun. W. L. Gore's secret is that people manage themselves by organizing around voluntary commitments. Some new hires are told to go find something interesting to do. "Commitment, not authority, produces results," says company founder Bill Gore. W. L. Gore & Associates achieves its money-making goal: Sales in the last ten years have grown at least 35 percent annually.

New Hope Communication, publisher of *Natural Foods Merchandiser* and *Delicious!*, invests heavily in personal growth for employees. Salaries are 25 percent above the going rate. Company benefits cover 50 percent of all wellness-related purchases such as running shoes or a bicycle and 100 percent of all medical and dental costs for the employee's entire family. New Hope pays for *any* education course or seminar for personal growth. The CEO's office was so nice, with such a great view, that the CEO moved out and it is now used by everyone. And, lastly (we love this—this is one we are introducing into our company), "We have a rule: We only do business with people who are pleasant." Dealing with pleasant people pays off: In 1984, New Hope grossed $2 million in sales, a 29 percent increase over 1983. In 1985, they are aiming for $5 million.

SAS, W. L. Gore & Associates, Inc., and New Hope Communication are among the most innovative companies, those which are already well into the process of re-inventing the corporation. These corporate pioneers are the leading lights, the new models that many corporations will choose to follow.

At a time when corporations are trying on quality circles

and open office systems as if they were new accessories to dress up their old industrial suits, these prototype companies and their leaders are digging deep into the process of corporate transformation. They are re-inventing today's corporation into a new structure we cannot yet define—the corporation of tomorrow.

Why Now?

These companies are now successful enterprises, but they originated as the experimental creations of individual geniuses who were intent on doing things a new way. Their founders never intended to formulate the new models of corporate America in the 1990s.

Nevertheless, that is what these companies have become. And their experimentation is about to burst into widespread innovation. Now and into the 1990s, three powerful trends are transforming the business environment and compelling companies to re-invent themselves. As corporate America searches out models and guidelines for re-inventing itself, companies such as People Express and Kollmorgen are filling that need.

These are the trends fueling the need for corporations to re-invent themselves:

1. The shift in strategic resource from financial capital in the industrial society to human capital in the information society

2. The whittling away of middle management

3. The labor shortages and coming seller's market of the booming 1980s and 1990s.

From Financial Capital to Human Capital

The new corporation differs from the old in both goals and

basic assumptions. In the industrial era, when the strategic resource was capital, the goal of the corporation could only have been profits. In the information era, however, the strategic resource is information, knowledge, creativity. There is only one way a corporation can gain access to these valuable commodities—that is, through the people in whom these resources reside.

So the basic assumption of a re-invented company is that people—human capital—are its most important resource. What used to be one of the radicals' favorite slogans, "People before Profits," is finding its way into the boardroom and being transformed into a more businesslike but equally humanistic "People *and* Profits."

In an information society, human resources are any organization's competitive edge.

American business has given this concept a kind of obligatory lip service in the past. Now it is time to understand the practical side: We will not see profits grow if we do not learn how to grow people.

One expression of the importance of human capital is the new corporate preoccupation with health and fitness. Corporations are treating their human assets with new concern, encouraging their people to stop smoking, lose weight, exercise, and learn to manage stress. What might have been considered an intrusion into one's personal life in the past is fair game when people are a company's strategic resource.

The new, re-invented corporations stress inordinate regard for the two most important types of people in an enterprise: employees and customers.

They have discovered that by being both pro-people *and*

pro-profits, a company can earn more than if it had targeted profits as its only goal.

Steve Jobs, cofounder and chairman of the board of Apple Computer, Inc., explains it this way: "The way we run Apple is by values. You've heard of management by objectives? We don't use that management system. Apple's the fastest growing company in American corporate history [People Express, another people and profits company, has since claimed that title], and when you're growing that fast, the only thing you can do is hire incredibly great people and let them go to it. In general, we hire people who tell us what to do."

It is not a question of being nice to people. *It is simply a recognition that human beings will make or break a company.*

The Whittling Away of Middle Management

We are witnessing the beginnings of a tremendous whittling away of *middle management,* a flattening out of those hierarchies that were the norm in industrial America.

Worldwide, middle management has shrunk more than 15 percent since 1979. And there is much more to come.

Middle managers—the people who collect, process, and pass information up and down the hierarchy—are losing out to smart technology in the race for productivity. Middle managers have benefited from the belief that people work better when they are closely supervised. But now those hierarchies which middle managers held in place are breaking into a wide array of largely self-managing structures— networks, multidisciplinary teams, and small groups.

The whittling away of middle management is accomplished in a variety of ways: early retirement, hiring freezes, outplacement. But it is all to the same end:

- Weyerhaeuser has let go 1,500 workers in the past three years. Half of them were middle managers.

- Western Airlines let go 13 VPs and 500 middle managers in December 1981 when it was in serious financial straits.
- Ford Motor Company has decreased the number of middle managers since 1978. They are seeking to expand the average supervisory control of the manager from three to five people, thinning out middle management.
- Brunswick Corp. cut its headquarters staff by 40 percent and division heads report directly to the CEO.
- TRW, Inc., is continuing its long-term strategy toward ''simplifying our organization.''

Much of this was done in the name of recession or tough times. But tough times sometimes give management an excuse to do what should be done anyway.

And new companies just starting out are building very flat pyramids where people, in effect, manage themselves.

Self-management is replacing staff managers who manage people; the computer is replacing line managers who manage systems.

What really enables us to shrink middle management is the computer, which gives top executives immediate access to the information previously obtained from middle managers.

And although many executives resist typing on the keyboard, computers are most definitely finding their way into the executive suite. United Technologies, for example, bought IBM personal computers for some 1,100 top managers and sent the managers to a three-day computer course. Firestone Tire & Rubber has given a personal computer to every corporate officer at the vice-president level or higher.

Ben W. Heineman, the seventy-one-year-old chairman of Northwest Industries, bought himself a computer in 1977 and analyzed his company's acquisition moves. Extraordinarily, he went on to write some 800 computer programs.

Now with the computer to keep track of information and people, middle managers are seen as disposable. These technological innovations ousting the middle manager are further reinforcing the new emphasis on self-management.

It is not happening just in the United States. West Germany has reduced middle management in small and medium-sized companies by between 30 and 50 percent. In larger companies, it is running around 30 percent.

Even in Japan, where there are half as many layers of management as in American companies, middle management has been cut deeply, despite the Japanese tradition of lifetime employment. A director of Japan Management Association, Takeji Kadota, foresees strong pressure on this tradition as the trend toward fewer middle managers continues.

Today, computers are replacing middle managers at a much greater rate than robots are replacing assembly line workers.

Once indispensable to senior executives, many middle managers are now watching computers do their job in a fraction of the time and at a percentage of the cost.

The whittling away of middle management presents serious problems for all those baby boomers about to enter middle management. The number of men and women between thirty-five and forty-six, the prime age range for entering middle management, will increase 42 percent between 1985 and 1995. Clearly, millions of baby boomers who aimed for middle management will never reach their goal. There simply will not be enough middle management jobs. It is a scary thought for some people. Corporations would suffer, too, losing talent and failing to reap the sizable investment already made in these valuable human resources—unless they can invent alternative ways to use people productively.

One way is to put talented people together in small groups— which are entering their own boom years. Others could work as entrepreneurs within a company. The whittling away of middle management is further reinforcing the trend for companies to smash the hierarchical pyramid and adopt new people structures such as networks, intrapreneurs, and small teams.

Millions of baby boomers who were squeezed out of the tight job market of the 1970s and early 1980s started their own businesses at an early age. The rest are entering their thirties and forties, the prime age at which people traditionally break away to start their own firms.

The baby boomers are fast becoming the most entrepreneurial generation in this nation's history.

The Coming Seller's Market

The new emphasis on the quality of personnel is occurring at a time when we are moving to full employment, moving to a seller's market, where we will soon see fierce competition for the best employees.

The return to full employment will occur much sooner than most people expect, for two reasons: (1) The new economy that has been overtaking the old is accelerating, creating millions of new jobs and (2) the number of people entering the work force is declining dramatically as we assimilate the last of the baby boomers.

During the 1970s, we created 20 million new jobs in the United States, setting an international record. (The reason unemployment still resulted in the 1970s was that we were losing so many jobs in the old industrial sector and the baby boomers were flooding the labor market.)

In 1983 and 1984, we broke our own record. We created 7 million brand-new jobs in just two years. Of course, it is not the Fortune 500 that are creating these new jobs, but the

entrepreneurs and small-business people in the information/
electronics/service sector.

For how long can we expect what Europeans call the
American economic miracle to continue? No one knows for
sure, but looking at the positive signs in the economy, one
cannot help being optimistic. Inflation and unemployment
are lower, productivity and GNP higher, while new businesses
and jobs are being created at record levels. And now there
are indications that Europe is pulling out of its economic
slump. Barring some unforeseen economic calamity, the
combined impact of all of these plus factors on the already
accelerating economy creates a healthy economic forecast.

The economists, of course, failed to predict this phenomenal growth.

**The economists always ignore the entrepreneurs, and,
fortunately, the entrepreneurs always ignore the economists.**

But just as the new information economy reaches unforeseen
heights (the economists, of course, failed to predict it
because they watch established companies in sunset industries instead of entrepreneurs in the sunrise sector), we are
about to run into a demographic glitch—the baby bust.

In fact, we are already beginning to feel the effects of the
baby bust: The number of teens in the work force *declined*
from 9.6 million in 1979 to 8.1 million in 1984, a 16
percent decrease. That is in sharp contrast to the 37 percent
increase in the teenage work force during the 1970s.

**The decade of the baby bust is the decade of full
employment.**

Most corporations have gotten used to the comfort of
operating in a buyer's market in labor, having their pick of
many competent, qualified applicants for each job. The
exception, of course, is in computers and other high-tech

areas where there are—and will continue to be—sizable labor shortages. But beginning in the late 1980s, there will be labor shortages in a growing number of jobs as the baby bust moves into the work force. The 1990s will bring the real crunch.

During the 1970s, though, because of the baby boom and the increase in women workers, the work force grew an unprecedented 2.5 percent per year, or 30 percent overall. Little wonder unemployment was such a problem in the 1970s and early 1980s. Between 1985 and 1990, the work force will grow by only 1.2 percent annually. Once we enter the 1990s, annual growth will shrink to only 0.8 percent. Now the boom has become a bust, and the entry of women into the work force, which will continue to be strong, is an anticipated factor.

Generally, corporations recruit their entry-level workers—practically everyone from file clerks to accountants and junior executives—from the eighteen-to-twenty-four age group. In the 1970s, the number of people in that age group increased 22 percent. Companies could afford to be very choosy. In the 1980s, that group will decline by 15 percent. Figured in real numbers, it is even more dramatic: By 1990, there will be 4.5 million fewer entry-level workers than in 1980, according to the Census Bureau.

It doesn't matter whether you make automobiles or software, this dramatic shift will force you to re-invent your company or be left behind.

By 1987, there will be a negative net gain in the labor force: More people will be leaving than will be entering. That, combined with the accelerating economy that is creating almost all the new jobs, will result in a return to full employment as early as two years from now.

The United States is in for labor shortages for the rest of this century that will drive the re-inventing of the corporation.

Look at it this way: All the people we will hire between now and the year 2000 are not only born, they are at least five or six years old. We can calculate almost exactly how many will be coming into the work force, and there will not be enough to fill all the new jobs being created.

The seller's market will present opportunities for groups which to date have not achieved their full potential in the corporation:

- Women will be treated fairly and paid what they are worth.
- Older people, rather than being squeezed into early retirement, will be considered a valuable resource and offered part-time, flextime, and job sharing.
- Poor and disadvantaged people will profit from the labor shortage as corporations demonstrate how swiftly and effectively they can train people when human capital is desperately needed. During World War II, the army taught illiterate recruits to read in six weeks. Corporations—which are already transforming themselves into universities of lifelong learning—can match that feat and surpass it.

This end-of-the-century seller's market is the key to understanding the process of re-inventing the corporation.

Corporations will aggressively compete for fewer first-rate employees. The most talented people will be attracted to those corporations that succeed in re-inventing themselves into companies that are great places to work for because the people in them grow personally while contributing to the company.

GM's Leap into the Information Society

But why should a successful, healthy company take on the

difficulty and challenge of re-inventing itself? That is what many observers are wondering about the recent actions of Roger Smith, chairman of General Motors. To create small cars that will compete with the Japanese in both quality and cost, GM has taken an unusual route—going outside its own corporate structure to create the Saturn Corporation. And the company's daring new acquisition is, of all things, a $2.5 billion computer services firm—Electronic Data Systems.

What is Chairman Smith trying to do? Re-invent General Motors?

"Smith has begun a restructuring of management and operations on a scale seldom seen in U.S. business, one that few giant companies have *willingly* undertaken [emphasis added]," writes Jack Seamonds in *U.S. News & World Report*.

GM's strategy is a model for re-inventing an established industrial company to survive and flourish in the new information society. And it is one that every large corporation should be studying.

First, it is doing the obvious—applying information technology to industrial production. "EDS knows computers, and computers will redefine the way cars are produced worldwide," writes Seamonds. EDS will help GM get the Saturn car into the marketplace more quickly.

Second, EDS will get the part of GM *that is already an information company* to work better. "Its merger has already streamlined GM's own data processing department," writes *U.S. News*'s Seamonds.

The combination of those two points about GM's actions underscore a key point about re-inventing the corporation.

As information technology is applied to industrial tasks, the people within industrial companies will increasingly work with information, thereby transforming industrial corporations into information organizations.

It is already happening. A large percentage of the half a million people working for GM in the United States, for example, get paid for processing information, not for making cars. There are the accountants, the managers, clerical and secretarial staff as well as the data processing people. The same goes for most other industrial companies.

And that sets the stage for the third part of re-inventing GM into an information company. Roger Smith is aiming to create at GM the environment of an information company. Saturn was specifically set up in writer Seamonds's words "to be free from the company's bureaucratic forest of ponderous corporate reports and committee meetings."

Instead of imposing GM's way of doing things on EDS, Smith wants GM people to learn from the computer firm, to become more entrepreneurial, to make decisions faster in order to create profit without paperwork.

Says EDS Chairman Ross Perot: "Roger told me, 'If anybody shows up with a GM procedures manual, I want you to shoot him.'"

GM is showing the kind of foresight that is rare in large organizations. It is not just responding to change, which is hard enough; it is anticipating it. "GM need not change to survive," says Seamonds. Having earned a total of $8.2 billion profits in 1983 and 1984, it may not seem that way now. But in 1995 when GM is the only surviving U.S. automaker, it will look quite different.

It is not too much to say that we are moving from an economy that rested on the motorcar to an economy that rests on the computer.

The Shake-Out Period

But in both the old and the new economies, we will continue in long periods of shake-out. In the old economy, we will continue to see companies contract, merge, and close down completely.

In the new economy, we will see thousands of failures in computer, in software, in cable companies during a long initial shake-out period. Osbourn Computer. Lisa. The PCjr— even IBM is not immune to the shake-out period.

To understand the current shake-out in information technology, we need only recall the early part of this century when we began making automobiles. We created more than 2,300 automobile companies. After a long shake-out period, we ended up with only three—four, if you count AMC-Renault, half foreign-owned.

It is the nature of the new economy that we will end up with thousands of new information companies. But we will have to go *through* thousands and thousands more to get there.

Vision

What is there about the new, re-invented companies that enables them to break the mold, to refuse to choose between a people policy and a profit strategy— but to achieve outstanding success with both? What guides an established company like GM through the maze of re-inventing itself for the new information society? What element will help a young information company emerge successfully from that long shake-out period?

We believe the first ingredient in re-inventing the corporation is a powerful vision—a whole new sense of where a company is going and how to get there. It is important to understand trends, such as the three important ones described above, but it is not enough. You must also discover the specific way that your company fits into the business environment. The company's vision becomes a catalytic force, an organizing principle for everything that the people in the corporation do.

Usually, the source of a vision is a leader, a person who possesses a unique combination of skills: the mental power to create a vision and the practical ability to bring it about.

To be successful, a CEO must create a "compelling vision of a desired state of affairs," says Warren Bennis, noted author, teacher, and former university president. Bennis studied eighty chief executive officers of major corporations.

"Successful CEOs see themselves as leaders, not managers," says Professor Bennis. "They were concerned with their organization's basic purposes, why it exists, its general direction . . . not with 'nuts and bolts' . . . not with 'doing things right' (the overriding concern of managers) but with 'doing the right thing.'"

Today's CEO must increasingly be a visionary. The entrepreneur must have a vision to start a venture. In established businesses, some CEOs have a vision for re-inventing the company, while others create a process to involve their colleagues in creating a vision.

William O'Brien, president of Hanover Insurance Companies of Worcester, Massachusetts, puts it this way: "We each are influenced by our own mental picture of what we are building with our efforts. I call these mental pictures visions and they play an important role in determining what our company becomes."

Hanover was nearly bankrupt in 1969 before the company developed a shared vision that all employees embraced. Now Hanover is a leader in property and liability insurance, and over the past six years, it has grown 50 percent faster than the industry average.

Belief in vision is a radically new precept in business philosophy. It comes out of intuitive knowing; it says that logic is not everything, that it is not all in the numbers. The idea is simply that by envisioning the future you want, you can more easily achieve your goal. Vision is the link between dream and action.

Whether you are a businessperson or an artist, your new creation must be real for you—even though there is no evidence to anyone else that it could succeed. Bill Gore had to "know" that a whole company could operate like a small task force. In his heart of hearts, Steve Jobs had to believe that the expensive, awkward, and unreliable computers of the early 1970s (was it really that recent?) could become the ubiquitous personal tools of the 1980s.

Ultimately, vision gets translated into sales and profit growth and return on investment, but the numbers come after the vision. In the old-style companies, the numbers are the vision.

The use of vision and visualization is better known today in athletics than in business.

"Research has shown that by picturing the successful completion of moves they want to make, athletes can improve their performance, especially if the mental picture is accompanied by physical practice," write Michael Murphy and Rhea White in *The Psychic Side of Sports*.

Jack Nicklaus claims his best golf shots depend 10 percent on his swing, 40 percent on his setup and stance, and 50 percent on his mental picture, according to Murphy and White.

Champion bronco and bull rider Larry Mahan says, "I try to picture a ride in my mind before I get on the bull. Then I try to go by the picture."

Bodybuilder Arnold Schwarzenegger says visualizing a particular muscle's contour helps the process to develop it.

But now visualization has entered the domain of business. CEOs are forming new images of their businesses and where they ought to be going and are bringing those visions into reality.

The leader who would create a vision sufficiently compelling to motivate associates to superior performances must draw on the intuitive mind.

People Express became a $1-billion company faster than any other corporation not because it had the rational, predictable goal of reaching that important benchmark (many companies had the same dream), but because the company's vision—MABW, "Making a Better World"—inspires People Express managers (they are called managers, not employees) to work harder than people in other airlines and to deliver such great service that customers keep flying People Express even though it might take days of annoying phone calls before getting reservations.

Intellectual strategies alone will not motivate people. Only a company with a real mission or sense of purpose that comes out of an intuitive or spiritual dimension will capture people's hearts. And you must have people's hearts to inspire the hard work required to realize a vision.

But vision is practical as well as mystical: It is easier to get from point A to point B if you know where point B is and how to recognize it when you have arrived. Without a goal, neither companies nor people get very far. But when people have a vision, they are motivated to make it a reality.

The vision of Cray Research is to build the world's fastest computer. And, according to CEO John Rollwagen, that vision creates enormous excitement. "If we lost track of our overriding purpose, all the other things we do would not be enough to guarantee our success."

Here are some other examples of forceful, well-defined visions which both compel and challenge each member of the organization to pursue goals that are lofty in purpose yet practical and achievable:

• SAS's president, Jan Carlzon, envisions a market where, in the words of *International Management*, "the cus-

tomer is always happy, costs are trimmed to the bone at
the head office while more money is spent on service,
businessmen are pampered without paying any extra on
the standard fares, tourists fly for the price of second-
class rail travel, and profits flow in like clear water from
a mountain stream.''

- The vision of Apple Computer cofounder Steve Jobs is
  to bring technology to nontechnical, everyday people.
  What distinguished Apple from the hundreds of other
  fledgling computer companies with dreams of becoming
  an IBM competitor was Jobs's insistence that partner
  Stephen Wozniak design features into the Apple that
  techno-peasants like the rest of us could feel comfortable
  with. Jobs has another vision: to become a $10-billion
  company by 1990.

- F. Kenneth Iverson's vision is to re-invent the steel
  industry into a high-tech business. Iverson, the chairman
  and CEO of Nucor Corp., was a pioneer in creating the
  minimill, the most productive dynamic element in the
  otherwise dying steel industry. Unlike other steel executives, Iverson is against import quotas and habitually
  undercuts the foreign competition.

- Control Data's simple, clear, and well-known vision was
  created by William Norris, the company's founder: "to
  address society's major unmet needs as profitable business
  opportunities." During the past fifteen years, Control Data
  has moved six plants to inner cities, created 100 small-
  business centers, trained 5,000 disadvantaged people, and
  offered computer-based education in twenty prisons.

- As an economics student at Yale University, Fred Smith
  outlined a vision of an air parcel service free from the
  problems of piggybacking air freight services onto pas-
  senger flights. Although he got only a C on his paper, he
  went on to realize his vision in Federal Express, the
  leader of a $3-billion industry that was previously
  nonexistent.

- W. L. Gore & Associates, Inc., founder Bill Gore set out in 1958 to create a profitable company where he could recreate the sense of excitement and commitment he had felt as a member of a small task force at the research labs of E. I. Du Pont de Nemours. "The task force," says Bill, "was exciting, challenging, and loads of fun. Besides, we worked like Trojans. I began to wonder why entire companies couldn't be run in the same way."

Alignment

Creating the vision is the leader's first role. Next, she or he must attract people who can help realize it by adopting the vision as their own and sharing responsibility for achieving it.

The name of this critical process is *alignment*. In its highest form, alignment creates a remarkable experience, whether it happens on the playing field, in the concert hall, or at work.

> Every so often we hear of a group of people who ... transcend their personal limitations and real-ize a collective synergy with results that far surpass expectations based on past performance. Anyone hearing a fine symphonic or jazz group hopes for one of those "special" concerts that uplift both the audience and the performers. ... In sports, the 1980 U.S. Olympic Hockey Team stunned the world by winning the gold medal against the vastly more talented and experienced Russian and Finnish teams .... *These occurrences, although unusual, are much more frequent in American business than is common-ly suspected.* [emphasis added]

That description of alignment at its best was written by
Peter Senge, professor at MIT's Sloan School of Management, and Charles Kiefer, president of Innovation Associates of Framingham, Massachusetts. Senge and Kiefer have
made it their mission to study both vision and that
special brand of high performance and workability called
alignment.

When people work to their full capacity, when they
feel in sync with their coworkers, when everything comes
together on cue though completely unplanned, alignment is
present.

In his autobiography, *Second Wind: The Memoirs of an
Opinionated Man*, Bill Russell, the famous Boston Celtics
basketball player, describes how alignment can reach meta-
physical heights.

> Every so often a Celtic game would heat up so
> that it became more than a physical or even
> mental game and would be magical. That feeling
> is difficult to describe, and I certainly never talked
> about it when I was playing. When it happened, I
> could feel my play rise to a new level. It came
> rarely, and would last anywhere from five minutes
> to a whole quarter or more. Three or four players
> were not enough to get it going. It would sur-
> round not only me and the other Celtics, but also
> the players on the other team, and even the
> referees.
>
> At that special level, all sorts of odd things happened.
> The game would be in a white heat of competition,
> and yet somehow I wouldn't feel competitive—which
> is a miracle in itself. I'd be putting out the maximum
> effort, straining, coughing up parts of my lungs as
> we ran and yet never feel the pain. The game would
> move so quickly that every fake, cut and pass would
> be surprising and yet nothing could surprise me. It

was almost as if we were playing in slow motion. During these spells, I could almost sense how the next play would develop and where the next shot would be taken. Even before the other team brought the ball in bounds, I could feel it so keenly that I'd want to shout to my teammates, "It's coming there!" —except that I knew everything would change if I did. My premonitions would be consistently correct, and I always felt then that I not only knew all the Celtics by heart, but also all the opposing players, and that they all knew me. There have been many times in my career when I felt moved or joyful but these were the moments when I had chills pulsing up and down my spine.

How many of us have experiences like Bill Russell's at work? In our collective hearts, we know that work and love, as Freud said, are potentially the most exciting forms of self-expression people can experience. Not just for scientists and artists, not just for champion athletes like Bill Russell, but for creative people in every walk of life.

We all know this, but now, for the first time, we are allowing this deep yearning to emerge as the dominant new work ideal. New companies like People Express are being created with this new ideal at their core.

Alignment transforms a leader's vision into a shared corporate vision—particularly challenging because many baby boomers want to work on their personal goals rather than the company's.

Yet when alignment exists, there is a fit, a meshing between the company's goals and the individual's.

When you identify with your company's purpose, when you experience ownership in a shared vision, you find yourself doing your life's work instead of just doing time.

You experience what all of us long to feel at work.

When corporations effectively define and publicize their intentions, they act as magnets for self-directed, talented people who seek a creative outlet for their personal goals within an organization which shares their values.

If your goal were to run a for-profit computer center in a poor Hispanic community, would you be attracted to work at Apple, Control Data, or the state employment service?

When there's a synergistic relationship between your goals and the company's, your power to achieve personal goals is amplified by the corporation.

When people experience alignment, they know it—and they yearn to repeat it. "Some find it so transforming that life becomes a search for duplicating it," say Senge and Kiefer.

Remember Bill Gore's vision: to run a company in a way that would foster the experiences of high performance he had known in a small problem-solving task force at E. I. Du Pont de Nemours.

Senge and Kiefer call organizations that achieve this state *metanoic*, a Greek word used by the early Christians, meaning the reawakening of vision and intuition. Metanoic organizations possess vision, alignment, mastery, and the ability to integrate intuition and rationality, to see the company as a whole and create structures that further that whole.

Achieving the Vision

A successful corporate vision links a person's job with his or her life purpose and generates alignment—that unparalleled spirit and enthusiasm that energizes people in companies to make the extra effort to do things right—and to do the right thing. That is what makes a corporation uncommonly successful.

But how often do companies achieve their vision? What happens when there is a discrepancy between the idealized vision and actual day-to-day conditions? Under the pressures of the average workday, it is tempting to react to the inevitable problems that arise by abandoning the vision, changing it, or ignoring it totally.

Senge and Kiefer believe this tension between what is and what ought to be is actually healthy: "The tension seeks resolution toward the vision. Each person is able to make decisions locally that are more consistent with the whole, while not necessarily knowing the details of activities in other parts of the organization."

But only, it would seem, *when the vision is not only powerful but persistent,* that is, when it is reinforced and reenergized until it becomes so compelling that the people prefer the structural tension to capitulation.

The only way to translate vision and alignment into people's day-to-day behavior is by grounding these lofty concepts in the company's day-to-day environment.

There are the rituals, stories, and heroes that express the organization's values, what some recent business books have called the "corporate culture."

At J. B. Robinson Jewelers, for example, the Cleveland-based retailing chain, the philosophy of the Golden Rule is reflected throughout training and sales efforts companywide. Too idealistic perhaps? "Pragmatic" companies, take note: Robinson Jewelers grew from two to eighty-two stores in fifteen years by being good guys.

Early in their training, salespeople learn that Robinson Jewelers expects them to treat customers in an honest, trustworthy manner. The company wants its sales force to be particularly sensitive to the customer's fear of being cheated when buying something the average person knows little about—expensive jewelry. The sales staff learns to empathize with the customers' fears and viewpoint by taking turns role-playing the customer and the salesperson.

Robinson Jewelers has a tradition of rewarding people who show special concern for customers. Corporate hero Lou Schwartz, now a regional supervisor, once delivered an engagement ring in the midst of a Midwest blizzard. Knowing their company has solid values enables Robinson's salespeople to feel good about themselves and about making money for a company that is not trying to screw the customer.

Not surprisingly, though, much of the task of reinforcing the corporation's vision falls to the CEO. Once people experience ownership in a company's vision, the CEO's job has only just begun. His or her challenge then is to reinforce, refine, and refocus the vision while supporting and inspiring the people aligned with it.

Donald Burr gets personally involved in People Express's orientation of new managers. Bill Gore, who has begun speaking to outsiders about his experiences creating W. L. Gore & Associates, circulates drafts of his thoughts and presentations to all the associates.

Clearly, SAS's Jan Carlzon, who often talks informally with managers and frequently attends staff parties in aircraft hangars, is deeply aware of his role in grounding the vision in everyday business.

"I have been traveling and preaching ever since I took this job," he says.

Carlzon formulated a skillful strategy for creating alignment: He released a fifty-two-page booklet to all employees detailing the airline's financial condition, his vision for the future, and his plan for delegating responsibility to frontline employees.

One year later, SAS's 7,500 employees boosted the airline to the number-one position in European air traffic.

SAS kept the vision alive with internal public relations.

Every employee receives reprints about SAS in Scandinavian and foreign publications.

This is not the trouble-free way to run a company, however, according to Carlzon. He claims it is much easier to use traditional top-down management than to put the workers in charge, as he did, and serve as a consultant to them.

The attraction of an authoritarian management style is almost irresistible—and wrong.

Bill Gore says, "The simplicity and order of an authoritarian organization make it an almost irresistible temptation. Yet it is counter to the principles of individual freedom and smothers the creative growth of man."

Clearly, both Carlzon and Gore want the financial results and reputation for excellence they and their companies have achieved by doing it the hard way, which they obviously believe is the best way.

"Instructions only succeed in providing employees with knowledge of their own limitations. Information, on the other hand, provides them with a knowledge of their opportunities and possibilities," says Carlzon.

In a company which once would not let flight attendants use their own words to greet or deal with passengers, Carlzon (known to be quite informal at times himself) approves of the pilot who got a good laugh from a plane full of businesspeople by opening his address with "Comrades!"

SAS applauds initiative on the part of its people. Another pilot, whose plane was grounded by a sit-down strike on the Copenhagen runway, responded by opening the bar, taking the passengers on a guided tour of the airport perimeter, and pointing out interesting sights.

Carlzon re-invented the corporation and dramatically increased profits at SAS with a powerful new vision: He turned the organization chart upside down.

Front-line workers with the *most* customer contact were formerly at the bottom of the chart. Carlzon put them on top. It became everyone else's responsibility, CEO included, to serve those who directly serve the customers. And he renewed and reenergized the corporate vision by communicating about it frequently.

To complete his masterful strategy, Carlzon needed to choose the corporate structure that best fit his plans for the company. He erased the pyramid and redrew his concept of the new organizational structure as a wagon wheel, with the CEO at the hub and operating departments revolving around him.

What Structures Will Realize the Vision?

Carlzon's last task—to select the right corporate structure—eventually falls to every CEO and entrepreneur engaged in re-inventing the corporation.

There is a growing recognition that yesterday's hierarchical structures do not work in the new information society. Yet the question is: If not bureaucracy, what? Most of us do not know how to organize ourselves any other way.

Many pioneering companies—both old and new—are experimenting with new structures.

The old bureaucratic layers are giving way to the more natural arrangements of the new information society.

It is as if all of the boxes in the organization chart were thrown into the air and programmed to fall into a new set of patterns that best facilitate communication—networks, hubs, lattices, circles, and wheels.

Computers and the whittling away of middle management

are toppling hierarchies, flattening the pyramid. At Apple Computer, for example, fifteen people report to CEO John Sculley.

When the best corporate talent has no corporate hierarchy to climb, what happens to their competitive energy? One answer is to transform it into a creative, enterprising spirit and channel it into small work groups where communication is quicker and more effective, and where the increasing number of baby boomers are experiencing the "small is beautiful" entrepreneurial environment that is consistent with their values—and highly productive for the company.

Networking is the baby boom's management style of choice. The millions of baby boomers who do make it into the smaller ranks of middle management and beyond—as well as the millions who have created and will create their own companies—will be in a position to influence the structures and management styles the rest of the corporate world will live within. Their choice is networks, small teams, and other decentralized structures.

In response to these changes, innovative companies such as CRS Sirrine, Advanced Micro Devices, and the others mentioned in the following pages are exploring a range of structures including cross-disciplinary teams, partnerships, and fellowship options—whatever promotes better communication, innovation, and increased productivity. Many of these companies are listed in *The 100 Best Companies to Work for in America* by Robert Levering, Milton Moskowitz, and Michael Katz.

Ultimately, there is no pat answer. It depends on the corporation. New structures, no matter how brilliantly designed, cannot be applied top down. Companies must experiment with them, and each new model must be custom-fit to the company and its specific needs. Here are some of the most innovative alternative structures.

The Small Team and Cross-Disciplinary Team

Flexible, fast, loaded with talent, the small-team model is the most popular and widespread alternative to bureaucratic organization. From the auto factories of Detroit to the software firms in Silicon Valley, corporations are successfully reorganizing the flow of power and communication within companies through this flexible new structure. One simple reason for their success is that people *like* working in small teams.

Advanced Micro Devices, the Silicon Valley–based silicon chip maker, has only 5,000 employees, but there are more than twenty company teams, from the Mail and Literature Distribution Team to the MOS Static RAM Design Team. Teams belong to "directorates" with their own engineering, manufacturing, and sales component and are led by a managing director who works directly with Jerry Saunders, the company's founder and head.

After Apple Computer's success in the personal computer market, IBM created its own version of the small-team structure, its IBUs ("independent business units"), to fight its own well-known bureaucratic tendencies.

Small teams can accomplish even more when people with different talents and perspectives come together to work on a problem.

Fortune magazine's eight most innovative companies in America—American Airlines, Apple, Campbell Soup, General Electric, Intel, Merck, 3M, and Philip Morris—are masters of the cross-disciplinary team.

"People in different disciplines are simply not allowed to remain in isolation," writes *Fortune*'s Stratford P. Sherman. "Business units are kept small in part to throw engineers, marketers and finance experts together into the sort of tight groups most often found in start-up companies."

That approach can work equally well in small to medium-sized firms. Jack Bares, president of Milbar Corp., a

$10-million specialty hand tool manufacturer, ran a contest in his company to reduce the production cost of a popular hand tool and devise ways for the company's tools to penetrate international markets.

Four teams competed against each other, consisting of six people from departments such as production, design, engineering, quality control, and accounting. The winners reduced costs 50 percent and discovered how to adapt Milbar's designs to tools already popular in Europe and Japan. Says company president Bares, "I've never seen a program generate so much enthusiasm."

At CRS Sirrine, an architectural team of six to eight people sees each project through from beginning to end. Instead of a design team, construction team, and client relations manager, for example, all the members of the team—who may have a background in any one of these specialties—get involved in everything from solving problems on the construction site to design work and meeting with clients.

"Biological" Organization

Advanced Micro Devices directorates are similar to Kollmorgen Corp.'s "productized" organization, where each product generates its own autonomous division.

Connecticut-based Kollmorgen Corp., a $326-million-a-year maker of printed circuit boards and electric motors and controls, has doubled sales every four years.

Kollmorgen evolved into a new model corporation by way of a painful but exhilarating metamorphosis in the early 1970s. Trusting his gut over conventional wisdom, Bob Swiggett persuaded his colleagues in top management to scrap a classic centralized management structure and reinvent itself into a series of autonomous decentralized divisions. Under that structure, the company has thrived.

"A lot of people have management structures where the

fellows who run the divisions have autonomy," says Robert Swiggett. "What we've done is work harder than anybody to make sure this really happens."

A lot of companies have "autonomous divisions," but in fact management pays only lip service to autonomy. As the old spiritual says, "Everybody talkin' 'bout heaven ain't goin' there."

Each of Kollmorgen's sixteen divisions has its own president—who reports only to the CEO—and a board of directors. A division's board consists of corporate officers, other division presidents, and top technical people outside the division. There is no additional layer of vice-presidents in between. Once a division grows larger than a couple of hundred people, it breaks into subdivisions.

Such a system renders profit sharing simple and equitable: When your product makes a profit, you get a bonus.

Minnesota Mining & Manufacturing Company (3M), with 87,000 employees, is a more likely victim of bureaucracy than Kollmorgen, which has only 5,400 people. Yet 3M uses a similar approach to preserving smallness and flexibility. 3M calls it a "biological" organization. When a new product sells well enough, a new division is born.

3M's commitment to decentralization is legendary:

- Median plant size is 115 people.
- Only five of the ninety-one U.S. plants have more than 1,000 people.
- 3M plants are found in small-town America—from Wahpeton, North Dakota, to Honeoye, New York.

The Partnership Option
Trammell Crow, the real estate development company, has done a splendid job of applying to business the

partnership model used in most law and accounting firms.

Simply put, each of the firm's eighty partners owns a sizable percentage of the properties he or she works on. All partners are paid the same, $18,000 per year. The rest—and partners make a *good deal* more—comes from sales commissions or ownership. That is how an estimated 5 percent of Trammell Crow's work force became millionaires.

"Partner" is also the key word at Hewitt Associates, the employee benefits consultant. Professionals who work there have just one job title—"partner." Structured like a law firm, Hewitt has ninety-two partners in its work force. Yet with an average income of $166,000 per partner, Hewitt partners made more money than the average partner in a Big Eight accounting firm.

Quad/Graphics, a printer of nationally known magazines, was founded by an ex-attorney determined to structure his company like a law firm. Quad employees are also called "partners." Potential partners are considered "students," hired by "sponsors" and directed by "mentors" (rather than bosses).

The Fellowship Option

Wasn't it the Peter Principle that said, "People keep getting promoted until they reach their level of incompetence"? It may sound funny, but in many cases it is painfully true.

In thousands of American corporations, career ladders have traditionally been set up so that competent technical people and other specialists must abandon the area they love—and in which they excel—in order to land a high-level job with more power, influence, and money.

Not all were promoted to their level of incompetence, by any means, but many would have been better off—and much happier—if they had continued doing the work they love and do best.

But this forced march into management inflicted the

greatest loss on the corporation itself. Its most creative, innovative people—the ones spearheading the critical areas like new product development and sales—were being pulled out and channeled into management. Maybe they were *good* managers. Nevertheless, the company was left wanting in the very areas that spur new growth.

In the 1960s and 1970s, several companies recognized the problem and experimented with new ways to solve it.

Today's high-tech companies are taking it one step further and making alternative career ladders an established part of corporate structure. Taking a cue from IBM, which started the practice some thirty years ago, they are developing a sort of fellowship option that lets engineers remain engineers yet progress in power, pay, and perks within the company.

ITT, General Electric, Analog Devices, Amdahl, and Wang Laboratories are among the companies with parallel career ladders.

The highest rung on IBM's parallel ladder is the title of "fellow." There are now fifty-five IBM fellows, people commanding high-level salaries without the managerial and administrative duties many creative people abhor. Their job is not to worry about how profitable their ideas are, just to be creative and chase after what interests them.

Analog Devices, Inc., based in Norwood, Massachusetts, has a number of division fellows. Analog's fellowship ladder begins with senior project engineer, moves up through staff engineer, senior staff engineer, culminating in division fellow—and the ultimate, corporate fellow.

The traditional path might instead be from engineering supervisor to functional manager to product line manager to director to vice-president.

There are a lot of advantages to this new structural model: Top brainpower stays where it is needed most—in new product development, which fosters the company's long-term growth. But equally important, the veteran engineer is free to become the re-invented manager—the manager as teacher, facilitator, mentor to the young and midlevel engineers and technicians, the company's talent bank for the future.

The Lattice Organization

This is the new organizational model developed by W. L. Gore & Associates, which has successfully used small-team management since it opened its doors in 1958.

Employees are called "associates," and everyone in the company deals with everyone else directly through a crosshatching of horizontal and vertical lines—hence founder Bill Gore's name for the company's management structure, "lattice organization."

We had read with great interest about W. L. Gore & Associates in *Inc.* magazine and in *The Tarrytown Letter*, a publication of Bob Schwartz's group in Tarrytown, New York. But we felt we would never really understand this lattice idea without visiting W. L. Gore & Associates.

After all, what does it really mean to say that people deal directly with everyone else?

In Newark, Delaware, we met Bill Gore and Vieve Gore, Bill's wife of fifty years and business partner for more than twenty-five years. In their early seventies, but much younger in their thinking, appearance, and energy level, they told us how the lattice structure works in transforming Bill's vision of work in a small task force into a companywide esprit de corps.

"Every [successful] organization has a lattice organization that underlies the facade of authoritarian hierarchy," says Bill Gore. "It is through these lattice organizations that things get done and most of us delight in 'going around' the formal procedures and doing things the straightforward and easy way."

Acknowledge the informal system that really runs a company and then throw away the hierarchical structure.

What W. L. Gore has done, it seems, is legitimize the essential—the informal structure—found in most organizations and eliminated the superfluous—the hierarchy. In Gore's lattice, people communicate person-to-person. No one holds any formal position of authority. Leadership emerges naturally when people attract followers.

But what really holds the lattice together is Gore's emphasis on commitment and its sponsor system.

All work assignments are voluntary, so tasks and functions are organized by commitments. At W. L. Gore & Associates, you make your own commitments and keep them, and you do not make commitments you cannot keep. Similarly, an important lattice precept is: "Objectives are set by those who must 'make them happen.'"

Gore's sponsor system is the second key element of the lattice. When a new person joins the company (which as it turns out is often because of the firm's extraordinary growth rate: 30 percent of Gore's 4,000 employees were new in 1984), an experienced associate volunteers to take responsibility for this new person learning his or her job. It is your sponsor, not a person in authority over you, who decides whether, after a three-month learning period, your contribution to the company equals your salary. If it does not, it is probably harder on the sponsor, whose responsibility it was to teach, than on the learner.

There are three different types of sponsors at Gore. The Starting Sponsor described above; the Advocate Sponsor, whose job it is to know about and appreciate a person's accomplishments and contributions in the organization and speak for them; and the Compensation Sponsor, who knows all the associates working on a team and consults with the Advocate Sponsor and, with other members of a compensation team, lists people's accomplishments and determines a commensurate salary.

Being people-oriented is not about being nice to people.

It is especially not about being nice to people who do not produce. At W. L. Gore, an associate's salary matches his or her contribution to the company. When after a three-month probationary period new associates fail to learn their jobs, they are not fired, but their salaries are reduced to equal their contributions to the company—zero. "Usually, they will leave then," says Bill Gore.

The CEO as Team

The small-group structure is percolating up from the office and shop floor to the ranks of top management. No longer is the top job in a company necessarily held by a single person. In the re-invented corporation, we are exploring the idea of the CEO as a team:

- Intel, the new economy silicon chip maker, is run by a triumvirate: vice-chairman Robert Noyce, president Andrew Grove, and board chairman Gordon Moore. Their job titles are different but they run the company together.
- At Nordstroms', the Seattle-based retailing chain, top management is "the five": three Nordstrom family members—cochairmen John and Bruce Nordstrom, Jim Nordstrom, (known as Mr. John, Mr. Bruce, and Mr. Jim)—John McMillan, executive vice-president, and Robert Bender, senior vice-president. Company managers are instructed to call up any one of "the five" and talk to whomever answers the phone.
- In late 1984, Kimberly-Clark Corporation announced it was creating an office of the chairman, consisting of chairman Darwin Smith, a chief executive officer, and

three vice-chairmen. It was the first time the company
had operated under this increasingly popular team approach.

Customized, Americanized QC Circles

While many American companies grafted the Japan-
developed quality control circle into their corporate culture
(some 10,000 people from 4,000 companies belong to the
Cincinnati-based International Association of Quality Circles), others called it a fad and rejected it out of hand.

But America had heard the message: The people who
know the most about any job are the people doing it. To
keep a business healthy, you have to get at that information
and apply it throughout the company.

And the best way to do that might *not* be with quality
control circles, so many innovative companies began to
experiment with other ways to exchange information and
custom-fitted these new forms to their company's needs.

- At Olga, the maker of women's undergarments, it is
  called a Creative Meeting, and it was originally the way
  designers brainstormed new fashion ideas. But Jan
  Erteszek, the company's cofounder (with his wife, the
  real Olga behind each Olga fashion), decided to try
  Creative Meetings companywide and ask people how
  they would run the company if they had his job. Now
  small groups of associates (they are not called employees at Olga) meet once a week for six weeks, usually
  two or three times each year.
- At the Portland-based Electro Scientific Industries, each
  spring groups of twelve to fifteen employees tell the
  company's president what is working and what is not, in
  their "Going Well/In the Way" meetings (as in "What's
  going well? What's in the way?").
- Drivers at Preston Trucking Co. meet in groups of

twenty every few weeks to discuss how to do their jobs better.
* Kollmorgen Corp. calls them People Meetings—the monthly get-togethers to discuss what is happening in the company.

In re-inventing the corporation, it is critical to choose the structures that work best for the company's particular needs, markets, and opportunities. These prototype structures represent some of the choices. There are many more. But in general, we are redesigning our hierarchies into networklike structures increasingly organized by product or service rather than function. The vertical hierarchy is giving way to the horizontal team where people from different disciplines and perspectives work together on a common goal. We are inventing new career ladders so that technicians and other specialists can advance their careers and the company's fortunes without moving into management. We are creating companies with just a single layer of management where all professionals have the same job title—be it partner, associate, or manager.

Bureaucracy Smashers

Sometimes, just a few key steps can start breaking down the barriers to effective communication and action within a company.

The following policies gleaned from a variety of companies are our list of bureaucracy smashers, simple but effective steps which help replace the industrial "us vs. them" mentality with the "we are all in this together" attitude needed to re-invent the corporation:

1. Set up a system of reverse reviews. Everyone who is evaluated gets to evaluate the boss, too (assuming there are bosses). That is the policy at Kollmorgen.

2. Call everyone by first name.

3. Try out the rule they have at Dana Corporation: "Use little paper; keep no files."

4. Call people associates, partners, managers—or just plain people—instead of employees (or workers!).

5. Decentralize authority absolutely. A cultural hero at Nordstrom, where decentralization is practiced with a vengeance, felt free enough to leave the store to drive a customer to the airport to be sure she caught a plane. That store clerk knew that the company trusted her judgment.

6. Eliminate executive dining rooms, executive rest rooms, special parking spots, and the like.

7. Insist everybody answer his or her own phone. (At People Express people also type their own letters.)

8. Get people to manage themselves: to set and monitor their own goals, to manage their work load and set their own priorities.

9. Adopt the policy they have at New Hope Communication: "Only do business with people who are pleasant."

10. Take a deep breath and throw out the old organization chart.

That last bureaucracy smasher reminds us of the oft-quoted story of how William McGowan, the founder and CEO of MCI, the long-distance discount phone company, has brought together new managers and, after his welcoming remarks, tells them, "I know that some of you, with your business-school backgrounds, are out there already beginning to draw up organization charts and starting to write manuals for operating procedures. As soon as I find out who you are, I'm going to fire every last one of you."

Forrester's Prophetic Idea

Re-inventing the corporation is not a new idea. Twenty years ago MIT professor Jay Forrester published a paper called "A New Corporate Design," which in effect prophesized the current corporate transformation.

"In technology, we expect bold experiments that test ideas, obtain new knowledge, and lead to major advances," Forrester begins boldly. "But in matters of social organization, we usually propose only timid modifications of conventional practice and balk at daring experiment and innovation. Why?"

Forrester does not go on to answer his insightful question. Instead, he describes in 1965 the characteristics of his "new corporate design" in a way that places him far ahead of his time, something of a habit with Forrester.

First of all, he says, we must eliminate the superior-subordinate relationship, the basis of control in a corporation.

The hierarchical structure where everyone has a superior and everyone has an inferior surely is corrupting of the human spirit—no matter how well it served us during the industrial period.

"A substantial body of thought, derived from several centuries of politics, national government, economics, and psychology," wrote Forrester, "exposes the stultifying effect of the authoritarian organization on initiative and innovation and suggests that, whatever the merits of authoritarian control in an earlier day, such control is becoming less and less appropriate. . . ."

In an authoritarian structure, he argues, people feel they cannot change the environment and thus are closed to the information which might change it.

In the new corporation that Forrester envisioned, individuals would *not* have a "superior," but "a continually changing structure of relationships," freely negotiated by the individual.

Here Forrester anticipates the "commitment over authority" approach of W. L. Gore & Associates as well as Gore's mentorlike "sponsor" system discussed earlier in this chapter.

Corporate policy, Forrester said, should be adjusted so that there is concurrence between "self-interest of the individual and the objective of the total organization." This is precisely the process we have come to call "alignment."

Forrester also anticipated the proliferation of profit centers within the corporation, advocating that "each man [only the masculine gender in 1965] or small team should be a profit center" and "have status similar to that of an owner-manager." He believed the corporation should be the counterpart of the larger economy outside.

Additionally, Forrester's "new corporate design" anticipated the restructuring through electronic processing and eventually the computer's role in smashing the bureaucratic pyramid. "Computers provide the incentive to explore the fundamental relationship between information and corporate success."

Education and training were (again presaged) at the center of corporate strategy. "Some 25 percent of the total working time of all persons in the corporation should be devoted to preparation for their future roles," he wrote.

Forrester ended his essay on what to contemporary readers must have seemed a practical note at last: "It does not seem likely that such sweeping changes could be implemented by gradual change within an existing organization."

Yet his practicality was an accurate prediction, too. "The only promising approach seems to be to build a new organization from the ground up in the new pattern."

Why has it taken this long—twenty years—for Forrester's vision to become reality? Why do we not—in Forrester's own question—take the bold leaps in social organizations that we do in technology?

The answer to that question is a fundamental theme of this book.

The point is this: Changing values—like Forrester's and so many other good ideas—and new notions of things do not in themselves negotiate change.

Change occurs only when there is a confluence of changing values and economic necessity.

Influenced by the works of Rensis Likert and Douglas McGregor, the new corporate humanists of the very early 1960s, Forrester's essay was an expression of changing values.

What was lacking in the booming 1960s was the economic necessity. Things were going fine. Re-inventing the corporation at that point sounded like re-inventing the wheel.

Not anymore. The turmoil of the 1970s—the stiff competition of a global economy and the declining industrial base—represents the economic impetus for change. And the new forces such as the coming seller's market, the whittling away of middle management, and the new definition of human resources as a company's competitive edge are reinforcing that economic imperative.

The economics of the 1960s did not necessitate change, so Forrester's vision for a "new corporate design" remained unactualized. Today, we can recognize it as a prophetic blueprint for re-inventing the corporation.

2

Ten Considerations in Re-inventing the Corporation

In beginning the process of re-inventing the corporation, we think there are at least ten considerations to bear in mind.

These are, in effect, guidelines to help you chart your course as you weigh which actions to take in your company and your career during the critical next few years, when the booming information economy comes face-to-face with the potentially threatening labor shortages of the coming seller's market.

These considerations can help you decide whether your company is re-inventing itself or whether you should think about working someplace else. You should use these guidelines to measure where you are and where you want to go, examining them to discover which apply most in your profession, business, or geographic area.

As you plot your next career move or shape your company's next policy (or consider throwing out the policy manual), remember these guidelines:

1. The best and brightest people will gravitate toward those corporations that foster personal growth.

2. The manager's new role is that of coach, teacher, and mentor.

3. The best people want ownership—psychic and literal —in a company; the best companies are providing it.

4. Companies will increasingly turn to third-party contractors, shifting from hired labor to contract labor.

5. Authoritarian management is yielding to a networking, people style of management.

6. Entrepreneurship within the corporations— intrapreneurship—is creating new products and new markets and revitalizing companies inside out.

7. Quality will be paramount.

8. Intuition and creativity are challenging the "it's all in the numbers" business-school philosophy.

9. Large corporations are emulating the positive and productive qualities of small business.

10. The dawn of the information economy has fostered a massive shift from infrastructure to quality of life.

1. The companies that create the most nourishing environments for personal growth will attract the most talented people.

If there is one factor that will make the difference in the seller's market, it is the opportunity for personal growth.

Traditionally, the assumption has been that you are hired to help the company grow. But the competition among companies for the best people adds a second dimension: *You have to be able to grow, too.*

You must invest your talent, your human capital, in the company that will bring you the best and biggest return.

In the best companies, your growth and the company's growth are compatible and mutually nourishing.

This is not about companies being altruistic. It is simply a good match, a win/win arrangement, another way of talking about alignment, which we discussed in the previous chapter.

Companies with the most nurturing environments for personal growth become known as great places to work—like the companies in *The 100 Best Companies to Work for in America*.

At companies like People Express, Hewitt Associates, Hewlett-Packard, 3M, and W. L. Gore & Associates, the corporate commitment to personal growth is reflected in a dynamic environment for work and learning.

- The credo at People Express is that "work must create a learning opportunity for the individuals involved. While certain aspects may be routine, the total work package must be varied enough to provide mental stimulus for personal growth."
- "You are your own manager. Rarely does anyone need monitoring. . . . If a mistake is made, it's everyone's mistake," says Linda Menees, a secretary at Hewitt Associates, the employee benefits consultant. Ms. Menees says she has always been treated the same as any of the company's partners.
- Hewlett-Packard has created such a positive environment for personal growth that a recent survey of some 8,000 HP workers about company practices placed HP in the top one-half of 1 percent of more than 1,000 U.S. companies.
- The strong point at Minnesota Mining & Manufacturing Company is its ability to nurture creativity, says *Forbes* magazine. 3M seems to have mastered the dictum "Grow or die." 3M's philosophy, as expressed by CEO Lew

Lehr, is, "Our concern for independent thinking and the entrepreneurial spirit is not just one approach among many. It is our only approach."

- W. L. Gore & Associates fosters personal growth by structuring people's tasks around commitment, not authority. Sometimes when new people join the company, they are told to "look around and find something interesting to do." (Of course, other times people are hired for specific tasks.) People grow when their work interests them and they are committed, rather than assigned, to it.

What specific actions can managers and companies take to create more nourishing environments? Here are some of the techniques followed by a number of companies, including "The 100 Best":

Get more of the most experienced, senior people out of their offices and working with younger talent.

CRS Sirrine, the Houston-based architectural and engineering firm, is known for getting senior management to work alongside new employees. Says Carter Rohan, a young architect, "You see the top people all the time here. You work directly with them. The concept is to understaff and give people lots of responsibility."

Hewlett-Packard's famous MBWA (Management by Walking Around) engages this same idea: Top management gets off its chairs and wanders around the office/plant looking for problems, ideas, people. Says personnel vice-president John Doyle, "It's not enough to sit and wait for people to come to see you with their problems and ideas—they probably wouldn't in many cases." Bill Hewlett concludes, "Men and women want to do a good job, a creative job, and if they are provided with the proper environment, they will do so."

Institute flexible hours.

When people choose their work hours, they are more committed to the work. Our next chapter will show many examples of flexible work schedules—job sharing, flextime, and permanent part-time.

Create an intellectually stimulating environment.

For instance, with a noon lecture series. Bell Labs, which employs some 9,000 people with either Ph.D.s or master's degrees, has kept the academic practice of a monthly lecture series. Bell's open-door policy encourages people from different disciplines to talk together. Chemists, mathematicians, physicians, psychologists, and computer specialists spend time with one another and the results are synergistic.

The Information Services Group at M & M Mar's Randolph, New Jersey, operation invites nationally known speakers to address a quarterly after-work gathering at a local restaurant.

Organize travel/learning experiences.

Kansas City–based Hallmark routinely sends artists to art exhibits in San Francisco, Santa Fe, and London, not as rewards, but for stimulation, learning, and inspiration. About 400 employees at Nissan's Smyrna, Tennessee, plant learned the Nissan way of doing things by working six weeks at plants in Japan. Molex, Inc., sent several employees from its U.S. headquarters on a ten-day working holiday at the firm's Japanese subsidiary. They spent their days working the same machines they use at home and learning from their Japanese counterparts. Back home they briefed coworkers and managers on their experiences.

Consider awarding sabbaticals to creative people.

This academic practice is finding its way into the corporation. More and more companies from high-tech firms to McDonald's are sending their people off for self-learning and relaxation—with full (or partial) pay, benefits, and the same or a comparable job when they return.

- Every full-time employee at McDonald's is eligible for an eight-week sabbatical with full pay for every ten years of full-time service.
- Tandem Computer Co. created a sabbatical program in 1979 after the people working there chose it over profit sharing and a retirement plan. After four years, an employee can take a six-week sabbatical. Some 75 of Tandem's 4,000 U.S. employees have already done so.
- After six years on the job at the ROLM Corporation, you are eligible for either twelve weeks off with full pay or six weeks off with double pay.

In a seller's market, companies will be offering many benefits—the sabbatical is special enough to attract the best, most creative talent.

Structure jobs holistically to stretch, develop, and integrate new skills.

Today's companies, whether they make automobiles or process information, are reversing the industrial practice of "Taylorism"—that is, breaking down jobs into their smallest, most simple parts, a practice named for Frederick Taylor, who introduced it into the early twentieth-century workplace.

The idea of reversing Taylor's approach started out with people like Frederick Herzberg in the 1960s and was known as job enrichment. A few companies were interested, but there was no widespread impetus behind the idea.

But the declining productivity of the 1970s brought back

the notion in the industrial sector in the early 1980s and the results were quite successful. A TRW aircraft components plant in Cleveland reduced job classifications from more than 200 to fewer than 100. A Chrysler plant in Indiana reduced annual costs by $2.8 million by getting skilled tradespeople to do one another's jobs.

It is equally important in the information sector. Today's well-educated work force, the coming seller's job market, and the need to create a work environment where people grow together are reinforcing the need to re-invent jobs holistically. It is an important vehicle for attracting competent people and creating an environment where they will remain interested in and stimulated by their work:

- In Northwestern Mutual Life's new business department, sixty-four distinct job descriptions were reduced to six. Clerical workers, who previously spent the whole day in front of a computer terminal updating applications, grew into service representatives who handle applications or respond to claims from beginning to end, including making phone calls to agents.
- At Continental Illinois National Bank, Christine Szczesniak performed the same function for seventeen years on a check processing line. Now she does practically everything herself: processing the check, depositing it into the customer's account by computer, telephoning customers, and mailing them data. The new system has improved productivity 40 percent.
- At Nissan's Smyrna, Tennessee, plant, employees in the Pay for Skills program learn advanced skills rather than stop and wait for a skilled craftsperson to come by and do a single task. Similarly, nine General Motors plants, including a Cadillac engine plant in Livonia, Michigan, have a pay-for-knowledge program under which production employees are encouraged to learn

all the jobs in their area. Both programs pay people more for their new skills.

This need to broaden work is just as important for highly skilled technical people. At 3M, for instance, scientist-inventors are trained to be more market-oriented, and salespeople more scientific.

Move people laterally to develop well-roundedness.

One eighteen-year veteran of Toledo's Dana Corporation has followed a typical Dana management path. He started out as a personnel clerk, became a buyer in the purchasing department, a production line foreman, and is now in industrial relations at corporate headquarters.

People at the prestigious Morgan Bank usually rotate jobs every three to five years, and most professionals work overseas at some point in their careers.

The ideal at People Express is for every manager (they are not called employees) to be familiar with every job in the company. Today's pilot might work in marketing tomorrow; the flight attendant may work in reservations next week.

Southern California Edison Company, an electric utility serving 8 million customers and known for its advocacy of solar and wind power, is also an innovative grower of people. It encourages people to move around laterally. In fact, the only way to get ahead at SCE is by moving from department to department.

Claire Spence, for example, was hired as a stenographer in the safety division, became a statistical clerk and then a safety specialist, spent a year and a half working on the company's United Way campaign, then became a conservation planner, and is now in corporate planning and budgeting.

The most distinguishing characteristic of the re-invented corporation is that it is a place where employees experience growth.

What does a nourishing growth environment actually look like? To summarize, it is a workplace where people are talking about their work, exchanging ideas, where top managers and newcomers know one another and often work together, where people are learning at company-sponsored events like lectures and concerts and through travel for specialized training or stimulation.

It is a workplace where people are working on what interests them most, although it also means stretching to learn new tasks related to your job or working in new departments to get a feel for the company as a whole.

We must re-invent the corporation into a place where people come to grow, instead of expecting people to satisfy the need for growth in their off-hours.

Procter & Gamble expresses that expectation this way: "We're looking for achievers . . . who possess the potential for rapid growth after they join us."

2. Inside the corporation, the manager's new role will be to cultivate and maintain a nourishing environment for personal growth.

If the corporation is the architect of this new environment for personal growth, the manager is the builder.

In the re-invented corporation, we are shifting from manager as order-giver to manager as facilitator. We used to think that the manager's job was to know all the answers. But in the 1980s, the new manager ought, rather, to know the questions, to be concerned about them and involve others in finding answers. Today's manager needs to be more of a facilitator—someone skilled in eliciting answers from others, perhaps from people who do not even know that they know.

This new role of the manager as facilitator has its roots in the beginnings of the first, and now the most successful, company of the information economy, IBM Corp. IBM's founder, Thomas Watson, began re-inventing the manager's role fifty years ago.

Aiming to create a workplace people could be proud of and aligned with, Watson started calling his foremen "managers" and said their job was "to make sure workers have the tools and information they needed, and to help them when they found themselves in trouble."

The manager's role is to create a nourishing environment for personal growth in addition to the opportunity to contribute to the growth of the institution.

This was the prototype of the manager as facilitator, the role companies will do well to advocate for their managers in the new information society.

The most successful companies of the new information era are committed to the manager's new role as developer and cultivator of human potential.

Ann Bowers, dean of Apple University, Apple Computer's in-house training arm and transmitter of corporate values, says Apple is interested only in this new type of manager: "We are looking for people who are coaches and team builders and expanders, not controllers of people."

"The role of a leader is the servant's role," argues Kollmorgen's Bob Swiggett. "It's supporting his people, running interference for them. It's coming out with an atmosphere of understanding and love. You want people to feel they have complete control over their destiny at every level. Tyranny is not tolerated here. People who want to manage in the traditional sense are cast off by their peers like dandruff."

This new manager is not just found in Silicon Valley or in high-tech companies. The new manager is growing people all across America.

For example, this is how Maryland's Preston Trucking Company describes its managers' jobs: "Preston people must be regarded as partners rather than adversaries. The person doing the job knows more about it than anybody else. It is the responsibility of managers to ask for suggestions, to listen to possible solutions to specific problems, and to help implement productive change. Each employee has unlimited possibilities."

PepsiCo has earned a reputation as a highly competitive environment which encourages individualism rather than the team approach. But the company is attempting to reshape its environment into a more people-oriented place without losing the competitive edge that made it a profitable, $8-billion company.

PepsiCo's change of heart came after a survey of 470 senior executives showed they did not feel the company cared about them as people, told them enough about what was going on in the company as a whole or about how well they were performing their jobs.

So now, among other things, Pepsi will encourage managers to be more like teachers and coaches—precisely the role managers should be playing now.

We have to think increasingly about the manager as teacher, as mentor, as developer of human potential.

The big challenge of the 1980s is not the retraining of workers, but the retraining of managers.

3. Compensation systems that reward performance and innovation are transforming employees into stockholders.

"The future of this company is to eliminate the differences between workers, managers, and owners by making them all capitalists,'' says Jim Pinto, a pioneer in the new incentives approach. Pinto founded Action Instruments, a San Diego electronics firm which distributed 20 percent of company stock to front-line employees.

Robert Metcalfe, chairman of 3Com in Mountain View, California, a builder of data networks, awards 11 percent of company stock below the officer level. He tells entry-level stock clerks that if they contribute to the company's growth, they can match their $10,000 salaries in stock gains.

Lotus Development Corp.'s Mitchell Kapor gave between 100 and 200 shares of the firm's stock to most of his employees.

The old definition of an adequate compensation package—benefits, salary, and security—is out of date in today's workplace. Now compensation is measured by company stock and profit sharing—which may be far more valuable than salaries.

In innovative companies throughout America, the key word today is "incentive." What kinds of new financial arrangements will give people the incentive to put out their best efforts?

A range of new models is being explored: bonus plans, stock-incentive plans, ESOP (employee stock-option plans), profit sharing, even outright employee ownership. These different, sometimes complex, financial models share two key characteristics: 1) They aim to offer incentives for loyalty and productivity; 2) they are moving from the executive suite to the average employee. Once the prerogative of a few top executives, stock options and bonuses are now widely dispersed throughout thousands of companies.

According to the National Center for Employee Ownership, there are more than 5,700 ESOPs covering some 9.6 million workers. That is up from 843 plans covering about half a million people in 1976. It's an old idea, but as these figures show, the time for ESOPs has clearly come.

"It's been good for us," says Jerry Knapp, vice-president for finance with CableData, a Sacramento, California, manufacturer in which employees own about 35 percent of company stock. "It puts ownership in the hands of our workers and we feel owners are better employees than those who don't share in the growth of a company."

In prototype new companies, people get paid not for their position on the organization chart, but for their productivity. Pay for performance is replacing pay for just showing up in the morning.

The profit-sharing plan at Cummins Engine Co. is a good example. Each quarter, all 14,000 employees receive a payment based on productivity (earnings as a percentage of return on sales). In November 1984, for example, each assembly line worker got a quarterly check for $700. Total profit sharing for 1984 averaged more than $2,000 per person.

Cummins's profit-sharing plan was put in place after several quarters of low profits and outright losses. By the third quarter of 1984, though, Cummins earned more than $65 million—up from only $1.5 million the previous year. The company credits profit sharing along with a stronger economy for its impressive turnaround.

Profit-sharing plans have been in existence since the turn of the century, but they have become increasingly popular in recent years. There are about 430,000 profit-sharing plans operating now, according to the Profit Sharing Resource Foundation. Unlike the Cummins plan, most defer payments until the employee leaves the company in order to reduce taxes.

But recognizing that employees are better motivated by an

immediate cash payout (even if that means a bigger tax bite), an increasing number of companies are profit sharing in cash.

Western Airlines, TWA, American Airlines, General Motors, Ford, Tektronix, and ROLM have cash profit-sharing plans. In 1984, GM paid out about $1,000 per employee in profit sharing and Ford about $1,600.

It is a good thing that companies have rediscovered the power of incentives. People on the "pay for attendance" model spend only about 50 percent of their time actually working, according to a study published by the American Management Association.

Perhaps large companies can afford this sort of institutionalized welfare—in the short term, that is. But the small businesses of the new information era certainly cannot (and even Apple and Hewlett-Packard were once small businesses). In their early days, these new businesses realized that people would make or break their companies and they created the financial incentives that got people working 100 percent of the workday (and often more).

If you spend only about half your day working in a small company (or a small team within a large company), it is obvious that you are not pulling your weight. And coworkers, who are also stockholders, resent it. Peer pressure replaces management pressure.

At Apple and Tandem Computer, where people bought stock or earned it through hard work, they were handsomely rewarded. As we all know (and love to hear again and again), twenty-five-year-olds became millionaires and many others held stock worth $500,000.

These new models of financial incentives have moved far beyond the experimental stage. They are beoming well established in a large number of America's major corporations and growing small businesses.

- About two-thirds of Dana Corporation's 18,000 employees own company stock. For each seventy cents the employee spends on stock, Dana contributes thirty cents.

- At Lowe's Companies, Inc., of North Wilkesboro, North Carolina, stories about people retiring rich on the company ESOP are legendary: the $125-a-week warehouseman who retired in 1975 with a $660,000 nest egg, the truck driver with $413,000. The company's ESOP plan has served as a model for similar plans being created all over the country.

- People Express, a company constructed around the ideal of self-management, requires all employees to be stockholders. About one-third of the company stock—a high percentage—is held by People Express managers (they are not called employees) who can buy stock at discount. Under a special bonus plan, People Express matches managers' purchases share for share.

- Procter & Gamble, the $13-billion-per-year personal products company, which is hardly a small new-age company, started a profit-sharing plan in 1887. It is the oldest profit-sharing plan in America.

- The bonus incentive plan at Raychem Corporation of Menlow Park, California, is easy to calculate. Every three months each employee gets a bonus based on one-half the company's return on sales. If the return is a healthy 10 percent, the employee gets 5 percent of his or her salary as a bonus. If you earned $5,000 per quarter in salary, your bonus would be $250.

The recognized need for financial incentives raises an interesting issue.

If a singer can participate in the sales of his product all his life, why can't an engineer?

That is the question raised by Jim Dietz, an engineering

vice-president at Wilson Laboratories, a $5-million computer test equipment maker in Orange, California.

But Dietz does not have to ask the question anymore. He and his fellow engineers at Wilson Labs stand to earn as much as $25,000 in royalties on the sales of each new product they design. In a seller's market for computer professionals, Dietz has turned down job offers that would have increased his salary 25 percent.

"Ordinary income is not enough for an employee who wants to feel that he's at least partially in business for himself," says Wilson president Randall Wilson. Turnover at Wilson Labs is just about zilch.

The ultimate in employee capitalism is, of course, outright ownership. And that model of financial incentive is growing increasingly widespread:

- At Linnton Plywood Association in Portland, Oregon, a $20-million-a-year worker-owned plywood manufacturer, workers earn more than $50,000 per year—much more than people at large mills such as Weyerhaeuser. But they must invest a substantial amount to buy a share and join the collective—$75,000 at this writing.
- Publix Super Markets, Florida's largest retail food chain, is completely owned by its employees. And it certainly has not hurt the bottom line: Publix profit per dollar of sales is twice that of Safeway, which has the country's biggest sales.
- At Ripley Industries, a St. Louis maker of shoe heels and cutting dies, and a publicly held company, the employee stock-ownership plan made a tender offer for all of the company's stock it did not own.

In 1984, Colorado's Fred Schmid Appliance & TV Co., with fifteen stores and $62 million in annual sales, transferred 100 percent of stock ownership to employees rather than sell the company to outsiders for nearly $10 million. Why such generosity?

"The employees built us to where we are," explains Karl Schmid, the founder's son.

The Fred Schmid ESOP had been operating since 1981, and company officers credit it for the sales increase from $27 million to $62 million in five years. The strong ESOP made it easy to attract top managers from Macy's, Maytag, and Sears.

Linnton Plywood, described above, represents a different type of employee stock ownership—not an ESOP, but a worker-owned cooperative. The two differ in that ESOP stock owned by workers goes into a trust and is voted on by that trust. But once you buy a share in a cooperative, you get full voting rights as a member.

This cooperative model, developed in Mondragon, Spain, is slowly spreading in the United States. There are now some 200 worker-owned cooperatives here, most with fewer than fifty employee-owners, according to the Industrial Co-operative Association in Somerville, Massachusetts.

When Weirton Steel of Weirton, West Virginia, became the nation's largest employee-owned company in early 1984, few observers predicted the success it now enjoys. But Weirton turned profitable almost immediately, earning $9.7 million the first quarter and $60 million in 1984.

It was the first profit since 1981. The company brought back some 1,000 employees when the employees took over. Nearly 8,000 work there now.

Says Eugene Keilen, the Lazard Frères partner and chief architect of the Weirton ESOP, "This is not industrial democracy, it's worker capitalism."

Weirton's turnaround under employee ownership is impressive by any standard. But it raises a question: Why is it that so many companies being sold to employees are in dying smokestack industries and are companies that no one else wants and are about to close anyway?

Imagine what employee ownership could do for a sunrise company.

Actually, that is what the new information companies and others cited in this chapter have imagined and that is why they have re-invented their corporations with new types of ownership models and financial incentives.

4. We are shifting from hired labor to contract labor, which is part of a larger trend of contracting out for a variety of services.

Employee leasing, or contract staffing, which can staff either a department or a whole company, is enjoying a phenomenal boom. In 1983, fewer than 4,000 people were "leased." In 1984, there were between 50,000 and 60,000 according to industry estimates. But that growth is far from having peaked. It will be the coming seller's market that makes contract leasing a widespread alternative to traditional employment.

We think that within a decade, as many as 10 million of us will be "leased" employees.

One reason behind this phenomenal growth is that employee leasing eliminates what small-business people, including doctors and dentists, hate most—paperwork. Many are firing their employees and leasing them back from Contract Staffing of America, National Employee Leasing Co., Omnistaff, and similar firms.

For a set fee, usually ranging from between 20 and 35 percent over payroll, these companies take the hassle out of running a small business—payroll, taxes, Social Security, unemployment insurance, and benefits.

"I am really pleased," says lumberman Tony James, who

fired his employees then leased them back from Unistaff, a large contract staffer, in 1983.

"We have better benefits at a cheaper cost," says James. "One of our employees is sixty-one years old. Most group insurance plans would not cover her at all. With Unistaff, it didn't matter."

Because they employ thousands of people, employee-leasing firms can offer excellent benefits—100 percent dental and medical, free life insurance, tuition reimbursement, and immediate vesting in pension plans—at low cost.

Employees who were understandably nervous about being fired and rehired by some strange new company are now giving the contract firms high marks.

"I was crushed when I heard they were going to lease us," recalls Marilyn Smith, who had been with Phoenix Bone and Joint Surgeons twenty-three years before she was fired and leased. "I figured it was the end of the world and my job. Now my doctors are much happier; we have benefits we didn't have before, and if there are disadvantages, I haven't found them," she says.

It seems to be a win/win arrangement. Leased employees enjoy top benefits, and business owners outwit the paperwork.

"I generally save employers enough to pay for my fee," claims Eugene Schenk, head of Staffco, an employee-leasing firm. "And I've taken away all of the headaches."

"What our clients can buy in the market for $100 [in benefits], we can buy for $80," says James Borgelt, general manager of Omnistaff, a Dallas leasing firm which handles some 7,000 people.

For well-to-do professionals, there are tax benefits that make contract staffing almost irresistible. Doctors and dentists, for example, who often want to shelter as much income as possible in pension plans, legally must set up an equal plan for their employees. Not a likely prospect. But by leasing employees, a professional may be eligible to create a generous 7.5 percent fully vested pension fund for employees and a separate pension fund to shelter personal income.

Is employee leasing, then, just a tax loophole for wealthy professionals? It might be except for extraordinarily better benefits that accrue to the leased employees.

One of the fine points: Legally, the leasing company genuinely employs the staff and has the right to hire and fire people. The way it works out, though, the owner tends to exercise that right because he or she can accept or reject a leased employee. Owners can recruit people and turn the final selection over to the leasing company for processing. If someone has to be laid off, the leasing company can often find work for that person with another client.

Supplemental staffing for assembly lines is a growing new business. Over the last year, for example, Norrell Temporary Services has been responsible for about 20 percent of the assembly line workers each morning at both the Vicks and Squibb plants in Greensboro, North Carolina. Both companies want to maintain a core employee group and expand their assembly lines, accordionlike, week to week, as product demand fluctuates. They pay Norrell for taking on that responsibility.

Not everyone is enamored with employee leasing, though. Unions and personnel professionals tend to feel it cuts into their turf, to say the least.

There are some 200 employee-leasing or staffing companies in the United States, mostly in the West and Southwest. Omnistaff in Dallas says it bills more than $100 million annually. A pioneer in the industry and one of the largest is Contract Staffing of America (CSA), based in Tustin, California. CSA specializes in staffing doctors' and dentists' offices.

When a question arose about the legality of employee leasing, CSA hired Sheldon Cohen, a former IRS commissioner, to lobby Congress to change a law concerning employee benefits plans. Mr. Cohen was successful and business has been booming ever since. CSA, for example, grew from 400 employees to 1,500 and earned some $26 million in 1983.

Employee leasing may be the best way for *small* businesses to attract the best people during the coming seller's market.

Brent Kidd, owner of an air-conditioning business—an industry where competition for labor is intense—says turnover is down sharply since he started leasing. "A lot of the competition doesn't have health and pension plans, so my company attracts the best people. Now the only people who leave here are those who are asked to leave."

In a seller's market where there is terrific competition for good employees, companies will have to accommodate a variety of work-style preferences—flextime, part-time, job sharing, and other arrangements described in detail in the next chapter.

Two things will help: Computers, and companies that specialize in providing people by contract. Computers will help keep track of the complexity of having many employees on uncommon schedules. And companies, which until now have provided temporary help, usually clerical, will also provide contract staffing of people who want permanent part-time and job sharing.

5. The top-down authoritarian management style is yielding to a networking style of management, where people learn from one another horizontally, where everyone is a resource for everyone else, and where each person gets support and assistance from many different directions.

At some corporations, the new cooperative ethic is challenging the traditional notion of "healthy competition" among workers. Employees are learning to ask fellow workers for help rather than competitively going it alone or turning to a manager.

At Wilson Learning Corp., for example, a new salesperson can save time and energy using the "field-intelligence network," an internal system that draws on the knowledge of experienced salespeople to link people and needs.

Key data about a sales rep's knowledge of company products and familiarity with different industries are stored in a computer. New salespeople can call up the data for advice about how to market the company's products to a particular industry. An additional benefit is the network's tendency to promote "player-coach" relationships within the sales force.

For example, an account manager with three years experience in telecommunications took up the practice of telephoning new account manager Teresa Zambo, on a weekly basis.

"I was preparing to serve a Bell company in a different sales region and a different state. She became my mentor, inviting me to accompany her on sales calls and sharing with me her best written proposals," recalls Jane.

The player-coach relationship helps ease corporate transitions, too. When the mentor moved to Wilson's western region, she asked if Jane would move to Chicago and inherit her clients—many of whom Jane had already met.

At some companies, networking is institutionalized. Workers and managers exercise together during the day and have drinks together after work. Far from just condoning this fraternization, many companies foster it.

New York advertising agencies, such as Batten, Barton, Durstine & Osborne, and J. Walter Thompson, operate after-hours membership clubs open to everyone from the CEO to the mail clerk. The clubs are considered productive because they encourage intermingling, further deepening the sense of corporate culture and communication. Clients get a sense of the company spirit and meet the people who work on their ads but do not attend regular business meetings with the clients.

6. Many companies are re-inventing themselves as confederations of entrepreneurs, operating under the main tent of the corporation.

Intrapreneurs are people with entrepreneurial skills employed in corporations. But instead of leaving the company to undertake their ventures, they create these new businesses within the company. It is a win/win arrangement. The company retains a talented employee and an innovative new business; the employee gets the satisfaction of developing his or her idea without having to risk leaving the company and going into business.

It is an idea we wrote about in *Megatrends,* and it is a critical part of re-inventing the corporation.

By allowing the creative, intuitive entrepreneur to maintain control and responsibility for a venture, the corporation produces both a deeply satisfied employee and a healthier bottom line.

Sensing the need for change, American business has already incorporated many intrapreneurial features, especially in some of America's new high-tech and information companies.

IBM has an unwritten rule permitting technical managers to allot 15 percent of their budget to pet interests called "off-the-record" projects.

Here is one way in-company entrepreneurship is promoted at IBM, according to CEO John Akers:

"We also encourage entrepreneurship internally by a policy of transfer pricing. Transfer pricing means that each plant is responsible for putting a firm price on what it makes or does including sub-assembly work headed for another IBM plant. The plant has to deliver at that price and make a profit. If the price is too high, the receiver of that work is free to look elsewhere—either inside or outside the company—to obtain an alternate source. In other words, every step of our manufacturing process is compared to what is going on outside the business. Each step has to compete as a source of supply."

3M, where the intrapreneurial idea is most fully realized in the United States, requires that managers not only provide a good bottom line but also introduce at least 25 percent new products every five years.

The whole principle behind intrapreneurship is to use a company's existing resources—human, financial, and physical—to launch new businesses and generate new income. So it is logical that mature industries facing a more competitive market such as airlines are ideal candidates for intrapreneurial innovation.

"This industry needs every cent it can generate. We've got to be creative about using our huge asset base to develop new revenues," says American Airlines president Robert Crandall.

That remark shows that Crandall is asking the right question—"What business are we really in?" Whatever the problems in the airline business, that is a good sign.

But what do airlines do that could grow into an intrapreneurial venture?

They maintain their aircraft, train flight crews, and mastermind enormously complex telephone reservation services—all of which have become intrapreneurial subdivisions of major airlines:

- United Airlines makes $15 million per year training flight crews for other airlines.
- American's training arm, American Airlines Training Corp., made $1.8 million in profits on $37.7 million worth of training sales in 1983.
- American, United, TWA, Delta, and Eastern lease computerized reservation systems to travel agents. The system generated $100 million of income in 1983 at American Airlines alone.
- American's phone system, American Airlines Telemarketing Services, has signed up a natural though unusual client—the system will be used to take pledges for a religious fund-raising telethon.
- Frontier Airlines leases its planes through Frontier Leasco, Inc., while USAir took in $25.5 million in 1983 as an aircraft broker selling twenty-one planes.
- Contract maintenance is becoming a growth area because of deregulation: American Airlines expects to gross $100 million in ground services by 1986.

Admittedly, airlines have been operating some of these inside businesses for some time. And, so far as we know, they are not doing anything special to nurture the inside entrepreneurs their industry needs. Nevertheless, businesses are accomplishing what intrapreneurs set out to do: use the company's existing resources to generate new products and services—and ultimately more income.

Airlines that creatively combine existing assets with the spark of new ideas will survive and flourish, while those which continually wail about the perils of deregulation—the loss of protected markets—will go out of business.

The intrapreneur concept can work equally well in small business.

Terra Tek is a small Salt Lake City–based high-technology firm engaged in research services, product development, and new energy ventures. It employs only 150 people but that does not stop Terra Tek from awarding its own "innovation grants" modeled after the National Science Foundation's Small Business Innovation Awards Program.

The two to five innovation grants of not more than $10,000 each are awarded annually. They enable employees to pursue their own projects while innovating and enhancing the company's research capabilities. When a project becomes commercially viable, the employee assumes control of the new venture, which in time may even become a separate company owned jointly by the innovator and the parent company; the equity, however, remains in the hands of the innovator.

School for Intrapreneurs

The first School for Intrapreneurs was created in Sweden in 1980 by the Foresight Group, Gustaf Delin, Lennart Boksjö, and Sven Atterhed, three very entrepreneurial Swedes. Now the Foresighters have started up a U.S. School for Intrapreneurs.

The school will teach would-be intrapreneurs how to turn fuzzy ideas into business plans. Its aim is to become an "incubator and nursery" for commercially viable ideas.

The School for Intrapreneurs will operate according to the principle of "voluntary commitment," the same idea Bill Gore of W. L. Gore & Associates talks about.

Self-selection is one of the three main criteria the Foresighters use to select candidates for their program. Next they ask, "Is she or he both a visionary and a doer?" These, they feel, are the three most important traits of entrepreneurs. They believe the right person is far more important than a good idea.

"Even a 'not so good' idea supported by an entrepreneur—a champion—is much more precious and potentially success-

ful than a 'good idea' with only an 'administrator' behind
it,'' writes Gustaf Delin.

The first phase of the Foresight program is working with
top management to prepare the company, its management,
and the corporate environment for the new intrapreneurial
ventures.

Over the course of the program, the intrapreneur students
are charged with developing a viable business plan. The
Foresighters work on growing him or her into the sort of
individual who could execute it. Intrapreneurs-to-be are
coached on visualizing their goal-picture or vision, networking,
idea refining, and basic accounting. At midsession, they
face a critical test—venture capitalists are invited to a
session to critique plans.

Some interesting projects have emerged from the Swedish
school:

- Rolf Ahlsgren, a shift worker at AB Iggesunds Bruk
  pulp and paper mill, is building a 5,000-square-meter
  greenhouse heated by the company's excess heat. The
  computer-controlled climate will produce 125 tons of
  commercial grade tomatoes each year.
- Bengt Jonssons, head draftsman of Surahammars Bruks
  AB steel mill, will start up an eel farm in an abandoned
  section of the plant. It will produce more than 100 tons
  of eels annually.
- Bror Andersson, a salesman with Forssells Knoststens
  AB, a manufacturer of specialized prefabricated concrete stairways, will oversee a new business within the
  company. He will develop prefabricated concrete eleva-
  tor shafts that can be installed in existing buildings
  without knocking down walls to get them into place.
  The new business is enjoying a great deal of success
  due to Swedish laws requiring handicapped access to
  upper floors in many buildings. He is swamped with
  orders.

For a more detailed discussion of intrapreneurship, we suggest Gifford Pinchot's *Intrapreneuring,* published by Harper & Row.

Putting Entrepreneurship into the Curriculum

As the idea of entrepreneurship within the corporation becomes more popular, American business and business schools are re-inventing the business curriculum to teach this new idea.

For example, there were only 6 universities with courses or research centers on entrepreneurship in 1967. In 1984, there were 150, including a course on entrepreneurial management at the Harvard Business School.

But the newest area of interest concerns entrepreneurship within the corporation. Leading business schools have introduced courses on how big companies can develop new products and adapt to changing markets. At Harvard and at Northwestern University's J. L. Kellogg Graduate School, the hot new subjects are about rewarding employees for risk-taking and turning ideas into products.

American corporations such as Aluminum Co. of America and AT&T already have shown their interest by funding research on how to foster entrepreneurship in corporations. Many more will follow.

Corporations will pressure business schools "to put more emphasis on corporate entrepreneurship," according to Karl H. Vesper, a professor at the University of Washington and an authority on entrepreneurial education.

Intrapreneurship is one of the hottest ideas in corporate America today. And if companies are smart, they will encourage women to play a strong role in inside entrepreneurship. They are certainly doing so in the larger society. Women are creating as many as one-third of these new companies in our entrepreneurially driven economy.

When most corporate managers think entrepreneur or intrapreneur, they see a man. That's very much out of date.

7. In the re-invented corporation, quality will be paramount.

Following World War II, we had rising incomes and declining prices for several decades. We didn't care very much that we bought a new washing machine or, later, a new TV set every few years because it was always cheaper and better. Those cycles are over, and today across the board, top to bottom, people are very concerned about quality.

"For successful products, services, and companies in the 1980s, quality is what's under the skin of beauty. To the consumer, value equals the sum of quality products, quality service, a quality environment, quality employee relations, and quality community involvement," says New York advertising man Steve Arbeit. "Consumers perceive quality in terms of the whole, not just the parts; a company must offer quality in the totality of its dealings with the public."

Author Tom Peters says, "We're watching a renewed focus in virtually every industry in this country on quality and quality products, aimed at somewhat special market niches." He quotes Campbell Soup chairman Gordon McGovern as saying, "Above all, we've got to teach our people to focus on quality first, cost second."

In their search for quality, people seem to be looking for permanency in a time of change.

Quality is represented in a changing ratio between mass and information in goods and services, as described by Paul Hawken in his book *The Next Economy*. For example,

Hawken points out that cars have shed up to 2,000 pounds of metal (mass), but they are now built with microprocessors in the engine and on the dashboards (information).

This shift in the mass/information ratio is a shift to higher quality and is characteristic of the new information economy. Homes are getting smaller, though they are becoming more intelligent as we apply microprocessors to functions of all kinds. And let's not forget the personal computer.

In the increasing demand for quality, the consumer is about to get a powerful new tool: computer software programs to evaluate the quality of goods and services. There are a few on the market today, but thousands are being worked on. We may be moving toward a truly consumer-ruled economy. Let the seller beware.

8. Intuition is gaining a new respectability in the corporate world, which has been run by numbers for so long.

Although it has not been talked about much, intuition has always been part of corporate life. The most successful CEOs use intuition regularly in planning and decision-making. Professor Henry Mintzbert of McGill University concludes from extensive study that the top CEO is a "holistic, intuitive thinker who . . . is constantly relying on hunches to cope with problems far too complex for rational analysis."

In a later chapter, we will discuss the new skills of the information society. One of these is creativity, the key element of which is intuition—the ability to perceive knowledge without reasoning.

But our formal education system has methodically excised the intuitive in favor of the rational. What little intuition remains after high school and college is drummed out in formal business schools.

Intuition becomes increasingly valuable in the new information society precisely because there is so much data.

In fact, there is so much information about such complex issues that it is often impossible to take it all in. One has to learn to rely on intuition.

In a test at Newark College of Engineering, eleven of twelve company presidents who had doubled sales in the previous four years scored abnormally high in precognition. A control group of presidents with average records showed no such special talents.

Similarly, Weston Angor, a corporate consultant on intuition and a professor at the University of Texas at El Paso, tested 2,000 managers at all corporate levels and found that *top* managers in every organization rated significantly higher in intuition than middle or low-level managers.

Peter Senge believes that intuition plays a key role in carrying out the CEO's all-important task of creating alignment, especially in dealing with complex, highly uncertain business decisions. He notes that successful entrepreneurs score well above average on tests of intuitive ability such as precognition and remote viewing.

Most businesspeople, however, usually do not call it "intuition," but rather "judgment." David Mahoney, former chairman of Norton Simon, credits his "judgment" with helping to make his most difficult business decisions.

Was it judgment or intuition that got People Express through the 1981 air traffic controllers' strike, which cut flights at home base Newark airport by 35 percent?

People Express, at the time a fledgling company, lost $6 million in a few months. "We were bleeding at a terrific rate. . . . We were going out of business," recalls CEO Don Burr.

The firm concocted a survival strategy—flying to Florida out of uncongested, unrestricted airports such as Columbus, Buffalo, and Baltimore—but the numbers were no help in deciding whether to risk it. The company's research failed to show whether there was a market for these flights.

Don Burr and People Express decided, in effect, to follow their hunch. "We had to bet the company a second time," says Burr.

The hunch paid off. People eagerly bought the airline's $59 tickets—to the tune of an 85 percent load factor. People Express stayed alive and went on to become the fastest growing company in U.S. history.

So much for the numbers, market research, and behaving rationally.

9. Large companies are discovering that to compete in a changing marketplace, they must adopt many of the values of small business.

John Kenneth Galbraith once said: "There is no more pleasant fiction than that technological change is the product of the matchless ingenuity of the small man forced to employ his wits to better his neighbor. Unhappily, it is a fiction. . . ."

It is a commentary on how much our values have changed in recent years that Galbraith's words ring so hollow and seem so archaic.

In a matter of a mere decade or so, the values of small business have become America's values.

The entrepreneur has become America's new hero. Two new magazines, *Inc.* and *Venture,* which began in spring 1979, now have subscriptions of 600,000 and nearly 300,000 respectively. *Inc.* and *Venture* have become the new *Forbes* and *Fortune* for a generation of Americans who are investing in their own businesses instead of in blue chips.

But equally noteworthy is the new homage being paid to

small business by Fortune 500 companies that previously
could not spare the time of day. The same is true of the
media that cover the big companies: *Forbes* does its own
version of the Inc. 500 fastest-growing small companies—
the Forbes Up & Comer 300, a list of highly profitable
small to midsize companies. This would have been almost
unthinkable at *Forbes* only five years ago.

Cheerleaders for small business (such as ourselves)
have long pointed to the studies that prove small is not
just beautiful but more productive. Inspired by the pro-
entrepreneurial values espoused in *In Search of Excellence*
and *The Spirit of Enterprise,* the big businesses themselves
are taking another look at what is making small business run
and what is attracting billions of investment dollars out of
the stock market and into embryonic ventures.

Many large companies watched small businesses get the
jump on them in the marketplace. IBM, one of the best
managed companies in the world, watched Digital Equipment Corp. take the lead in minicomputers and Apple in
personal computers. Clearly, the strategies that once worked
so well are out of date in a new marketplace and an
economic environment that seems to favor small businesses
and individuals who can move fast.

For IBM, It's Back to the Garage

As a result, a host of companies from IBM to Xerox and
NCR are forging new strategies aimed at applying what is
best about small business—its knack for innovation, team
spirit, and swiftness—to their own virtues of stability, financial muscle, and security.

IBM's response to Apple was to duplicate as nearly as
possible the same environment that fostered the creativity
behind Apple's success. IBM spun off a number of "independent business units" (IBUs), teams designed to be small
enough and flexible enough to move in the volatile high-tech

markets. As is well known, the computer giant developed the phenomenally successful IBM PC in one of these IBUs outside the company's hierarchy.

"If you're competing against people who started in a garage, you have to start in a garage," says Don Estridge, who led the group that came up with the PC. Estridge's Boca Raton–based outfit started in August 1980 with twelve hungry people on a limited budget, highly unattractive surroundings, a lot of zeal, and freedom from IBM headquarters in Armonk, New York.

IBM people think this approach combines the best of both worlds. Says the marketing director of one IBU, "It's like having a fighter who can move like a lightweight and hit like a heavyweight."

In the book *The Soul of a New Machine,* author Tracy Kidder painted a vivid portrait of this kind of high-energy small-team innovation at Data General in Westborough, Massachusetts.

NCR re-invented itself into a more entrepreneurial company made up of independent units after a McKinsey & Co. study showed that NCR's functional organization style— which separated development, production, and marketing— was holding back product development and creating barriers against innovation.

Reorganizations, of course, are nothing new, but in the past they have been inspired mostly by financial considerations, rather than by a new "small is beautiful" philosophy.

NCR's new system promotes autonomy. A unit within the company, for example, is now free to buy components from the outside if they are cheaper or better.

Don Coleman, NCR's vice-president in charge of the 3,000-person Data Entry Systems Division, thrived under the new system. His division was responsible for NCR's entry into the competitive personal computer market.

Describing himself in the old system, Coleman says, "I didn't put ideas forward as an individual. I did think things could be improved, though, and now I find myself in a position where I have been told to put up or shut up. . . . Now if you screw up, they know it's you, and if you win, they know it's you.''

One of Coleman's notable wins is NCR's self-service terminals for gas stations, hotels, ski lifts, and airlines, a concept which grew from idea to installed product within five months—impossible under NCR's old regime. Another measure of success: 50 percent of his division's annual revenue came from products it did not sell the year before.

New Big- and Small-Business Alliances

Noticing that start-up companies are attracting venture capital for the simple reason that they stand to make a lot of money, large companies such as Xerox, Exxon, Monsanto, and Standard Oil (Indiana) are seeking the benefits of small business by creating ''special relationships.''

General Electric is an excellent example. When GE decided to get into biotechnology, it invested $3 million to fund Biological Energy Company, a start-up biotech firm. By 1984, GE had invested a total of $100 million in some thirty start-up companies.

In these new alliances, the larger company might own a minority interest, say between 20 and 40 percent, in exchange for putting up capital like a venture capitalist.

But whatever the terms, they are emphatically not the acquisitions of the past, which tended to drain away the very vitality the large company was seeking.

''There is a natural temptation to go in and overlay your own reporting procedures, your own benefit plans, sometimes your own management people,'' says Wayland R. Hicks, a Xerox vice-president. Xerox watched as the founders of two key 1970s acquisitions quit their jobs to start their own business away from Xerox's watchful corporate eye. Says Xerox's Wayland, "You create frustration, and, to an extent, you stifle creativity."

Instead, these new relationships are designed to foster the entrepreneurial spirit and independence of a small company, which, the larger firms admit, their corporate environment could easily destroy.

"These are brilliant, independent individuals we could more than likely never employ," says the president of one firm that has started investing in smaller companies.

One secret behind the continued success of re-invented companies such as W. L. Gore & Associates and Kollmorgen is their success in preserving structures in which people feel they are working in a small company. These companies kept the spirit of their early years while growing into successful firms that could have been threatened by bureaucracy.

W. L. Gore starts planning to open a new factory whenever there are more than 150 associates at the same place. Two hundred is the maximum number. It is expensive, Bill and Vieve Gore concede, but worth it. Gore now has thirty plants and eight more under construction.

In plants and units limited to 150 people, everyone knows everyone else, but more important, everyone knows what everyone else's role is in relation to the whole.

At Kollmorgen Corp., corporate fission occurs whenever an operation grows too large.

"We believe that divisions which get too big lose vitality, family atmosphere, and easy, informal internal communication," says Robert Swiggett. When there are more than a couple hundred people, a new unit breaks away to form an autonomous profit center run by a small team.

Kollmorgen's philosophy is that "freedom and respect for the individual are the best motivators, especially when innovation and growth are the objectives."

10. In the information society, we are shifting from infrastructure to quality of life.

During the long industrial period, when we wanted to locate a plant, we looked to the infrastructure, transportation, natural resources, water (for both energy and transportation), proximity to market. In this new information/electronics economy, we can locate a facility anywhere we want, and do not have to be concerned with infrastructure.

So we look to the quality of life: good climate, good schools, cultural opportunities, recreational opportunities, and, increasingly, opportunities for two-career couples. It is an old industrial idea to persuade a big company to locate a plant in our backyard. The big companies are no longer creating the new jobs or the new wealth-creating capacity. This is an entrepreneurially driven economy.

The new strategy in the competition for economic development is to create an environment that is nourishing to entrepreneurs.

The Boston area has such an environment. And it is the biggest city by far to have shifted from the old industrial economy to the new information economy. Today in the Boston area, there is already that seller's market that is soon to come to much of the rest of the country. Boston has achieved this in the face of the extraordinary economic and population momentum to the Southwest and in Florida.

The quality-of-life point is made here. While Boston's winters leave something to be desired, the ambience otherwise is hard to match. There are sixty-five universities and colleges in the Boston area. It is arguably our greatest concentration of culture and has great recreational opportunities. All in all, a great environment in which to grow information companies.

And now the Massachusetts High Tech Council (167 companies, most around Route 128) wants to push on to even higher levels with a new high-tech agenda for the rest of the 1980s. The new agenda proclaims as its goal a Massachusetts that would be the "world's most attractive location for creating, operating and expanding high technology business."

Boston's Route 128 is "America's high-technology highway"; California has Silicon Valley, but few of us realize that Oregon's great quality of life is attracting new ventures in record numbers.

One of the most beautiful states, Oregon faces the Pacific rim where there will be enormous opportunities for growth in the decades ahead. There is a two-hour overlap between the Portland and Tokyo workdays, a great advantage for joint ventures with the Japanese. It will come as a surprise to some that Portland is ranked tenth among U.S. cities for electronics companies; the Japanese call it Silicon Forest. Since Oregon repealed its unitary tax in 1984, four major electronics companies—NEC, Seico, Kyocera, and Fujitsu— have announced plans to invest hundreds of millions of dollars in building manufacturing plants in the Portland area by 1987.

Importantly, Portland has a large pool of entrepreneurially minded engineers. Home-grown Tektronix, Inc.—a $41.3-billion computer instrumentation company—has lost scores of its employees who have started new companies in the Portland area. Many of its citizens are worried about the effect of all this economic growth on the area's quality of life, which of course is what attracted the growth in the first place.

Companies are increasingly locating offices where creative people say they want to be. Amdahl Corporation, the computer company, opened a Dallas office to attract research engineers. IBM has recently opened research offices in Boca Raton, Florida; San Jose, California; Austin, Texas;

and Boulder, Colorado. All these cities have an ambience, a quality of life, that is attractive to creative people who can locate pretty much where they want to. And that is a most important factor.

Rating Places for Quality of Life

A sign of the times: all the controversy created when Rand McNally's *Places Rated Almanac* named Pittsburgh the best place to live in the United States and Yuma, California, the worst. The last time the almanac came out in 1981, it was hardly noticed, but now that we are more deeply entrenched in the information society, the ambience factor is recognized as a key factor not just for individuals, but for corporations.

The *Almanac* evaluated 329 metropolitan areas according to eight factors—climate, housing costs, health care, crime, transportation, education, recreational and cultural opportunities, and economics—all very appropriate criteria for measuring quality of life.

What is interesting to note about Pittsburgh's rating is that it did not rank first in any of the eight categories, but it ranked relatively high in enough categories to win the top score. On the other hand, a community that rates very high in a few categories—education, cultural opportunities, health care, for example, and is above average for most of the others—might well be considered a better place to live than Pittsburgh. Philadelphia, New York, Chicago, Los Angeles, and Washington, D.C., fit that profile.

Communities, like companies, can discover their market niche in the quality of life market and develop a strategy for specializing in those areas of ambience.

In summary, these are the most important considerations in re-inventing the corporation:

To attract the brightest people, companies will have to

consciously create an environment for learning and growth. Central to this will be the manager's new role: to coach, to teach, to nurture. To keep people motivated and productive, the best companies are exploring a range of new financial incentives from performance bonuses to employee stock-option plans. The people in the re-invented corporation, however, will not all be employed there, but many will increasingly be leased from contract staffing firms.

We are re-inventing the corporation from a top-down bureaucracy into a network where everyone learns from everyone else.

The new economy is once again an entrepreneurially driven economy. That has inspired and instructed established companies to emphasize entrepreneurial activities inside the corporation—or intrapreneurship.

Add to these considerations the growing consumer demand for quality across the board, the need to foster many of the values of small business, as well as the need to get away from running companies strictly by the numbers and to learn to use intuition effectively. Today's new information company can locate in America's (or the world's) most attractive cities and towns—places where the most creative people would enjoy living.

3

Re-inventing Work

There is a new ideal about work emerging in America today. For the first time, there is a widespread expectation that work should be fulfilling—and that work should be fun.

Thirty years ago, that would have been an outrageous notion. And in the parts of corporate America still run according to industrial values, it still is. Nevertheless, people know intuitively that work ought to be fun and satisfying, even when it is not.

Today, however, the same forces which are re-inventing the corporation are transforming this deep human need into a realistic expectation in the workplace. The economic demands of the information society together with the new values of the baby boom generation are fostering the ''work should be fun'' idea.

For millions of baby boomers, this new ideal is not outrageous; it is natural. Affluent and extremely well educated, they grew up believing life should be fun—and work, too. Who put this strange notion into their heads?

Oddly enough, it was probably their own parents, who grew up in the Depression and toiled in the factories of industrial America. For the parents of the baby boom, work was quite possibly *not* fun. Determined that their children would have more education and more of everything, parents sacrificed for their children's sake. And succeeded in giving them what they had lacked.

But the education and affluence change people's expectations. Result: The "work should be fun" ethic has begun to displace the puritan ethic, which holds that work is honorable and valuable in and of itself, that work must have some drudgery attached.

That new value is becoming the dominant attitude in today's workplace. Some 40 percent of the work force has adopted (at least in part) the notion that work should be personally satisfying rather than valuable for its own sake, according to Stephen A. Zimney of Yankelovich, Skelly & White, the New York market research firm, which has studied people's attitudes toward work for the past thirteen years.

Though appalling to traditionalists, that new value is remarkably suited to the needs of the information society. People doing information work, for example, are far more difficult to supervise than those performing manual tasks. Yet they are by definition more committed. When you work in your head, do thinking work, you cannot leave it behind at the office with the punching of a time clock. When people enjoy their work, they do a better job and need less supervision. In effect, they manage themselves.

Furthermore, when your company depends on human capital rather than on equipment and financial capital, you want people to be happy. That way they are more productive. People who are having fun at work are aligned with their company's goal. And in a seller's market, companies where people enjoy their work attract the best new talent.

The New Worker

The exciting thing about work today is that there is a growing new compatibility between the needs of people and the needs of companies in the information society.

But you would never know it by looking at most of the American workplace—which today is still organized to fit the industrial society of thirty years ago. Then the average worker:

- was a white male breadwinner with a wife and children to support,
- who worked full-time either in an office or in a factory,
- who either belonged to a union or would join one,
- who was about forty and would retire at sixty-five,
- who was motivated by job security and steady pay,
- and who, though he might work in an office, lived in an industrial society.

But this "average worker" is no more. As the industrial society became an information society, the U.S. labor force changed dramatically.

There is a new minority in the American work force: white males.

"For the first time, white males, the prototype of the American worker since the beginning of the nation, no longer make up the majority of the country's workforce," writes William Serrin in *The New York Times*.

In 1954, white males were in the majority, 62.5 percent of the work force. By June 1984, they had become the minority, only 49.3 percent.

The profile of today's average worker looks something like this:

- a thirty-four-year-old baby boomer with two children and a working spouse,
- who plans to work past retirement (and expects to because of the insecurities of the Social Security system),
- who does not belong to a union and would not consider joining one,
- who is willing to accept a certain amount of risk in exchange for the possibility of being rewarded for superior performance,
- who is increasingly likely to have some sort of flexible work schedule—or would prefer one.
- increasingly, that "average worker" is a woman.

Into this new business environment has come a new work force motivated by considerations that did not apply in the 1950s.

There is some good news and some bad news about the new worker.

The good news is that he or she possesses the exact talents needed by today's newly re-invented corporations—an entrepreneurial spirit, the ability to nurture others, and the desire for self-management.

The bad news is that the workplace is so poorly organized to take advantage of these valuable qualities that she may not stick around long enough to discover that fit.

The unspoken factor behind the entrepreneurial boom is that working for most companies is so demeaning to the human spirit that many talented people are forced out the door.

The only way to have a nurturing work environment, they reason, is to create it themselves.

*   *   *

The New Work Contract

The information economy in which all that entrepreneurship
is happening plays to the importance of the individual,
whereas in the industrial society, the focus was the group,
the assembly line—which contributed to the growth of
unions. When people work together now, in small teams, for
example, the idea is to cooperate as individuals, not to
blend into a group where everyone is the same.

Today, we are re-inventing the world of work to shift
from unions—that industrial creation which demanded that
everyone be treated the same—to individualized work contracts. Flexible benefit plans, flexible scheduling, and computers make it possible.

Instead of collective bargaining, people are negotiating
unique arrangements based on a coming together of the
company's need for human capital to achieve corporate
goals and the individual's desire to grow and develop his or
her talent while earning income and enjoying a set of useful
benefits.

The union movement is dead. Today, only 17 percent of
the U.S. work force is organized. In the private sector, only
15 percent is unionized. And in the economically dynamic
South and West, only 5 percent of the work force belongs to
a union. Because unions don't understand the need to
re-invent themselves to fit the information society, their
decline and eventual demise seem certain.

The New Ideal: Self-management

We are shifting the ideal of the model employee from one
who carries out orders correctly to one who takes responsibility and initiative, monitors his or her own work, and uses
managers and supervisors in their new roles of facilitators,
teachers, and consultants.

Throughout corporate America, there is evidence that people are increasingly expected to manage themselves.

At the General Motors plant in Fitzgerald, Georgia, self-managing work teams make many decisions that management made in the past.

Honeywell vice-chairman James Renier let go of some 1,400 middle managers within weeks of assuming control of the firm's computer division. Summing up this corporate shift from middle management to self-management, he expressed preference for a management style which "lets people do their jobs and tell you what expertise they need."

The same refrain is being echoed across corporate America. John Welch, chairman of General Electric, puts it this way: "If you pick the right people and give them the opportunity to spread their wings—and put compensation as a carrier behind it—you almost don't have to manage them."

Self-management presumes independence, self-confidence, and competence, values which are increasingly important in the new worker because of several trends:

1. Computers are taking information out of the hands of middle managers and placing it into the hands of individuals. And people who use their brains at work cannot be managed the way foremen supervised industrial workers. So management must rely on the individual to be motivated to produce high-quality work.
2. The whittling away of middle management, discussed in an earlier chapter, will mean, quite simply, that there will be fewer people around to manage others.
3. The shift from hierarchies to networking means that it matters less who your boss is (or how well the boss "manages" you), more how well you make the right connections with a supportive mentor or a sponsor to champion your ideas and contributions.
4. There is a growing recognition that the person who

knows the most about a job is the one doing it as expressed in the rise of quality control circles.

5. The new corporate structures—cross-disciplinary teams, partnerships, independent business units, and "skunkworks" (highly motivated, entrepreneurial teams)—emphasize innovation, not seniority or position.

These factors are pushing us toward the inevitable: Companies today do not have the time, the personnel, or the resources to monitor people carefully. People have to manage themselves. Besides, people perform better when they manage themselves.

People cannot be supervised into getting it right. They have to bring the spirit of getting it right with them to the job.

The company's job is to create an environment which fosters that positive attitude and reinforces it with recognition, financial incentives, and opportunities for personal growth.

Hewlett-Packard vice-president Bill Parzybok says, "I tell division managers if they have a profit problem, I give 'em about two years to fix it. But if they have a people problem, I give them about two weeks."

Don Burr, president and chairman of People Express—where each individual holds the job title of manager and is expected literally to manage him- or herself—says, "People are the glory and frustration of People Express. We thought longer and harder about building our people structures than anything else."

Self-management: How Close Are We?

But how many of us know how to manage ourselves?

America's great strength is people, well educated, ethnically diverse, still full of the incentive to achieve economic success.

Yet today, people seem confused about work.

We say we want to work hard, but we often work just hard enough to get by. On the one hand:

- A 1980 Gallup poll showed that 88 percent of Americans want to "work hard and to do the best on the job."
- More than half of the people interviewed for a 1983 Public Agenda Foundation study coauthored by Daniel Yankelovich of the research firm of Yankelovich, Skelly and White said they have an inner need to do the very best job *regardless of pay*.

On the other hand:

- Half of the same people said they worked just hard enough to avoid getting fired.
- Seventy-five percent said they could be "significantly more effective on the job."

When asked why they do not work hard, they had two answers: (1) They do not get paid any more for working harder, and (2) managers provide little incentive to work hard.

Are people confused about work or is the workplace confused about people? It is becoming clearer and clearer that it is the workplace that is out of step with today's workers.

People want the satisfaction of knowing that their work is competent, respected, and effective. The vast majority of our workplaces are not structured to offer that satisfaction. What do people want in a job?

The 1983 Public Agenda Foundation study came up with these top ten qualities people want in a job today:

1. work with people who treat me with respect
2. interesting work
3. recognition for good work
4. chance to develop skills
5. working for people who listen if you have ideas about how to do things better
6. a chance to think for myself rather than just carry out instructions
7. seeing the end results of my work
8. working for efficient managers
9. a job that is not too easy
10. feeling well informed about what is going on

Notice that job security, high pay, and good benefits are not even on the top ten list (they made the top fifteen, though). Yet most companies deal with people as if security, pay, and benefits were the only ways to motivate them.

That is ironic, since those psychic rewards people want—challenging work, personal growth, learning new skills, autonomy, participation, respect, acknowledgment, effective management, and information—are exactly what business needs now.

If people did not already want these things, business would have to find a way to sell them these ideas, because these are the qualities corporations need to flourish in the new information era.

The problem is that we are still running our offices in the old industrial mode where people used to punch in their time clocks and get paid for showing up.

We should be re-inventing the workplace to take advantage of the natural alignment that exists unfulfilled between the corporation's economic needs and the new worker's values.

The new models and guidelines discussed in this chapter

facilitate that natural yet largely unrecognized confluence between people's desires and values and the needs of today's companies. Like the considerations listed in Chapter 2, they are tools to use in re-inventing the workplace.

The New Strategy: Life/Work Planning

The new American work ethic holds that work should be fulfilling and fun, an integrated part of a whole life plan. More and more of us believe that work should accomplish a personal or social mission.

"Americans are weighing the rewards of conventional success against less lucrative but more satisfying personal achievements and are seriously considering the latter...if they can afford to...," writes Daniel Yankelovich in *New Rules: Searching for Self-Fulfillment in a World Turned Upside Down.*

Today, work must provide more than just a paycheck. We want it to express ourselves and our values, to make a difference in society, and to fit harmoniously with other priorities—family, health, spirituality.

That challenging new ideal is fueling the growth of a new breed of career consultant whose special mission is helping people integrate life and work. Today's career gurus share one simple precept: Deciding what you want to do is the first step—only then can you plan how to do it.

"You don't start out saying, 'I need a job,'" says John Crystal of the John Crystal Center, one of the leading teachers of life/work planning. "You start by asking, 'What do I want to do with my life?'"

That stands in sharp contrast to the average job hunter, a stereotypically humble soul who does not know what he or she wants to do and "will take anything" or will take a job because it "sounds interesting."

Life/work planning is not just for people out of work. It can also benefit companies by supplying the missing piece in the puzzle of re-inventing the corporation. The only way that corporate metamorphosis can come about is from the bottom up through people who are self-motivated and self-directed.

"From the organization's standpoint, the most difficult person to manage is the person who has no idea what he or she wants to do," says Buck Blessing, who consults on employee career planning with Exxon, Johnson & Johnson, Sperry Univac, and others.

Planned or not, America has become a job-hopping society—an added boon to the new life/career consultants. One-third of all Americans switch jobs each year!

"All over the country, a generation of professionals is career hopping. . . . Lawyers are becoming teachers, teachers are becoming accountants, doctors and dentists are going into real estate," says *Newsweek*.

To be sure, changing technology and the shift to an information society propels many job changes. But the new "work should be fun" ideal plays a role, too.

"It's more like divorce," says Susan Manring, assistant director at the Center for Management and Developmental Research, the Weatherford School of Management. "People realize that unhappiness is not their lot."

The life/work planning model is designed to eliminate much of that unhappiness by getting you to envision your perfect job, inventory your skills exhaustively, discover how to transfer those skills to the job of your dreams. Only then can you take the next step and negotiate with a company to hire you, perhaps for a job that does not yet exist.

But is the job market ready for this new self-assured job seeker?

The world stands aside for the person who knows where he or she is going.

That is what John Crystal says. Crystal is a former

intelligence officer who discovered the life/work planning system working on his own job search in the early 1950s, when he tried to transfer his cloak-and-dagger skills to the business world. Eventually, he was spending all his spare time coaching his friends in the job process that had worked for him.

Millions of people learned about life/work planning in *What Color Is Your Parachute?* by Richard Bolles, an Episcopal priest who came across John Crystal while trying to discover how to help out-of-work clergy.

"A genius named John Crystal emptied his file drawers (via the mails) onto my desk," says Bolles. *Parachute* became a classic. After five years on *The New York Times* best-seller list, it still sells 20,000 copies per month. Bolles and Crystal later collaborated on a life/work planning workbook called *Where Do I Go from Here with My Life?*

A small but growing number of trained counselors teach life/work planning. Richard Bolles's organization, the National Career Development Project in Walnut Creek, California, provides a list of their graduate instructors.

John Crystal was the principal consultant when Hal and Marilyn Shook founded Life Management Services (LMS) in McLean, Virginia, in the early 1970s, the decade when the work force swelled with all those baby boomers and new women workers. Crystal left Virginia to start a New York office. Hal and Marilyn Shook, an energetic, enormously supportive husband-wife team, have taught their life/work planning course to thousands of people throughout the United States.

Through the LMS program, for example, Leia Fransisco charted new goals to combine her experience in communications, management, and personal development. Within four years, she had shifted from academia to career development. Today she directs the Reentry Women's Employment Center in Fairfax, Virginia.

In 1977, Bill Fox left Admiral Rickover's navy with high expectations and dreams about his new freedom. Five years later, he was disappointed, dissatisfied, and ready to confront his future at an LMS weekend class. "It was tough at first, but then the process started to work. I knew these tools would help me identify my values and realize my goals for the rest of my life," Bill said.

Using those "tools," Bill found an exciting new job in his company, becoming a project leader for implementing a formal management control system which transformed the way an electronic manufacturing company operates.

"The focus here is on the whole person," says Marilyn Shook. "People look at their lives and ask, 'Where does my job fit in?'" They ask those questions during a five-week class or an intensive weekend course at a local mountain retreat.

At the LMS course, you write your autobiography and read it to classmates who often point out skills you have missed. You think about what you would do if you had no financial worries—an exercise designed to draw forth your deepest interests. You determine the environments where you would be most productive. In a structured, systematic way you find which companies best match your work style. To get an idea of where the society is going and plan your life accordingly, you read books like *The Aquarian Conspiracy, Encounters with the Future,* and *Megatrends.*

What Do I Really Want to Do with My Life?

But most important, you explore the big questions: Who am I? What are my personal priorities? What are my values and strengths? What do I really want to do with my life?

Once you decide where you are going in your life and work, you develop a game plan for getting there by answering questions like: What further learning or job experience do I need? What is the ideal company for me to work for? How do I research a company's needs? How do I write a proposal to create a new position which synthesizes the company's needs and my work objective? You become, in effect, your own entrepreneur. And companies that hire entrepreneurs know they have productive people.

This fancy notion that work should be something more than work emerged during the late 1960s and 1970s when the baby boom generation came of age. The affluence of the baby boom's parents bought the education that opened their minds to the dual goals of doing your own thing and contributing to society. The happiest, most successful people have synthesized those potentially contradictory goals.

The parents of the baby boom rarely expected so much from work. Work was not supposed to be fun; work was, well, work. That was their attitude. And the theme of many a generation-gap squabble. Nevertheless, sending their children to college opened the door to the "work should be fun" ethic and ushered in the beginning of life/work planning.

Will Flexible Work Scheduling Become the Norm?

The industrial model of regular, full-time, eight-hours-a-day work was perfectly suited to the needs of a male head of household with a family to support and a wife to run the home.

In addition to cooking, child care, and keeping house, the wife handled all the family and personal business—shopping, laundry, the dry cleaning, the bank, conferences with teachers, and on and on. No wonder the industrial man could work full-time—he had nothing else to do!

(Hence the declaration of the early feminists, "What I need is a wife.")

But in today's work force of single adults and two-career families, everyone has two permanent full-time jobs, the one you get paid for and the one you do for free—life, which the wife used to do and which is the reason why people want and need flexible work schedules.

As early as 1978, a survey by the National Commission on Employment Policy showed that some 65.5 percent of the American work force wanted to work fewer hours and would accept a smaller paycheck to do so.

Now more than one-fifth of the American work force have job sharing, flextime, or permanent part-time jobs. But in the coming seller's market, more companies will have to offer these alternatives to get the labor they need. That is why we agree with Work in America Institute's projection that half of us will be on alternate work schedules by the end of this decade.

Flexible scheduling is the work style of the self-managing information worker.

Several important trends are reinforcing the push for flexible job styles.

- Most important, the trend toward dual-earner couples means more people can *afford* to work less than full-time. We are moving toward what Swedish scholar Lennart Arvedson calls the "total employment society," where more people want to work—but less than full-time.
- In this society of lifelong learning, more and more of us will want to work part-time to upgrade skills and retool for new careers.
- In this entrepreneurial society, the part-time option helps pay the bills while starting a new business.

That people need more time is not news to anyone in a two-career family or to anyone trying to balance school, work, and family. What is happening now, though, is that companies are discovering or soon will discover that alternative work patterns are not a fad, but a key direction in which the workplace is headed.

Like the rest of the social change described in this book, the new models are being fueled by a confluence of personal values and economic necessity:

The seller's market in human capital (economic) will force companies to accommodate to vastly different work styles (values).

Just in time to help that trend is a body of corporate experience showing that workers in flexible jobs come to work alert, refreshed, and ready to perform.

Flextime

Quite simply, flextime is the cheapest yet most appreciated benefit a company can offer. People on flextime can usually vary their arrival and departure times but not their core work hours when the employer needs their presence.

It is a win/win arrangement. People get to manage their own time, and companies get better morale, increased productivity, and less absenteeism and tardiness. As of 1980, 12 percent of the work force used flextime, according to the Bureau of Labor Statistics. Unfortunately, BLS cannot provide a more recent figure on flextime. But Stanley Nollen, a Georgetown University professor who wrote a book on alternative work schedules, estimates that 15 to 16 percent of the workplace now operates on flextime.

It may come as a shock to learn that one of the great pioneers in flextime is the United States government: People in nearly all federal agencies can vary their schedules within each two-week pay period. After a three-year trial, flextime won acceptance from a majority of government supervisors.

If the conservative, stodgy U.S. government can embrace flextime, so can your company. Some of the most prestigious corporations have successful programs.

- At Hewlett-Packard you can start work at 6:00 A.M., 7:00 A.M., or 8:00 A.M.
- Control Data notes that tardiness and absenteeism decreased since the advent of flextime.
- Metropolitan Life of New York, a flextime employer since 1974, reports increased productivity when workers schedule their hours.
- Conoco in Houston switched to flextime in 1976. People there like arriving as early as 6:45 because they can get a lot done before the telephone starts ringing.
- Meredith, the Des Moines–based publisher of magazines such as *Better Homes and Gardens* and *Metropolitan Home,* used flextime in the office and the compressed workweek in the pressrooms.

In that extreme variation of flextime—the compressed workweek—people work four 10-hour days, or even three 12-hour days. It works best when companies want to maximize the use of equipment and/or cover unpopular shifts and when the people in companies really want large blocks of free time (and less commuting).

At Quad/Graphics, for example, people work three 12-hour days per week and alternate getting three or four days off. When the company switched to this new schedule, productivity increased 20 percent—this at an already highly effective firm known for self-management.

Firestone and Goodyear pay people for 36 hours of work if they work two 12-hour shifts on the weekend. They are then entitled to take the rest of the week off.

Compressed workweeks are not everybody's cup of tea. In 1980, Georgetown's Stanley Nollen studied 215 companies that used compressed weeks and found that 59 later declared the experiment a failure. Employees grew tired, car pools were difficult to organize, and family problems resulted.

But that was in 1980, and although we know of no more recent studies, the positive experience of Quad/Graphics makes one wonder why compressed schedules are not more popular. The key may be in how effectively people can use leisure time. There is a big difference between the stereotypical auto- or steelworker sitting around the house and drinking beer all day, watching TV and driving the family crazy, and the new worker who might be attending school, starting a new business, or training for a marathon.

Beyond Flextime

In Europe, where thousands of companies use flextime, the "flex-week" model—in which hours are rearranged over a week's time—has become a "flex-year."

Munich's Beck-Feldmeier KG department store contracts with employees to work a certain number of hours during the year. Small groups within each department arrange a schedule that fits their needs and the department's.

Department store managers report that people come to work more willing and able to concentrate on their jobs, and there are fewer problems with absenteeism and tardiness. Because of the dependability of its work force, the store has been able to cut back on backup personnel.

Of course, the ultimate version of flextime is deciding what hours you want to work and setting your own schedule, the way millions of self-employed people from writers to taxicab owners to real estate agents already do. Because of the decentralized nature of information work, this is not such a farfetched idea. In the industrial economy, however, it would have been. To operate an assembly line, everyone had to be there at the same time.

Permanent Part-Time

Part-time work has traditionally been associated with a low hourly rate, a low-skilled job, and zero benefits. The assumption is that people work part-time only because they cannot get full-time work.

But more than 14.4 million Americans—about 14.7 percent of the work force—worked part-time by choice in 1984, according to the Bureau of Labor Statistics. For people who want a serious career for twenty to thirty hours per week—new fathers, working mothers, students, older workers, two-career couples, single parents, entrepreneurs, people who are more interested in their hobby than their job—it is a very desirable arrangement.

One leading employer of part-timers is Control Data Corporation (CDC). Paul Jones, CDC's personnel coordinator, says every effort is made to make part-timers feel part of the company. The company's superior benefits, including medical and dental plans, sick leave, and life insurance, are one reason CDC attracts high-caliber part-timers.

Other corporate innovators in permanent part-time arrangements are Hewlett-Packard, New York's Metropolitan Life, Chemical Bank, Citibank, Manufacturers Hanover, Levi Strauss, and the New York State government.

However, most professionals who want to work part-time careers still feel the onus is on them to convince employers to try this new schedule.

One professional woman who has succeeded, though, is Judy Fishman, who works three days per week as vice-president of personnel at Citibank. When she negotiated her part-time arrangement some ten years ago, it appears she started a trend at Citibank—which now has twenty part-time executives.

Several associations have sprung up as support groups and information clearinghouses for people who want good jobs part-time. Two very active ones are San Francisco's

New Ways to Work and the Association of Part-Time Professionals (APTP), based in the Washington, D.C., area.

Speaking at an APTP national conference in 1983, Helen Axel, senior research associate with the Conference Board, advised would-be part-timers, "Get yourself a full-time job, prove your worth, and then negotiate part-time hours from a position of strength."

That is the same strategy used by many of the estimated 1 to 2 million pioneers in job sharing, a form of permanent part-time work, where the responsibilities and benefits of one full-time job are shared by two people.

Job Sharing

Job sharing has worked for executive secretaries, college presidents, engineers, computer programmers, physicians, social workers, personnel administrators, and many others, according to Barney Olmsted and Suzanne Smith, cofounders of San Francisco's New Ways to Work and authors of *The Job Sharing Handbook*—must reading for anyone interested in job sharing.

Like flextime and part-time, job sharing will become increasingly common in the seller's market of the late 1980s and the 1990s, when companies will have to adjust to the various work styles people want.

Atlantic Richfield used job sharing to help older people phase into retirement, but younger workers can share jobs there, too.

Laurie Forster, at New York's Pfizer, Inc., shares her job as executive secretary with another woman. "This is the perfect setup," she says.

Within the next few years, more than 800 major American corporations will include job sharing as a job style, according to the American Society for Training and Devel-

opment. Those companies will gain double the creative and
productive capacity in one job. Individuals come to work
more alert and are more productive, particularly important
traits in high-stress jobs where fatigue might cause a serious, costly error.

A wide variety of different *types* of jobs lend themselves
to sharing:

- At Pella, Iowa's Rolscreen Co., fifty pairs of employees—
  mostly assembly line workers—now share jobs.
- Two telephone receptionists share the hours between
  7:30 A.M. and 5:30 P.M. at San Francisco's Wells Fargo
  Bank.
- At San Francisco's New College, Mildred Henry and
  Peter Gabel share the job of college president.
- Two Wisconsin parole officers share one job, alternat-
  ing every six months.

Job sharing works remarkably well in education. More
than one-third of the school districts in the bellwether state
of California have had experience with job sharing.

Teachers, students, and administrators are enthusiastic
about job sharing.

"We bring in new spirit, new blood, new enthusiasm,"
says Dr. Robert McLean, assistant superintendent of the
Palo Alto Unified School District.

In the Mount Diablo school district, 97 percent of the
children said they felt lucky to have two teachers. All thirteen
principals in the program asked for more coteaching candidates.

"It helps to keep your sanity," says one job-sharing
teacher in the Santa Clara school district.

Job Sharing in Action: A Case Study

For more than a year, Maureen Feldman and Peggy

Gillette have shared the job of business systems manager at Levi Strauss. They are enthusiastic about how well it works.

"I had just had my first child and was coming into work exhausted," explains Maureen Feldman. "I was just running around trying to do too many things and not getting time with my child."

She decided it was impossible to have a full-time job and care for an infant, too. At the same time, Maureen's assistant, Peggy Gillette, was beginning to think of phased retirement.

"I was recovering from an illness and had just moved into a retirement community, I wanted to get to know my neighbors but still keep my hand in at work."

After discussing the possibility of combining their two jobs into one and sharing it, the two women decided it would work. Levi Strauss, which is known to encourage job sharers, went along with the idea, because of positive experiences with job-sharing experiments.

"We complement each other," says Maureen. "Otherwise, it wouldn't work."

"We don't point fingers," adds Peggy. "Each of us accepts full responsibility for the whole job."

The two women work three days each week, overlapping their schedules to both work Wednesdays, when they catch up with each other, solve problems, and coordinate future plans.

Clearly, the job sharers have gotten what they want. But Levi Strauss got the better bargain: two highly skilled, experienced managers who would have left without the job-sharing alternative. That will become increasingly important in the coming seller's job market.

An important fringe benefit for the company: Job sharers can cover for each other during vacation and in case of illness.

How to Share Your Job

- Pick someone whose skills complement your own.
- It should be someone who is extremely well organized. If you are not orderly yourself, forget job sharing. It is an essential trait.
- Never job share with someone you do not know.
- Do not overlook either your immediate supervisor or your assistant as a possible job sharer.
- Schedule one person to work Monday through Wednesday, the other Wednesday through Friday. It is vital for both to work the same day once a week.
- Guard against workers playing you off against each other.
- Expect to be responsible for the whole job, not just your part. In job sharing, there is no dividing line of responsibility.

Flexible Benefits

What sense does it make to offer today's work force a benefit package designed to fit less than 20 percent of them—male breadwinners with a family to support and a wife who does not work?

And yet most companies still draw up their benefits packages ignoring the 80+ percent majority—women, singles, and people in dual-earner households. What is even crazier is that it is costing the *company* a fortune to do so.

Today's variegated work force needs different benefits:

- Older people need comprehensive health care, while younger folks, especially single parents and two-career families, want time off for family or personal matters.
- Two-career couples gain nothing when their employers

duplicate expensive health coverage for the whole family while unnecessarily paying out a fortune on insurance premiums.

• Women with young children, the fastest-growing segment of the work force, show greater loyalty to companies that offer child care.

• In this era of training and retraining, almost everyone expects tuition reimbursement but may use it only every few years.

No company can afford to offer *all* the above benefits. But many companies can and do offer people a choice of benefits—that is, a fixed amount of benefit dollars to "spend" on a menu of various benefits, aptly named a "cafeteria" of benefits.

Some 325 firms have flexible benefits plans or are in the final stages of putting one in place, according to Hewitt Associates, the leading benefits consulting firm. There will be 500 plans by the end of 1986, predicts Hewitt Associates. That figure may grow even more rapidly, since flexible benefits plans are becoming so easy to administer that they are making their way into small business.

Clo Ross, administrative vice-president of Clairson International, a $20 million manufacturer with a flexible benefits plan, puts it this way:

Where once we had one plan, we now have four hundred— one for each employee.

Cafeteria plans are very popular with workers. But in reality, it is the *company* that profits most from this new prototype plan, which increases benefit *options* without increasing benefit *costs*. In fact, companies often save money. How?

The most expensive benefit, and the one employers think employees value most, is low-deductible health insurance.

Cafeteria plans save companies money because a surprisingly large number of people—an average of 50 percent according to Hewitt Associates—do *not* take this benefit. Some are covered by their spouse's plan; others prefer a high-deductible health plan, while others simply prefer other, less costly benefits.

This win/win arrangement saves corporations money while giving people the freedom to elect the benefits they want.

In addition to health plans, cafeteria benefits could include extra vacation time, health club memberships, tuition reimbursement, day care, homeowner's insurance, or even legal counsel. Attractive options often cost the company very little.

An interesting new benefit is the IRA- and Keogh-like portable pension plan, which accompanies its holder from one company to another without lost benefits.

Thanks to the Section 401(K) pension plan (named for the IRS code that allows it), your pension plan can follow you as you move from company to company. Under current rules, employees can make tax-deductible contributions to their accounts of up to 15 percent of their salaries.

In some cases, benefits options are just plain good for morale. According to benefits consultants, child-care reimbursement is very highly valued among single parents and two-career families, although only a small percentage actually use it.

Similarly, people are often pleased just to have a choice. At American Can Co., 89 percent of employees like the option of selecting new benefits each year; 74 percent rate the program "excellent" or "very good."

As the cafeteria menu grows larger to attract an increasingly diverse work force, computers will make it easy to track the more and more complex benefits options.

Without computers, we could not keep track of the complexity of each employee having a different benefits package—another example of new technology in confluence with changing values.

Expect to see benefits reemerge as a recruitment tool in the coming seller's market for a shrinking labor pool. Notice how, for example, with the shortage of nurses, hospitals are using day care as a way to recruit more nurses.

Computers Transform the Industrial Worker into an Information Manager

Frederick Taylor's concept of scientific management, which broke jobs down into their tiniest components, and industrial structures such as the assembly line made it possible for a work force of illiterate immigrants to make America the strongest economic power on earth.

But the Industrial Revolution has given way to a revolution in information technology which is reasserting the need for individual workers to use their brains rather than their brawn in the workplace.

"In an automated process, the worker switches from being an operator to being a programmer," writes Peter Drucker. "Each worker has to be pretty much in control of the process, has to understand it, know how to program the machines he is responsible for and reset them."

Just as the Industrial Revolution streamlined agriculture, computers are transforming manufacturing.

- Pratt & Whitney's Columbus, Georgia, plant produces aircraft engine disks and compressor blades under computer control from the time raw materials enter the production process through final inspection.
- At John Deere's $500-million Waterloo, Iowa, plant,

computers now control all materials-handling functions, match parts to orders, and manage inventory.

- Inland Steel's No. 3 line in Chicago, which uses more than 100 microcomputers, can process a coil of steel strip in ten minutes instead of the five to six days it used to take.

Those changes are transforming yesterday's blue-collar worker into a full-fledged information worker and blurring the distinction between worker and foreman, foreman and manager.

At Best Industries, an oil field equipment producer, foremen now have direct access to the information heretofore reserved for white-collar managers. With the touch of a computer button, a foreman has instant access to information on inventory, orders, and future shipments.

"Before, you had a vice-president in an ivory tower sending out directions," says Robert Dintenger, vice-president for material and manufacturing at Best. "Now the factory manager can make decisions unilaterally."

Northrop is also breaking down the barriers between engineers and production people. At the company's Hawthorne, California, plant, which makes the Tigershark fighter plane, engineers work alongside production people making changes directly on the plane instead of sending memos back and forth. As a result, it took 30 percent less time to make the second Tigershark plane, and the third had zero defects on the fuselage, which is unheard-of, says Welko Gasich, Northrop's senior vice-president for advanced projects.

At Tandem, the Cupertino, California, computer company, the people who actually make computers are getting at the information they need just the way company executives are—from on-line terminals. Production people have complete access to more performance data and other information than management could have tapped in the past. To prepare for their new jobs as information managers, the Tandem workers took short courses in statistical analysis and measurement.

As the Tandem example shows, yesterday's production worker needs the skill and training of an information worker. Companies need fewer supervisors and middle managers, whose importance rested on their access, processing, and control of information.

Despite the stereotype of workers as technology-fearing Luddites, there is evidence that American workers have welcomed technology into the workplace.

Three-quarters of the workers interviewed in the Public Agenda Foundation study said that technology made their jobs freer and more interesting, rather than more routine, and that the subsequent challenges motivated them to perform better.

"Robots and the microprocessors that control robots have altered the rules for success in manufacturing," says Dennis Wisnosky, a vice-president with GCA Corp., a robot supplier.

As the work force becomes more educated and sophisticated, hierarchical management from the top down will have to be replaced by a participative system of relatively autonomous computer operators organized from the bottom up.

We have recognized the inefficiency of authority to motivate and lead people in the new information environment. "We can no longer control people by authority, by bureaucracy, and by rules," says Thomas N. Gilmore, associate director of the Wharton School's Management and Behavior Sciences Center.

Ford's Edison, New Jersey, auto plant has instituted the now famous Japanese model "stop button," a powerful example of self-management. Assembly line workers can stop the whole line anytime they find a defect that does not allow them to do their job properly. In the wake of the stop button, Ford reports quality and employee morale are up while turnover, absenteeism, and tardiness are down.

Similarly, GM's Orion plant was designed to "put more responsibility into the hands of the worker," according to a GM spokesperson.

By 1990, more than 80 percent of the work force will hold jobs requiring more thinking and decision-making than traditional blue-collar jobs.

Almost all jobs will require sophisticated high-tech tools and the advanced skills to operate them. That kind of complexity makes supervision almost impossible. Result: Supervision will give way to self-management.

The Older Worker Reemerges in the Seller's Market

Virginia Coulter, 80, is a pasteup and layout artist at Boston's Warren Publishing Corp. She has been with the company for 63 years. Her work is not easy; she often spends hours on her feet bent over a drawing board.

But when she gets tired, she can count on Winifred Church, 83, who runs the mail room, for inspiration. "Age is only a number," says Church. "It is no indication of a person's ability. Sure there may be a few older people who are no longer capable of holding a job, but I've also known some people who were pretty decrepit at the age of thirty."

Warren's president, Tim Warren, Sr., encourages the eight people eligible for Social Security (out of a staff of thirty-five) to stay on the job. "Why should we tell anyone to stop working when we can provide a flexible environment that supports them?"

That flexibility includes letting older people set their schedules to work as much or as little as they like; Warren just adds more workers as business picks up seasonally.

Warren Publishing is a prototype company from which

we can all learn a lot, at a time when more older people will begin rejoining the work force.

During the 1970s, when the labor market swelled with the baby boomers and new women workers, the number of older people in the work force decreased substantially. In 1970, 26.8 percent of males and 9.7 percent of females over sixty-five worked. By 1980, those percentages had decreased to 19 and 8 respectively.

But between 1985 and 1995, we will see that trend reversed. Economics and demographics will encourage an estimated 100,000 older workers to come back into the work force each year.

America will need these workers. By 1990, when 4.5 million fewer youths aged eighteen to twenty-four are entering the work force than in 1980, the new information economy will need skilled, able workers. There will be literally nowhere to turn but to the experienced ranks of retired workers.

But most corporations are still encouraging older workers to retire early—a policy that made sense during the 1970s and earlier but needs to be reevaluated and maybe reversed for the late 1980s and 1990s.

Companies that anticipate this need for older workers and set up model programs to accommodate them now will reap great advantages from their foresight and may even ensure their companies' survival in a time when the cost of human capital will reach an all-time high.

At Varian Associates, Inc., in Palo Alto, California, for example, people over fifty-five can work as few as twenty hours per week and still keep full fringe benefits. This policy helps the company retain people who would otherwise retire, according to Varian's personnel director.

Fortunately for business' sake, most retirees want to work at least part-time, according to the National Council on Aging.

Although many companies are still pushing early retirement, many farsighted companies have never instituted the practice. Others are retiring outdated policies rather than senior workers.

At Polaroid, which has never had mandatory retirement, 30 percent of people over sixty-five have stayed on the job. Chicago's Bankers Life and Casualty is another company which never had mandatory retirement. "Our policy toward older workers is the same as it is toward employees of any other age. The ability to perform the job determines whether or not the individual is hired or retained," says human resources vice-president Anna Marie Buchmann.

"The wisdom, judgment, and experience [of older workers] are invaluable to the corporation. They are a vital future manpower resource over the long run," says Blair Hyde, the head of Atlantic Richfield's Senior Worker Policy and Program Group.

Some companies are taking a lead that many will follow—rehiring workers who have already retired:

Grumman Corp., the aircraft maker and defense contractor, fills its seasonal needs from a pool of retired people who know the territory and have proven themselves more productive than new hires. In 1983, some 300 retirees worked temporarily.

At Hartford's Travelers' Insurance, the Office of Consumer Information is staffed entirely by retired Travelers' employees. Sixteen job sharers fill four positions and field 36,000 calls each year.

But there is also a good chance for older people to be hired by companies they have never worked for.

Texas Refinery Corporation in Fort Worth, which makes building protectants and heavy-duty lubricants, employs 500 salespeople whose ages range from the sixties to the eighties.

"The company gets the benefit of a lifetime of experience," says company president Wesley Sears. "It's like a baseball pitcher. When he is young, he pitches hard because that's all he knows. As he gets older, he pitches maybe not so hard, but now he's got the skill to get it across the plate more times.''

Western Savings Bank in Phoenix, with $2.5 billion in assets, sixty-five branches, and nearly 1,000 employees, has 80 people over sixty-five in either full-time or permanent part-time jobs. Fifteen older workers are available on call. Older workers staff the bank's ''customer clubs,'' for elderly people with large deposits.

Avanti in South Bend, Indiana, a manufacturer of custom-built cars, hires older workers because ''they are on the job every day; they are meticulous and dedicated and take pride in their work,'' according to a company spokesperson. None of Avanti's 124 workers is younger than forty-five.

What does a company have to do to accommodate older workers? In most cases, simply put in place the flexible work arrangements discussed in this chapter which appeal to all workers—part-time, job sharing, and flextime.

Chicago Title Insurance Company, which has branches in forty-two states, employs older workers in job-sharing teams as interoffice messengers. But instead of working half a week, they work alternate months, an option which reportedly attracts retired people from other companies.

Corning Glass Company reports that older people tend to use flextime more than younger people.

As companies hire more older people to combat labor shortages and adjust to the work styles those older folks want, it may be that older workers pioneer the work options that many of the rest of us want, too—flextime, job sharing, and permanent part-time.

When the baby bust hits the job market in full force, where will fast-food companies find their teenage staffs? Imagine a McDonald's staffed by octogenarians. What a delightful change.

The Decade of the Entrepreneur

For millions of us, having our own business is still the best way to work in the information/electronics/service society. Whether you start a home-based business or raise millions in venture capital, the classic advice applies, "Find a need and fill it."

What is behind today's entrepreneurial explosion?

Again, the key point is this: In this information economy, the strategic resource has shifted from capital to information, knowledge, creativity.

Access to the economic system is much easier.

In the industrial society, it took megabucks to build a plant or factory. Now you need a telephone, a kitchen table, a customer, and you are in business. Provided you have a vision, belief in yourself, and the unique ability to turn your vision into a reality.

More people than ever before are realizing the dream of independence by working for themselves:

- Nearly 11 million Americans work for themselves, compared with 5.7 million, in 1970, according to the Internal Revenue Service.
- People are starting new businesses at the rate of 700,000 per year—double what it was a decade ago and eight times what it was in the 1950s at the height of the industrial period.
- From 1982 to 1983 alone, Dun & Bradstreet reported an 11 percent increase in receipts of inquiries (an indicator that newly formed corporations are really doing business).
- The number of self-employed people (nonagricultural) reached more than 7.5 million in 1983, a 38-percent increase in ten years.

Filling a Need and Having Fun

Entrepreneurship in the new information society can range from a predictable business such as word processing or computer software to a whole cluster of offbeat products and services that are fun and profitable:

- Houston's Tom Schooler founded Petmobile Veterinarian Ambulance Service, Inc., to ferry pets to kennels and the vet's. Schooler, a former art gallery owner, got the idea on vacation in Italy, where he saw a vehicle transporting a horse and cow.
- Scott Alyn sells greeting cards containing packets of seeds and sayings, such as, "I'd like to hug you till you're squashed" and "Curry up and get well." Turned down by venture capitalists, he now sells more than 1 million cards internationally each year.
- Gary Gygax, inventor of the immensely popular Dungeons and Dragons game, turned his love of games ("I've been playing chess since seventh grade and Parcheesi for longer than I can remember") into a $22-million-a-year business.
- Richard LaMotta, a former CBS video engineer, is the entrepreneur behind Chipwich, the sandwich of ice cream held together by two chocolate chip cookies.

New Entrepreneurial Forces

The shift in strategic resources from capital to information is the main factor fueling the entrepreneurial boom. But there are others.

Corporations no longer provide the security they once did.
The whittling away of middle management, global competition, and the trend toward lean, flexible people structures mean that your corporate job will not necessarily last forev-

er. Would-be entrepreneurs figure, "If there is going to be risk anyhow, why not up the ante a bit and possibly reap some big rewards?"

The new information society has created new markets and new business opportunities. And in this new environment, individual entrepreneurs hold a key advantage over corporations: They can act faster. Entrepreneurs can respond to rapid technological change without wading through layers of bureaucracy.

There is a billion-dollar fund of venture capital looking to invest in the right entrepreneur. By the end of 1984 New York State had attracted $2.6 billion; Massachusetts, nearly $1.5 billion; and California, $3.7 billion. Although most entrepreneurs finance their ventures with savings and loans from friends and relatives, an enormous pool of capital exists for the entrepreneur who sells the right idea to a willing venture capitalist.

These three factors encourage entrepreneurship generally, but the decision to become an entrepreneur or simply to work for yourself is motivated by personal needs.

At New York's Tarrytown School for Entrepreneurs, which we both attended in January 1979, we learned that (despite numerous claims to the contrary) there are no magical ways to predict who would become an entrepreneur.

Nevertheless, entrepreneurs must possess a combination of vision and the ability to act to achieve that vision. Entrepreneurs are seeking independence, challenge, achievement, fair compensation.

COMPENSATION. People sometimes start their own company because they feel their efforts within a corporation have not been fairly compensated.

"I once made a decision that increased the profit of my employer, a retail tire store, by $100,000," recalls California's Hank Heeber, the owner of four tire stores, three shoe stores, and a cattle ranch. The company responded by giving me a raise of fifty dollars per month. I looked at it and said, 'This isn't a raise, it's an insult,' Then I left."

INDEPENDENCE. Though they seek equitable compensation, most entrepreneurs are not obsessed with making money. Today more than 50 percent say they are in business for themselves because they "do not like working for someone else," according to a study by Joseph Mancuso of the Center for Entrepreneurial Management. That represents a big change from ten years ago, says Mancuso, when they were in business primarily for the money.

Typical of this attitude is Philip Bredesen, founder of HealthAmerica Corp., which manages Health Maintenance Organizations: "Your mistakes are your own . . . there is a sense of controlling your own destiny."

CHALLENGE. Some people work for themselves because it is the only way they can satisfy their need to be challenged. Betty Barkyaumb started a skating rink, a golf driving range, and several other commercial ventures. "I guess I always want there to be a new challenge," she says.

A psychological study of entrepreneurs sponsored by Control Data in conjunction with *Venture* magazine concluded that entrepreneurs are excitement junkies, people who flourish taking risks. "Work lacks sufficient thrill unless it is imbued with risk," the report states, noting that entrepreneurs also enjoy gambling.

But others disagree. Nancy Flexman and Thomas Scanlan, authors of *Running Your Own Business*, believe it is a myth to portray entrepreneurs as excessive risk-takers.

"Most entrepreneurs take moderate, calculated risks; they are not just gambling," the authors assert.

ACHIEVEMENT. "The entrepreneur wants achievement, not power," says Robert Kuhn, professor of corporate strategies at New York University Graduate School of Business. It is generally agreed that entrepreneurs seek achievement, while successful managers want power.

These are the classic needs said to motivate entrepreneurs. Yet there is a simpler explanation: Working for yourself may be the best way to find the perfect job. Carl Hathaway, for example, gave up a vice-chairmanship at Morgan Guaranty Trust Co. to be near his great love—sailing.

Hathaway manages portfolios totaling more than $200 million from a dock on Long Island Sound. "The highs are higher and the lows are lower . . . [but] every time I hear the halyards making that musical pinging sound when they slap against the masts of the sailboats, I know I made the right decision."

The Entrepreneurial Woman

The search for the perfect job is also behind the surge in women entrepreneurs—who now own some 30 percent of all American businesses and are increasing that share at a rate five times that of male-owned firms, according to the Office of Women Business Owners, United States Department of Labor.

Sandy Kurtzig, who started Ask Computer out of a spare bedroom and built it into a $65-million business, is a great and well-known women's entrepreneurial success story. But millions of other women are achieving success and independence in small businesses—especially in products and services designed for women.

Eliane Kesteloot turned her hobby of painting on silk into a very successful dressmaking business with a twist: Working with Carol Jackson, author of the phenomenally successful *Color Me Beautiful*, Eliane designed and made a line of scarves for each of Carol's "seasonal colors—bright winters, warm autumns, soft springs and summers." How many male entrepreneurs would develop that business idea?

Tricia Fox, a computer salesperson, arrived in Chicago with her three children and a need for a good day-care center. Amazed that she could not find one, she started her own. Now she operates six and is franchising Fox Day Schools nationally. "With the number of women who work and have children today, there is a need for 50,000 day-care centers," she argues. "There are only 9,000 in the whole country."

The need to care for children is the reason so many women entrepreneurs operate out of their homes—combining business and motherhood. Most corporations have not begun to acknowledge that dual need.

"Home-based businesses are growing and they are going to expand terrifically," says Phyllis Gillis, author of *Entrepreneurial Mothers*. The National Association of Homebased Business-women has 1,200 members throughout the fifty states.

Although it is difficult to determine the number of home-based businesses, there were an estimated 5 million in 1983.

Peggy Boston, for example, operates a cookie company in her McLean, Virginia, home. For $28, she will make you a "Mammoth Monogrammed Munchie," a 4½-foot-tall cookie in the shape of your favorite letter. "It's wonderful," she says. "I wouldn't work this hard for anyone else."

Barbara Isenberg grosses $5.5 million designing toy bears—like William Shakesbear and Elvis Bearsley—in her Greenwich, Connecticut, home. (She also has a factory where the bears are made, packed, and distributed.)

Would you succeed as an entrepreneur? You will never know until you try, but you probably should not even try unless you possess these attributes:

SELF-DIRECTION. You should be thoroughly comfortable at being your own boss, self-disciplined.

SELF-NURTURING. You must believe in your idea when no one else does, and be able to replenish your own enthusiasm.

ACTION-ORIENTED. Great business ideas are not enough. The most important thing is a burning desire to realize, actualize, and build your dream into reality.

HIGH ENERGY LEVEL. You must be emotionally, mentally, and physically able to work long and hard.

TOLERANT OF UNCERTAINTY. Successful entrepreneurs take only calculated risks (if they can help it). Still, they must be able to take some risk. Venture capitalists, in fact, look for people who are psychologically capable of handling risk, while at the same time making things happen.

Here is a collection of advice from successful entrepreneurs:

- Research your market, but do not take too long to act.
- Start your business when you have a customer.
- Try your new venture as a sideline at first.
- Plan your objectives within specific time frames.
- Surround yourself with people who are smarter than yourself—including an outside board of directors.
- Do not be afraid to fail.
- Hire a great accountant.

Today's worker is more and more likely to be self-employed or an entrepreneur. As futurist Barbara Marx Hubbard put it, "For the job you want, no one is hiring and the pay is nil. That is why we must all learn to be entrepreneurial."

Family Business

Family business, which is hardly a new work model, is making a strong comeback in this new information economy.

People who would never have dreamed of joining the family business are flocking to seminars to learn about the right—and wrong—way to succeed Mom or Dad in the family business. Today's business-minded women have doubled the pool of family talent and are re-inventing family business with company names like W. R. Smith & Daughters.

The reason is simple: This is the age of the entrepreneur. Children of successful business owners, who previously might have entered medicine, banking, or law, have now caught the entrepreneurial fever.

Today's entrepreneur has a glamorous new image in complete contrast to the old days—when it was considered a mark of underachievement, sometimes even a stigma, to take over the family business.

Furthermore, given the predictions of labor surpluses in the prestigious areas of law and medicine, the family business looks downright alluring.

"People are returning to family-perpetuated proprietorships; it's no longer considered coattail hanging. It's even prestigious," says consultant Leon Danco, head of the Center for Family Business, the residing guru to, and adviser of, American family business.

But with the upsurge in family business have come its legendary problems.

Psychologist Harry Levinson, president of the Levinson Institute in Cambridge, Massachusetts, says, "Family business is the most difficult business in the world and no family ought to be in it."

He is just kidding, sort of.

Nevertheless, millions of people thoroughly ignore his advice, including the owners of the grocery at the corner, the local automobile dealership, the stockbroker downtown, the wholesaler on the highway, and the contractor who renovated your house:

- Experts estimate that between 12.1 and 14.4 million of the nation's 15 million businesses are family owned.
- Family businesses contribute half of the GNP.
- They employ half of all workers in the nonfarm private sector.
- Family businesses account for 99 percent of all construction firms, 94 percent of all wholesalers, 96 percent of

all retail and distribution companies, and 94 percent of all manufacturing firms.

Not all are small businesses, though. Some of the largest and best known corporations in the world—Cargill, the international grain company, Hallmark Cards, Estée Lauder, Perdue Farms, and Mars, Inc.—are family owned.

According to *Fortune* magazine, in thirty-five of the fifty largest private industrial companies, the majority of the shares are held by a single family.

Family business is a world apart with its unique set of advantages and its equally compelling set of problems.

Clearly, the greatest attraction is the sense of freedom and flexibility.

With no stockholders hounding them, family-owned businesses are free to follow long-term strategies that build successful futures, rather than being held slave to quarterly profits. Without stockholders, family businesses are in a favorable position to take advantage of market opportunities.

That is the way family-owned Stroh's Brewing Company in 1982 acquired Joseph Schlitz Brewing Company, a larger, public company, and rose from the seventh to the third largest U.S. beer maker.

The twenty-seven family members who own Stroh's were willing to accept lower dividends to finance the deal. ''Family sacrifice is one reason we operate successfully,'' says company president Peter Stroh.

Freedom, flexibility, the opportunity to build a business.

Why does Harry Levinson have such harsh words for family business?

Because the advantages are often wiped out by the tangle of personal and emotional problems that destroys the relationship among parents, children, and other family members as well as the dream of a successful business empire.

Only 30 percent of all family businesses survive into the

second generation. The average family-owned business lasts no longer than the founder's lifetime.

Family business consultant Leon Danco thinks it is because so many founding fathers (and increasingly mothers) commit the number-one sin in family business: failing to plan for the CEO's succession.

"Most owners don't plan because they don't think they are going to retire or die. . . . The fate of the business will probably be decided by the banker and the attorney, on the way back from the funeral about four cars back from the flowers," says Danco.

The excuse, of course, is that the owner is too busy. In reality, most owner-entrepreneurs are unwilling to delegate—especially to their child—preferring to think of themselves as indispensable and immortal.

Groups like Danco's Family Business Center and the National Family Business Council have dished out a lot of sensible advice about succession in family business, a problem that has been dealt with in some rather outlandish ways.

One New York son removed his father from his office at gunpoint . . . in another instance, a father had his son kidnapped and held hostage until the son agreed to leave the firm . . . a wife sided with her son in a succession battle and hired a professional hit man to do away with her husband . . . the twenty-one-year-old head of a clothing firm filed suit to prohibit his father from entering the business.

Those are some of the stories, and people in family business do not doubt their authenticity. But several new models can help smooth the transition, strengthening families and their businesses.

A key problem with succession is that the child enters the business at about twenty-five—young, inexperienced, raring to go—and convinces the parent that he or she will destroy the business.

The best way around the problem is for the child to get his or her basic training outside the family firm. And come into the company in his or her thirties, a little older and a lot wiser.

That plan succeeded at Allied Supply Company, a California supplier to the oil and chemical industries. Allied owner Charles W. Smith and his wife told their two sons that if they wanted to work for Dad, they would have to work for someone else first, "to get the spots knocked off them," as Smith, Sr., puts it. Then they would have to come and ask to join the company.

After ten years with other businesses, Smith's two sons are Allied's president and vice-president.

Gerald Slavin, a young man who had problems with his father's nonsuccession plans, founded a group in 1969 with the marvelous name of SOBs (Sons of Bosses). Soon there were 600 chapters nationwide. (In 1976, the name was changed to the National Family Business Council. How boring.)

Slavin's group runs an innovative "swap" program in which sons and daughters are loaned to outside firms to broaden their skills. The Associated General Contractors of America has a similar program operating among noncompeting companies. In some cases, the swap is for as long as five years.

W. R. Smith & Daughters

In the past, family business succession and the accompanying internecine battles were about fathers and sons. Not anymore.

"Increasingly, daughters by choice are entering family businesses and wrestling with their brothers for control and a place at the top," contends Danco.

In 1982, Cleveland's Center for Family Business knew of only 500 family businesses run by women, but estimated that the number would skyrocket by 1990. Some 500,000 daughters are potential owners of family businesses, the group calculates. There has been a 30-percent increase in the number of women attending its seminars on family business succession. More women are joining the National Family Business Council.

"In many cases they tend to do a better job than their brothers because they are better trained and have more outside experience," says Donald Jonovic, vice-president of the Cleveland Center.

Business literature is beginning to fill up with stories about father and daughter businesses: the father who trained his nineteen-year-old daughter to take over his contract painting business . . . the newly graduated MBA who'll take over her father's six travel agencies . . . the former attorney who is learning her father's $58-million women's sportswear company . . . the daughters who have taken over their father's retread tire franchise or glove-manufacturing company.

Christie Hefner, the daughter of *Playboy*'s Hugh Hefner, is president of Playboy Enterprises, but father Hugh is not the only publishing mogul with a daughter to run the family business.

John Johnson, chairman and president of Chicago-based Johnson Publishing, the second largest black-owned business in the United States, expects his daughter, Linda, twenty-eight, to take over his multimillion-dollar business within the next few years.

One of the best father-daughter business stories comes from Häagen-Dazs, the ice-cream company. Typically, the founding father resisted his child's bright idea—and later learned to admire it. It took Doris Mattus a year to convince her father to let her open the first Häagen-Dazs retail shop in Brooklyn in 1976. The rest is history.

Some experts believe daughters are often better prepared to take the helm because they do not automatically assume the business is theirs. They expect to have to prove themselves, work harder at earning their job, and learn more in the process. And there's an added plus: Women do not provoke macho battles with their fathers.

No, Her Husband Works for Her

The upsurge in daughter-led family business parallels the growing phenomenon of husbands and wives going into business together, but with a twist—the wife is boss.

Says *Business Week,* "Role reversal in family-owned businesses is becoming more common all the time. A growing number of couples are entering business together—in fields far removed from the mom-and-pop candy stores of yesteryear—and, ignoring yesteryear's customs, they typically name the best qualified partner as boss even when the best qualified partner is the wife."

For example, Susan Nichols is president of Communico, Inc., a passive-solar-home–building company in Santa Fe, and her husband, Wayne, is vice-president in charge of marketing.

"I'm better at being the boss than Wayne," says Susan. "He's wonderfully creative but I'm extremely disciplined."

Sandra Bracy, thirty-seven, is president of Bravince Electrical Contracting, while her husband, Gerald Vincent, forty, is general manager. Bracy was put in charge after her husband's previous venture with a male partner had failed. The new company is "a marriage of my administrative abilities and my husband's technical skills," she says.

In some cases, men leave their jobs to join their wives' successful ventures. David Howie, once a Fulbright professor, is secretary-treasurer at his wife Helga's successful high-fashion apparel company.

To re-invent the workplace, we must recognize the new work force—women, minorities, entrepreneurs, two-career couples, and, soon, many more older people. They are the best educated people in the nation's history. And they have this strange notion: They want work to be fulfilling and fun.

Companies could not ask for a better potential match between corporate goals and people's needs.

Today, people want to make their company successful— but they want to work where they can have psychic ownership as well as literal ownership.

Re-inventing work in the information society means shifting from the union contracts of the industrial period—where everyone is treated the same—to the individualized contract negotiated through flexible benefits, flexible job schedules, flexible careers.

The rigidity and regimentation of the industrial company are being replaced by the flexibility and fluidity of the information company.

As the information economy progresses, more of us may choose to imitate the work style of the computer hacker, a young professional who is often so involved in work he might stay at the office until 3:00 A.M. and not show up until noon the next day.

Gradually, companies have had to learn to accommodate to the strange ways and wacky hours of creative people like hackers. As a result, these creative types may be leading the way for millions of information workers who could set their own hours without upsetting the company's ongoing business. As the labor shortages in the computer business spread to the rest of the information economy, we will all gain more clout to bargain for the schedules we want. Having become used to computer hackers, corporations will more readily comply.

Some of us, on the other hand, firmly believe the best way to have fun and make money is to start our own business. Others are taking another look at their parents' businesses and asking themselves, "Why not skip the start-up phase and jump into a full-fledged company?"

There are great lessons to be learned about self-management and productivity from people who work for themselves.

The first step is to define a day's work in terms of tasks rather than time—that is the only way to be free of the industrial time-clock mentality, which is totally inappropriate in an information society.

What if information workers and their supervisors or team members set specific daily goals:

- Draft a ten-page report that passes muster with Ms. Brown, or
- Get Alex's program to run, or
- Get the client signed up on ten talk shows.

We have not discovered any companies that operate this way, but our experience as self-employed people with many self-employed friends tells us that people who are on their own do it all the time.

Corporations committed to re-inventing themselves are employing more creative, self-managing people who are paid for performance, not for showing up. As these companies recognize that flexible schedules increase both commitment and productivity, the workplace will look more like clusters of self-employed people and entrepreneurs.

4

The Skills of the New Information Society

The corporation's competitive edge is people—an educated, skilled work force that is eager to develop its human potential while contributing to the organization's growth. Yet as we enter this literacy-intensive society, this data-drenched society, there is growing evidence that the people joining our corporations are less skilled than ever before.

Unskilled people are the one obstacle to the promise of prosperity in the new information society, the one threat to successfully re-inventing the corporation.

But what skills should we be learning now? What *are* the skills of the new information society which all of us—from schoolchildren to executives—should begin acquiring?

There is little doubt: If we aim to re-invent the corporation, we must give some thought to re-inventing education, too.

And midway through the 1980s, there is evidence that

people *know* we must do something about education. That is a positive sign for students and for the companies that will hire them. But we think it is a mistake to believe that reform will solve our problems.

Today's education system—the one some reformers want to elevate to a level of excellence—was never meant to serve the needs of today's information society; it was custom-made to fit the industrial society—a time when it made sense to treat everyone the same.

Uniformity, control, centralization in the factory and in management were the ideals of industrial society. And the schools were modeled in the image and likeness of these industrial values—right for their time, but horrendously wrong today.

Individuality, creativity, the ability to think for one's self—the values we treasure now—were hardly considered assets on the assembly line or even in the executive suite.

Were we to, in effect, freeze our children in the educational paradigm of the industrial society, we would condemn them to being as ill-equipped to function in the information society as their grandparents would be.

Furthermore, much of today's search for educational excellence sounds suspiciously like the old movement to reindustrialize America: "Back to Basics." What sense does it make to reindustrialize an economy that is no longer based on industry, but has shifted to an information economy?

Similarly, what good does it do us to achieve excellence in an education system that no longer fits our society?

We have essentially the same education system we had in the industrial society and we are trying to use it to equip us for the information age.

That is the real problem with education today. And making the system better is not going to help.

Instead, we must ask ourselves, "What would education

look like if we were to invent it right now?" "What skills does the information society demand of its members?"

We must be willing to hear the answers to those questions and if necessary let yesterday's education system die along with the industrial era it was created to serve.

People *know* the system no longer works. Like the pioneering companies that are re-inventing the corporation, the most creative schools and educators are experimenting with new models, groping for the new ways and the new arrangements that make sense now.

Once we accept the challenge of re-inventing education, we are free to stop justifying our failures and to move ahead to the creative part, which asks, "Where do we go from here?"

Back to Basics vs. High Tech

Where *do* we go from here? Is it back to basics or forward to high tech?

We say neither. It is time to give the kids a little TLC. Only, in this case, TLC does not mean "tender loving care" (though we all need that). TLC is shorthand for learning how to *Think*, learning how to *Learn*, and learning how to *Create*. These are the new basics, the three Rs of the new information society—Thinking, Learning, and Creating.

Do we mean that the old basics—reading, writing, and arithmetic—should no longer be taught? Hardly. There is no doubt that students need to learn to read, write, and do math. The point is that to stop there is to equip them only with skills their grandparents had—which is like giving them a wrench to fix a computer. There is nothing wrong with a wrench, but it will not fix a computer.

When we make the old reliable basics the be-all and end-all of education, we reduce the three Rs to remedial, repetitious, and rote.

Alongside the three Rs, it is time to give our young people a little thinking, learning, creating—the high-tech/high-touch skills on which the new information society and the new corporation need to be built.

Before describing the specific ways in which today's education innovators—both in schools and in corporations—are incorporating TLC into the curriculum, we want to notice the powerful bottom-up trend toward reestablishing quality in education.

Though we believe that educational reform will not equip our students for the new information society, we applaud the grass-roots demand for accountability and competence in education.

Quality: A Bottom-Up Education Trend

Today's education-reform movement is no doubt the most ambitious effort since 1957—the year the Russians launched *Sputnik* and the United States launched its drive to catch up in space and in education. Baby boomers in grade school then were challenged with math problems "any Russian child your age could do."

But there is a big difference between 1957 and today. That earlier reform movement started with the federal government. Today's reform is coming from the bottom up, from local school boards and state legislatures.

Long before the now famous damning report of the National Commission on Excellence in Education, parents and educators all across America had drawn their own conclusions about the declining quality of American education.

In our business offices, we found recent graduates who could not read or write well. In retail stores, clerks were hard-pressed to calculate the right change. Merchants purchased "idiot-proof" cash registers. In fast-food establishments, the keys on cash registers had pictures of hamburgers or french fries, which, when pressed, recorded the price. News stories about declining scores on college entrance exams and other standardized tests only reinforced what we already knew.

Just after the commission's findings were published, the American people had a chance to express their own opinions about education, to give the schools a report card from the American public. The results of *Phi Delta Kappan*'s annual Gallup poll on education were published in September 1983.

The schools did not do well. Thirty-two percent gave the schools a C grade and 20 percent a D or F. Thirty-one percent gave the schools an A or B, the lowest percentage since the question was first asked in 1974.

By any standard, a bad report card. On the other hand, these critical views were energizing people to act. State by state, school district after school district, parents, teachers, and local officials were already weeding out the second- and third-rate courses from the local curriculum and again requiring that students take the more traditional courses— English, science, math, languages, social studies.

This ground swell of support for better education has since become so powerful that the return of quality standards became a sort of educational megatrend all its own.

Still, the Excellence Commission's report was shocking. Although we knew education was not what it should be, few of us were prepared to have our worst fears documented and confirmed:

- Compared with students of other industrialized countries, American students rated last on seven different test scores.

- Some 23 million Americans are functionally illiterate.
- The navy reported to the commission that one-quarter of its recent recruits could not read at ninth-grade level—which is necessary to understand written safety instructions.
- Combined SAT scores dropped some 90 points between 1967 and 1982.

"A rising tide of mediocrity," the commission concluded, made us "a nation at risk."

Several other major education reports followed, reaching many of the same conclusions.

"Each weekday morning more than 13 million young people stream into America's 16,000 public high schools. One in ten receives an education as fine as any in the world; twice as many are condemned to schools that mock the name. The majority glide through with the understanding that they won't demand too much from school, and the school won't demand too much from them," wrote *Newsweek* in summarizing the results of *High School: A Report on Secondary Education in America,* sponsored by the Carnegie Foundation for the Advancement of Teaching. Its main author was former U.S. Commissioner of Education Ernest Boyer, who was far more optimistic than the authors of the Excellence Commission report.

"We see a different patient and a different prognosis," says Boyer. "America is turning once again to education."

The Boyer report among other things recommended:

- less emphasis on SATs, which are a poor measure of college aptitude, and the creation of a new SAT to measure achievement
- active recruitment of and better schooling for teachers
- a new partnership between schools and colleges and universities

- a 25-percent pay increase for all teachers
- a career track for teachers: associate teachers, full teachers, and senior teachers
- writing required in every course. (See the section in this chapter on learning how to think/learning how to write.)
- eliminate "tracking," which segregates students into groups of bright, average, and poor learners. Instead, everyone would take the same course, with no watered-down versions.

Some 270 smaller commissions and task forces set to work in all fifty states, and the reform movement, already established at the grass roots, galloped to a feverish pitch. By spring 1985:

- Twenty-one states were pushing for better textbooks.
- Thirty-five states had enacted proposals to increase high school graduation requirements, while at least thirteen others were considering such moves.
- Thirty-four states had created or were considering minimum competency tests for high schools.
- Another thirty-four states were in the process of tightening college admission criteria.
- Thirty-eight states were looking for ways to lengthen instruction time, including fourteen which lengthened either the school day or the school year.

"The stage is set for recovery," believes Bill Honig, California superintendent of public instruction. "Now comes the hard professional work—developing good curricula, attracting and holding good teachers, working on the textbooks, testing, involving the community."

That kind of optimism, it seems, is catching. Only one year after the 1983 Gallup poll on education (the worst in the poll's ten-year history), Americans showed an impressive increase in confidence in education. Forty-two percent gave local schools an A or B (up from just 31 percent the year before).

"Americans are more favorably disposed toward the public schools today than at any time in the past decade," wrote George Gallup, analyzing the poll's findings.

Mr. Gallup thought the higher ratings meant that the public believes schools have "heeded the criticisms . . . and have instituted reforms."

Furthermore, the Gallup poll shows evidence that people are willing to pay for better schools. Although three out of four adults do not have children in school, 41 percent of the Gallup respondents in 1984 would vote for higher taxes to support local schools—an 11-point increase since 1981.

A *New York Times* poll in February 1983 showed that 51 percent would pay as much as $200 more a year in taxes to help the schools.

In some communities this has already started to happen.

More than half the states have passed tax increases to fund school budgets.

Many more local communities will take that lead, seeking ways to fund, among other things, merit pay increases for teachers—an increasingly popular way to attract and keep the best teachers. Six states have some sort of incentive pay plan, while twenty-seven others are considering proposals to pay teachers based on performance.

It is essential to bring quality and accountability back into education, but it is not enough. We must go further and introduce the new skills that are appropriate to the information society, skills that are equally valuable in the classroom and in the corporation—thinking, learning, and creating.

Learning How to Think

How valuable is an education that does not teach you how to

think? That is the question on the minds of many people who are appalled at the poor thinking skills of today's students.

We all know that scores on college entrance exams and other standardized tests have plummeted in the past twenty years. But the experts who analyze individual test questions say students are especially weak on the questions that require thinking.

This is not a surprise for groups like the National Assessment of Educational Progress, which reported that problem-solving ability in math declined throughout the 1970s. Inferential reading ability dropped in 1981 for both junior and senior high school students. Tests from 1983 and 1984 are still being analyzed.

But what has caused this monumental thinking slump? Part of the blame goes to the Back to Basics movement. Pressured to raise scores on SAT and other standard tests, some teachers succumb to "teaching the tests" and downplaying the important reasoning skills behind the basics.

In today's information society, that is a disastrous error. As many forward-thinking educators are recognizing, the ability to think and reason logically and coherently *is* the new basic skill.

"It's not so much that basics are out, it's that we're reexamining what the basics are," says Carol Kuykendall, assistant superintendent of Houston's public schools. She puts it this way:

In a world of rapid technological change, the basics of 2000 will not be the basics of 1984.

But what exactly is this new basic skill called thinking? Thinking is the ability to synthesize and make generalizations, to divide into categories, to draw inferences, to

distinguish between fact and opinion, to put facts in order to
analyze a problem.

Traditionally, however, most of us have put thinking
ability into the same category as creativity, believing (quite
incorrectly) that either you are born with it or you go
through life doing without.

The educational innovators of the new information society, however, are rejecting that clichéd approach and
experimenting with a host of new programs that teach
thinking.

"Thinking has to do with the way information is arranged
and rearranged to make decisions, solve problems, create
opportunities, and raise human potential," says Edward de
Bono, founder and director of the largest program in the
world for teaching thinking as a specific skill.

"Thinking is the most fundamental and important skill.
Like all human skills, it can be learned and developed," he
believes.

De Bono's Thinking Megamodel

Edward de Bono is an Oxford-educated professor at
Cambridge University in addition to running his own thinking institute. He is probably the world's leading advocate of
teaching thinking.

It is a function of the clarity of de Bono's approach that
his thinking courses work equally well with schoolchildren
or executives.

In the United States, de Bono has taught thousands of
Fortune 500 executives how to improve their thinking skills,
yet his courses have also been used in more than 5,000
schools worldwide in industrialized, developing, even
communist countries.

In Venezuela, for example, 106,000 teachers have been
trained to teach de Bono's thinking techniques as part of

that country's extraordinary national program to increase the intelligence of its people.

Writing in *Phi Delta Kappan*, the nation's leading education magazine (with an audience that could spread his thinking course to millions of American students), de Bono made the strongest argument we have heard for teaching thinking in the new information society:

Information is no substitute for thinking and thinking is no substitute for information. The dilemma is that there is never enough time to teach all the information that could usefully be taught.

De Bono is absolutely right. The more information we have, the more we need to be competent thinkers. This is the quandary of the information society: We have an over-abundance of data. But we lack the intelligence, the thinking ability, with which to sort it all out. That is why thinking is now as basic as reading.

De Bono's program consists of sixty different thinking lessons which a student can follow with an individual instructor, by mail, or in arranged small classes.

The first lesson, called PMI, is a simple exercise which illustrates de Bono's approach.

PMI stands for "plus, minus, interesting." It is a way to scan and map out the ramifications of an idea or possible action, instead of reacting the way we usually do with a snap judgment about whether we like or dislike an idea without really exploring all the possible outcomes.

PMI works with any idea—going back to college, asking the boss for a raise, seeing a movie with Joe. Whatever idea you want to explore, make a list of the plus points (P), a list of the minus points (M), and a list of the points that are neither plus nor minus, just interesting (I).

With executives, the idea might be, "What if everybody

in the company wore badges to show what sort of mood they were in?''

Some of the responses to the badge idea might be:

(P) "We'd know the boss was in a bad mood and would not ask for a raise.''

(M) "Declaring one's moods might be an invasion of privacy.''

(I) "It might be fun to get up in the morning and decide your prevailing mood for the day.''

It sounds easy and it is. But exploring an idea objectively requires discipline. It really *does* make you think. If you do not like an idea, it is extremely difficult to look for the positive points.

One of the characteristics of a thoughtful person is hopefully the ability to be broad-minded. Though we talk a lot about how valuable it is for people to be open and tolerant, it is usually a vague hope. PMI is a specific tool which directs you (or a family member or coworker) to explore an idea.

Millions of people have improved their thinking skills with de Bono's program, which is not, of course, the only approach to thinking. There are many other innovative models.

New Jersey's Philosopher Kids

"In our view, critical thinking and the ability to solve problems are the most important skills we can give youngsters today,'' says Nat Giancola, superintendent of schools in Totowa, New Jersey, where philosophy is a required course for students in grades one through eight.

The children at Memorial Middle School, for example, read stories designed to raise questions that have puzzled philosophers for centuries. They are encouraged to express ideas freely and openly and are not judged to be right or wrong.

Totowa's program, called Philosophy for School Children, was developed by Dr. Matthew Lipman, a professor at New Jersey's Montclair State College. It is already showing results.

In a 1981 experiment, 2,500 philosophy students in grades five, six, and seven tested 80 percent higher in reasoning skills than a control group. The Lipman program is now taught in 4,000 school districts in every state and in some foreign countries.

When young people study thinking, does their academic performance improve?

That is the question the University/Urban Schools National Task Force will try to answer with a major new study funded in part with a $300,000 grant from the College Board.

The study will compare the careers of thousands of students from Chicago, Detroit, Memphis, Minneapolis, San Francisco, and New York who learned reasoning and thinking skills with other students who did not.

Thinking Your Way into Medical School

The teaching of thinking is finding its way into the college curriculum as well. At Xavier University in New Orleans, a private black college, premed students take a four-week course in reasoning designed to improve their performance in science and math and to raise scores on the Medical School Admissions Test. According to the school's premed adviser, the course is credited with getting eighteen seniors into medical school each of the last three years, more blacks than were admitted from any other school except Howard, Harvard, Morehouse, and Michigan.

Learning to Think/Learning to Write

"Clear thinking becomes clear writing: one can't exist without the other. It is impossible for a muddy thinker to write good English," writes William Zinsser in his excellent book *On Writing Well*.

The best writers have known it all along and now teachers are catching on. Good writing and clear thinking go hand in hand.

If our students' thinking skills have deteriorated badly—and we know they have—perhaps it is because their writing skills have grown equally slack. More and more educators have reached that same conclusion and come up with the same solution: Strengthen the writing curriculum as an avenue to sharpen thinking.

In a national survey of more than 1,200 colleges, nearly one-third reported that large numbers of their students were poor writers.

Perhaps the main reason students do not write well is that they rarely practice. Appallingly, only 3 percent of classroom time and 3 percent of homework in high school require writing so much as a paragraph, according to a study commissioned by the National Council of Teachers of English. Today's students are getting a multiple-choice "education," and the written essay, once an educational mainstay, has become an antique.

A new emphasis on writing, however, is bringing the venerable essay back into service. With its revival comes a welcome new attitude: Writing should be fun and creative for both students and teachers.

That is in stark contrast to the traditional obsession with grammar, punctuation, and the other rules of the writing game which grind away the enthusiasm of all but the most persistent and gifted student. With so much attention on our faults, it is little wonder so few of us learn to write clearly and well.

The Thinking/Writing Process

The new writing revival stresses the creative over the mechanical. It focuses on the writing process—what happens before, during, and after writing—rather than looking only at the written product.

At New York's City University, for example, Dr. Sondra Perl's students keep a journal to jot down ideas and notes before starting an "official" writing assignment.

Journal writing gets students to *think* out loud before the act of writing. "There is a kind of mental rehearsal as the student asks himself what he really wants to say," says Dr. Perl.

There is a growing consensus that new approaches work better than conventional techniques.

"Every bit of research shows that instruction in traditional grammar for its own sake doesn't improve writing," says Skip Nicholson, a Burbank, California, English teacher and chairman of the secondary school section of the National Council of Teachers of English.

The University of Chicago's Dr. George Hillocks reviewed seventy-two research studies on writing instruction and concluded that the traditional approach—lecturing students and expecting them to produce a piece of writing—is the *least* effective way to teach writing.

But even these new techniques do not solve the major problem: Most teachers—English teachers included—have not the foggiest notion about how to *teach* writing.

The Teacher as Writer

One group, however, the National Writing Project, is devoted to solving that basic problem.

"About ten years ago, people began to realize that children were writing not just poorly, but terribly," says Richard Sterling, director of the New York City Writing Project, part of the National Writing Project. "We discovered then that before we can teach students, we have to reteach teachers,'' says Sterling.

The goal of the National Writing Project is to teach teachers how to teach writing by teaching the teachers to be better writers. The group operates in 116 sites in forty-four states and is capable of training 70,000 teachers annually.

While writing and rewriting their own pieces, the teachers experience the writer's frustration and loneliness, all the while gaining empathy for their own students.

''I was frustrated most of the time,'' says Lillian Rossi, a high school English teacher from New York. ''I kept trying to find a lesson plan or a purpose in the whole thing.'' Mrs. Rossi's writing about the death of a loved one provoked a breakthrough that helped her better understand her own students. ''We don't write in structured ways and we can't force students to, either,'' she discovered.

Back in the classroom, Lillian Rossi decided to bend the rules to encourage creativity: Students in her three writing classes are now allowed to sit on either the windowsills or the floor and to munch on cookies while writing.

Teachers who have completed the program report better quality writing, higher attendance, and more enthusiasm about writing. ''They are much more anxious to write,'' says one teacher. ''They don't moan anymore when I ask them to write.''

Writers-in-the-Schools

The success of the National Writing Project leads to an interesting question: If it takes a good writer to teach the subject, why not have professional writers teach creative writing in the schools?

The answer is that they do. Four thousand writers have participated since 1972. It might be the ideal model for certain communities to beef up the writing curriculum.

Writers-in-the-schools is not a new model, yet it deserves

a second look because of the new appreciation for writing and the relationship of writing to thinking, learning, and creating—TLC.

Writers are often willing to do what many teachers are not—experiment. They are more likely to try the offbeat: writing while listening to music or viewing photographs or writing television commercials and songs. What makes the programs so successful? Writers can often view the creative process from the child's vantage point.

Writing-across-the-Curriculum

"How did we ever forget that schools are a place for reading, writing, and thinking?" asks Dr. Elaine Maimon, a professor at Beaver College, Glenside, Pennsylvania. Dr. Maimon, who has organized writing workshops for colleagues outside the English department, is a prime force in a new movement called writing-across-the-curriculum.

The idea is not to "teach" writing as such but to *use* writing to teach all subjects.

Other colleges are taking the same approach. Yale, Michigan Technological University, and the University of Texas at Austin have used similar approaches. Minnesota State University is using a $1-million grant from the Bush Foundation to give professors intensive training in how to incorporate writing into their courses.

What are some examples?

- History students write the history of an American family through the centuries.
- One teacher started a science and math journal and challenged students to compete for the honor of being published in one of the journal's nine slots.
- In a sex education class, students wrote letters to the imaginary editor of a sex education text.

The popularity of writing across the curriculum in high schools is growing steadily. Requests for workshops on the subject have increased threefold in the last two years, according to Mary Kay Healy, coordinator of the Bay Area Writing Project in California.

Learning How to Learn

Whenever one of us lectures, the question that always seems to come up is, "What subject should I (or my child) study in order to be really prepared for the future?"

People half expect a high-tech answer like "computer programming" or "fiber optics"! But we answer with a very old-fashioned idea:

In a world that is constantly changing, there is no one subject or set of subjects that will serve you for the foreseeable future, let alone for the rest of your life. The most important skill to acquire now is *learning how to learn*.

If you know how to learn, you can adapt and change no matter what technological, social, or economic permutations occur.

If you know how to learn, you will not be completely devastated if, like many U.S. autoworkers, your job has moved overseas, or like many steelworkers, your equipment has grown obsolete.

If you know how to learn, you possess the necessary tool—your learning ability—to study new fields and acquire new knowledge.

How do you learn?

Learning requires openness and curiosity.

"What we have to learn first is 'how to unlearn,' " wrote

the English explorer and scholar Richard Burton some 100 years ago.

Learning how to learn requires humility.

"You have to be able to concede . . . that there are those who are better and cleverer than oneself," wrote author Doris Lessing in an article entitled "Learning How to Learn" about her experiences studying Sufism.

Learning sometimes requires finding the right teacher and becoming a proper apprentice or surrendering one's previous conceptions to create the openness needed for real learning.

It might mean discovering by trial and error where to look for information. A child gets a taste of learning how to learn when the teacher says, "There is the library. Find out about the Civil War."

Journalists with new assignments about which they know absolutely nothing learn how to learn by gathering information piece by piece, source by source, formulating and testing hypotheses.

Learning how to learn requires self-knowledge. It means answering questions, such as, "How do I learn best?" and "Where do I learn best?"

Many of us, for example, have discovered that we have learned more in a weekend seminar than in an entire semester at college. At one such weekend format, for example, we learned a wealth of new concepts about this very subject—learning how to learn.

In summer 1984 we visited one of our own favorite places to learn, the Tarrytown Executive Conference Center, which hosted a weekend seminar called "The Coming Education Explosion," known more informally as "The Education Tent Show" because of the huge tent which housed the audience and speakers and for the festive rather than academic atmosphere that permeated the entire event.

These are some of the ideas we learned about—which are themselves new models of learning how to learn:

- From Reuven Feuerstein, a brilliant Israeli teacher of children with learning problems, we learned that the more people have taught or interacted with a young child (what he calls "mediated learning experience"), the greater the child's learning capacity. This important insight is at the core of Feuerstein's Instrumental Enrichment (IE) program, 500 pages of problems and exercises with a difference: Teachers are specifically trained to interrupt students frequently to guide and help them find the answers. IE is used in thirty-nine states and several countries.

- With Donald Campbell, we experienced the power of sound in the learning and teaching process. Campbell, the author of *Introduction to the Musical Brain,* showed us a series of exercises using sound, music, and visualizations. Music has the power to awaken millions of neurons in the brain and is a far more powerful learning force than speech, he believes.

- Howard Gardner, a Harvard psychologist, explained his theory of seven different types of intelligences or completely different ways of knowing:

  mathematical (in scientists and mathematicians)
  linguistic (in poets)
  musical
  spatial (in architects, sculptors, pilots, and painters)
  kinesthetic (which dancers, surgeons, and athletes possess)
  interpersonal (understanding others and what motivates them)
  intrapersonal (knowing yourself)

Gardner believes the intelligences operate quite independently of one another and have different life cycles. Musical intelligence, for example, can appear in very young children; mathematicians and lyric poets often peak in their twenties, while interpersonal and intrapersonal insight grows over a lifetime.

One could easily devote a whole college course to studying any of these ideas, yet in that one weekend we learned (and will remember) the equivalent of a graduate course in a subject that might be called Introduction to Learning How to Learn.

But instead of reading books by the authors the professor would have assigned, we met and talked with the dozen speakers and met scores of other audience participants as illustrious as the program's featured speakers. And we did all of this in an uplifting and beautiful environment of the beautiful New York countryside.

The weekend conference/seminar is an important model concerned with learning how to learn and lifelong learning.

Learning to Be Creative

The realm of creativity is one place where few businesspeople feel competent, even comfortable. In this society, we think creativity is for the scientist, the artist, or the musical genius, not for the typical corporate manager.

But in the new information-rich, decentralized, global society, creativity will be increasingly valued in business. Creativity is the corporation's competitive edge. It is the special talent that discovers the right market niche.

Creativity finds that final bug in the new computer system, writes the proposal that gets the company into Saudi Arabia, redesigns the organization chart into a decentralized network, and meets the other challenges the megatrends bring.

The need for creativity in the re-invented corporation is a relatively new phenomenon.

The mass production–oriented industrial society relied on uniformity to produce results. No creativity or individuality on the assembly line—please.

In the new corporation, creativity and individuality are organizational treasures.

But even if we accept the notion that we all need to be more creative, the question remains: Can creativity be taught?

We believe the answer is yes. So do many corporations which are experimenting with a wide variety of ways to stimulate creativity in the corporation. They are hiring creativity consultants, teaching employees to meditate, even encouraging people to listen to relaxing music—all an acknowledgment of the growing importance of creativity, part of TLC.

Corporate Creativity

Roger Von Oech, the author of *A Whack on the Side of the Head,* is stimulating idea-spawning sessions for companies like Amdahl, ARCO, Wells Fargo, IBM, Lockheed, and Xerox by teaching employees to break out of their traditional modes of thinking and approach problems creatively.

At Varian, a $600-million Palo Alto electronics firm, Von Oech's mission was to help the company create a more efficient solar cell made out of a new material called gallium. A week after his seminar, engineers there had increased the cell's efficiency from 22 to 24 percent. To techno-peasants like us, 2 percent does not sound like much of an increase. In reality, it was a big breakthrough.

At Du Pont, Von Oech taught his techniques to accountants. Result: They saved the company millions of dollars by finding sources of money at a couple of points below the prime interest rate.

"One of my key ideas is this," he says. "It's really hard to see the ideas that are right on the side of you or behind you. It's really hard to see fresh ideas by looking twice as hard in one direction. Often, what people need is a whack on the side of the head."

How do you give yourself a "whack on the side of the head"? Von Oech suggests the following:

- Challenge the rules.
- Inspect your own rules.
- Fall out of love with your own rules and ideas.
- Think frivolously. Make jokes about the problem you are working on.

That last suggestion recalls the advice of the famous advertising man David Ogilvy, who wrote a series of rules for creative thinking. His first rule was, "The best ideas come as jokes. Make your thinking as funny as possible."

The Corporate Muse

What about a musical whack? It has long been believed that music stimulates creativity while relaxing the body and mind. Senior managers at Singer are taking that belief quite seriously. They can be seen daydreaming in their offices while listening to Chopin or Bach on the Walkman.

Moreover, they have learned this unusual behavior at company-sponsored seminars featuring Richard Larenz, European sales manager for Singer's Link division. Larenz, who trained to be a professional violinist before becoming an electrical engineer, calls it "imagineering," and his seminar is based on the premise that certain types of music can provide mental relaxation and stimulate creativity.

Imagineering got its start in the U.S. *Apollo* moon flight program where Larenz, then an engineer on the Apollo project, used music to help astronauts to relax. While spending an hour on the beach did little to relieve the tension of the sixteen-to-eighteen-hour days, Larenz found that exposing them to harmonic music significantly aided relaxation. And they could use it whenever they needed it.

Musicologist Steven Halpern of the Spectrum Research Institute in California has reached the same conclusion. Halpern composes haunting mood music for relaxation. Sales of his recordings, which doubled every year for three years, reached the $1-million mark in 1984. Kitaro and George Winston are even better known with sales between five and ten times Halpern's, according to Todd Broadie, director of sales and marketing at Neruda, a music distributor.

Halpern reports that orders for his music have come from corporations such as Bell & Howell Education Group, Inc., Dow Chemical, the Upjohn Company, the Coca-Cola Bottling Co., and the American Red Cross.

"Even after the first few sessions, people say they never realized what a storehouse of relaxation there was in music," says Larenz. "It is far easier than meditation. The music gets you going sooner, supplying intellectual stimulation and magnifying the relaxation."

The Corporate Mantra

In a letter published in *International Management*, Reino Avela, a Finnish management consultant of twenty-two years, wrote, "I find managers are often so stressed in their work that they are increasingly unable to cope with new ideas or start anything new unless forced to it. I have found meditation to be a real help."

American companies are discovering the benefits of meditation, too. Though some offer meditation courses for stress management and as part of a wellness program (see Chapter 6), there is also a payoff in increased creativity.

Among the companies that have taught meditation are Adolph Coors Co., General Motors, Transco, AT&T, Connecticut General Insurance, and Ampex Corp.

The basic assumption of the human potential movement is that we utilize only a fraction of our full potential. The starting point in releasing creativity through practices like meditation, daydreaming while listening to relaxing music, and even brainstorming in creativity seminars is to move beyond ordinary consciousness.

Our most creative scientists and artists speak about their experiences in altered states of consciousness—dreams, meditativelike trances, daydreams, intuitive flashes, deep relaxation, and visualization. Developing creativity means learning how to be at home in these strange new settings.

Dr. Tom B. Roberts, professor of educational psychology at Northern Illinois University, believes we will ultimately define the "fully educated person" as one who "can select the appropriate state of consciousness for his/her purpose, voluntarily enter it, and use and develop the abilities that reside there."

Creativity in the Classroom

But have these special applications found their way into the educational mainstream? For the most part, the answer is no.

Our schools are perfect models of rationality—desks lined all in a row and school bells ringing to mark the end of each class. As Alvin Toffler pointed out in *The Third Wave*, the schools are organized like factories in order to socialize people to work in factories.

Young people brimming with creative potential are run through a system that recognizes and deals only with the linear, logical, rational side of human and social reality.

How do we engage the whole person, the whole brain, in the process of education?

Today's innovators in education are taking up that challenge. And one of their most interesting discoveries is that of going way beyond the basics to visualization. They are teaching children to close their eyes and mentally rehearse a skill or activity before actually doing it—the same technique Olympia athletes use. Visualization helps students improve their ability to read, write, and do mathematics.

Dr. Beverly-Colleene Galyean, director of the Center for Integrative Learning in Los Angeles, has introduced students in the Los Angeles public schools to what she calls the four Rs—relaxation, reflection, re-creation, and renewal. She persuaded administrators that the four Rs can improve the three Rs. Dr. Galyean synthesized English, music, and art with relaxation, deep breathing, focusing, concentration, guided imagery, visualization, and sensory awareness.

"In every project, we saw impressive gains in the cognitive areas being treated...areas of self-concept, and appreciation, self-starting, creativity, expanded comprehension, warmth, openness with others, and introspection," she concludes. High school students used visualization to improve athletic performance, personal relationships, and job performance, she says.

Washington State's Dee Dickinson, coordinator of New Horizons for Learning, shows teachers in Washington, California, and Connecticut, all bellwether states, how to use visualization and guided imagery.

At Mead School of Byram, Connecticut, and Walden School of Pasadena, California, Dickinson's colleagues have taught teachers the kinesthetic approach—using psychophysical exercises such as those used in T'ai Chi, the ancient Chinese discipline. First thing in the morning, students focus and center their attention through deep breathing and slow, flowing movements.

Students are more stimulated, engaged, and curious to learn when they are taught to learn with all their senses rather than just to read or listen, says Dickinson. At some schools using these techniques, math and reading scores have risen 20 points after one year.

Even the business schools are getting the idea: Stanford has a course called Creativity in Business, which is designed to teach right-brain skills.

Lifelong Learning

In the new information society where the only constant is change, we can no longer expect to get an education and be done with it. There is no one education, no one skill, that lasts a lifetime now.

Like it or not, the information society has turned all of us into lifelong learners who must periodically upgrade our marketable skills and expand our capacity for knowledge.

During the industrial era, to have one's job become obsolete was like the end of the world. Over the next decade, job obsolescence will become increasingly commonplace and people may even welcome the opportunity to engage in four or five different careers over the course of a lifetime.

The Adult Education Boom

It is already happening today. The economic and political megashifts of the past decade have brought a tidal wave of adults back into the classroom.

These new lifelong learners include would-be career changers, upwardly mobile MBA types, engineers and technicians in fast-changing fields, homemakers reentering the job market, executives, and former auto- and steelworkers.

"Virtually everyone who comes in the door to take a course is doing so for job-related reasons," says one continuing education director. "Very little of it is for enrichment."

For college administrators, it could not have happened at a better time. The baby bust—that generation which is about to create a seller's market in labor because of their small numbers—recently entered their college years. The sharp drop-off in the number of students could have brought extremely rough financial times for colleges and universities.

But then came the adult boom. And the schools which made the most of change—by catering to today's thirtyish collegian—turned a demographic challenge into a profitable opportunity. Instead of restructuring themselves to handle fewer full-time students, they geared up to handle many more students—but on a part-time basis.

The change is still unfolding. By 1993 the number of eighteen-year-olds who would be potential college students will have declined 25 percent nationwide since 1977.

But the adult education boom shows no signs of letting up: The number of people taking some kind of adult education courses rose from 13 million in 1969 to 20 million in 1982, a figure representing four times the number of full-time students.

This colossal continuing education boom is taking place in colleges and universities, community colleges, for-profit trade schools, businesses, publicly funded job-skills centers and night schools, agricultural extension services, and the armed forces.

Once dismissed as second or third rate in academic circles, adult education has gained a new respectability. One-third of the nation's colleges will accept for credit the nearly 2,000 training programs offered by businesses and the government—unheard-of just a decade ago.

Community colleges are in the midst of the movement. A story in the *Chicago Tribune* put it this way:

> Community colleges in Illinois and the nation are shedding their image as "glorified high schools" to become leaders in the retooling of American society for a postindustrial, high technology economy.
>
> Low tuition, accessibility, flexible hours and innovative job training programs have made the nation's 1,231 community colleges magnets for a record number of job-hungry students.

The most revolutionary aspect of the new adult education boom, however, and the most interesting, is *where* and in some cases *when* all this new learning is taking place.

We are re-inventing education for adult lifelong learners by scheduling courses at the convenience of the student, not the school.

To make the most of today's educational renaissance, schools must go where the students are: in the office, in front of TV, in the Silicon Valleys of America—even on commuter trains.

The adult education programs that will be most successful now are those that have decided, in reconceptualizing what business they are in, to be in the "learning on the run" business.

Today's over-twenty-five student will sign up for the course that helps him or her balance work, family, and school. The best way to attract that student's educational dollar is by making it as convenient as possible to go to school.

More than 700 students go to the Illinois Institute of Technology without ever leaving their offices. The institute televises courses in computer science, engineering, finance, and management to a group of some twenty-four Chicago-area companies. In Philadelphia, 150 employees of CIGNA Corporation study for their liberal arts degrees every day on the job site from 4:30 to 7:10 P.M.

Another way to go where the students are is by decentralizing—opening branches in areas like Silicon Valley, which are filled with upwardly mobile employees who are virtually all potential students. Silicon Valley has attracted branches of the University of San Francisco, Golden Gate University, the University of Phoenix, and Pepperdine University. All that in addition to San Jose University and the University of Santa Clara.

But perhaps the most intriguing place to learn (and certainly most convenient) is on either the 6:59 A.M. Port Jefferson or the 7:55 A.M. Seaford/Babylon train from Long Island to Manhattan. More than 300 commuters have participated in Adelphi University's University on Wheels program.

5

Education and the Corporation

American business has begun playing an extraordinary dual role in education today. In society at large, American corporations have become this nation's leading education activists. Furthermore, within themselves, corporations are undergoing an extraordinary metamorphosis that is, in effect, transforming them into universities in their own right, so vast, so competent, that they begin to rival the traditional education system.

The new corporate role as educator-activist illustrates the ever-deepening connection between education and the corporation.

The job of education is to prepare students for life—a large portion of which is work. Yet today there is a profound mismatch between what the workplace needs and what the schools are providing. So wide is that gap that business feels compelled to enter the education arena in a big way.

Today's ill-prepared graduates become tomorrow's corporate burden. Three-quarters of U.S. large corporations teach remedial education and basic skills. Remedial reading programs alone cost companies $300 million annually, according to the American Society for Training and Development. Corporations lose millions of dollars more because of mistakes by workers who cannot read. That factor alone is behind much of the shift into the new corporate role as educator-activist.

But most important, as we approach the seller's market, a shrinking labor pool of entry-level workers will bring companies face-to-face with the prospect of hiring graduates who are even more poorly qualified. This represents a far-reaching threat to the promise of prosperity in the new information society.

This chapter describes the corporation's two new roles—the activist and the educator. The activist seeks to improve education; the educator provides it as a university of lifelong learning.

The Corporate Education Activist

The corporation as education activist is visible all across America. Businesspeople are entering the neighborhood classroom in unprecedented numbers to teach, contribute equipment, and offer role models for today's young people. And corporations are playing a leading role in the fight against illiteracy.

High-tech companies are American education's secret weapon against the critical lack of science and math teachers. A cadre of engineers, computer scientists, and other specialists are putting aside their corporate obligations to teach in innovative cooperative exchange projects.

To the chagrin of the education establishment, some businesspeople are enthusiastic about vouchers—the radical proposal to take school budgets away from the schools and put them into the hands of parents in the form of vouchers. Schools would then compete for vouchers, which would then constitute their school budget. Schools that could not attract enough vouchers would be forced to close.

American corporations are engaging in unprecedented educational experiments offering outlandish proposals such as contributing a computer to every classroom and guaranteeing a job for every high school graduate.

Even though corporations are emerging as potential rivals in the education business, cooperation between universities and corporations has never been stronger.

How do educators feel about this growing partnership? Some of our best are its greatest supporters. Ernest Boyer, former U.S. commissioner of education and author of *High School*, is a notable advocate of corporate involvement with the schools.

"In every major urban area, there is at least some collaboration between school systems and the network of businesses around them," says Boyer, who understands that this new relationship benefits both the schools and the corporations.

"This reflects enlightened self-interest by firms that realize that their futures are tied to having adequately trained manpower," says Boyer.

For educators, this new interest on the part of business could not come at a better time. Since the federal government is growing less and less supportive of education, educators are wisely encouraging all sorts of new partnerships between business and the schools.

Along with their innovative actions, American business is doing more. It is contributing to the schools in that important basic way—by giving money.

Corporations contributed more than $1.23 billion to education in 1983 (the last year for which figures are available) according to the Council of Financial Aid to Education. Companies in the bellwether state of California are in the vanguard: Bank of America contributes $1 million annually to education. Crocker National Bank invested $800,000 to bring courses on the "fourth R"—reconciliation of bank statements—into the schools.

Corporations and corporate foundations are contributing an increasing amount to secondary and even primary schools. As of 1984, some 400 companies, twice as many as in 1970, had provisions for matching what their employees contribute to schools. Some, like Meredith Publishing Co., double their employees' contributions.

Private schools do very well under this system, since the parents of private-school children are more inclined to make donations to their schools. St. Ignatius High School in Cleveland got $28,000 in matching grants in 1983—14 percent of its entire contributions.

"Everybody talks about the schools. Now some businesses are doing something about them," noted the *Los Angeles Times*.

The Allegheny Conference, a Pittsburgh business group, contributes $1 million annually to Pennsylvania schools. John Hancock has given $1 million to the Boston schools. In Hartford, Connecticut, local businesses tripled their contributions to the public school system between 1981 and 1983. The Travelers Insurance Company, for example, will contribute $500,000 for computer equipment to the Hartford Catholic school system between 1983 and 1987.

"Business leaders say they realize that if their companies are to thrive, Hartford must thrive also. And they realize a city can be only as healthy as its schools," concluded the *Hartford Courant*.

All across America, businesses have become the new local activists in education.

Adopt-a-School

In May 1984, American Can Company held its annual shareholders' meeting in the auditorium of the Martin Luther King, Jr., High School on New York City's Upper West Side.

Strange site for a shareholders' meeting? Of a company based in Greenwich, Connecticut? Not really. American Can Company has "adopted" the high school under a growing model program of business/education cooperation.

The White House Office of Private Sector Initiatives has identified 10,000 corporations involved with about 20,000 schools.

The Chase Manhattan Bank adopted Murray Bergtraum High School for Business Careers.

Frito-Lay Corp. adopted Dallas's Caillet Elementary School.

Booker T. Washington High School in Memphis, Tennessee, was adopted by Federal Express.

The adopt-a-school idea is a simple one: Rather than contributing to "education" in some vague way, individual companies link up with specific schools to create a personal relationship based on the schools' needs. Company employees tutor students, for example, or act as role models. It is not a new model, but an extremely successful one that deserves to be recognized and replicated.

Half the schools in New York City have been "adopted," as have thirty schools in the Nashville area.

Adopt-a-school has been particularly successful in Dallas. More than 1,000 area businesses and civic groups have adopted nearly all of the Dallas school district's 189 schools.

Rich Pachere, the Dallas Chamber of Commerce's adopt-a-school manager, cites the main reason businesses all across the United States are participating in various programs: "If we don't save the schools, it will erode the quality of life in Dallas."

When Dallas businesses ask Pachere, "What's in it for us?" he answers: "The company is the ultimate beneficiary of the educational enterprise. We're preparing a worker the company will not have to reeducate.

"Last year, U.S. business spent $30 billion to retrain and reeducate employees coming from the public schools. We are nipping that problem in the bud."

The Dallas program began the way many others did, through networking. Someone in Dallas heard about a longstanding relationship between a Detroit high school and the local phone company, Michigan Bell.

"We brought the principal down to pick his brain," says Larry Ascough, special assistant to the superintendent for communications in Dallas, and soon the Dallas program took off.

Adopt-a-school is a highly decentralized program and therein lies much of its success: Schools and companies work out unique relationships based on local needs and resources. Every locality, of course, is different. Some programs are undoubtedly superficial and in name only. But in other cases, there is real engagement.

- Chase Manhattan Bank set up a management training institute for principals.
- Fairchild Industries brings high school seniors into its boardroom as junior directors and hires teachers for part-time summer jobs.
- Bechtel, Shell Oil Co., and IBM have sent technical staff to work with students at their adopted schools.

It all depends on the individual local needs. The *Chicago Tribune* reports, for example, that the brainchild of predominately Hispanic Juarez School and Illinois Bell was a "bilingual call squad." The principal's top priority was improving attendance, so the phone company recruited thir-ty Spanish-speaking employees to call parents of absent students. Average attendance rose from 81 to 86 percent.

Says Mose Walker, principal of Booker T. Washington High School, "Federal Express is the best thing that has ever happened to Booker T. Washington and I mean that. It has had the most telling effect that any kind of community agency or outside agency has ever had on the school—period."

Bring in the Computers—and Let Companies Pay

If companies want to upgrade American education, why don't they contribute computers? Everyone agrees that com-puter literacy is a critical skill now and for the future. Isn't it a natural for companies—especially computer companies—to contribute this new high-tech tool which many schools cannot afford?

Apple Computer tried—and failed—to contribute an Ap-ple computer to every primary and secondary school, both public and private, in America.

Apple's failure shows there are lessons to be learned, problems to be resolved, if education is to derive the full benefits of a corporate community dedicated to re-inventing education.

The background to the story is this: Apple's chairman, Steve Jobs, ran into Congressman Fortney H. Stark on (where else?) an airplane between Washington and San Francisco. The two got to talking about the problems in American education, the need for computer literacy, and that sort of thing.

Jobs proposed contributing the computers—$200 million worth; Stark was enthusiastic. Back at Apple, though, the lawyers and accountants had a fit: Under current laws, companies can get a tax deduction for contributing scientific equipment to colleges and universities, but not to primary and secondary schools.

The Apple Bill

The solution seemed easy enough: Rep. Stark would introduce legislation to change the law. It easily passed the House of Representatives but ran into trouble, Big Trouble, in the Senate Finance Committee.

The Apple Bill, as it became known, aimed to increase the maximum percentage of taxable income a company could contribute—and get a tax break for—from 10 to 30 percent. The computer company also wanted its deduction based on the market value rather than manufacturer's cost, similar to the way scientific equipment contributed to U.S. colleges and universities can be deducted.

The Finance Committee, which regularly enacts tax loopholes for various special-interest groups that make the Apple proposal look like kid stuff (which it was intended to be), thought these provisions overly favorable to Apple and vetoed its plan.

Lawmakers, nurtured by the system where politicians pat each other on the back, are apparently incapable of understanding how to work out "win/win" resolutions. Apple's motive—to benefit itself while benefiting America's schoolchildren—was considered highly suspicious.

In the old line, old paradigm, win/lose framework, there must be a winner and a loser. If Apple is winning, somehow the American schoolchildren must be losing.

One big objection: Schoolchildren would get hooked on Apples, get their parents to buy Apples or buy their own, giving Apple an unfair advantage over other computer firms.

Apple's response: Other computer companies can contribute their machines, too. No unfairness there.

Congressional opponents calculated that Apple would be

the only company to take advantage of the tax break. "It's a gold mine," said one.

As the Congress confirmed its own obsolescence, the states, in true decentralist form, took responsibility for the school/computer revolution. The bellwether state of California (Apple's home base) legislated the tax break Apple sought and California children reaped $21 million worth of computer equipment during the 1983-84 school year.

Of course, Apple is not the only computer company trying to get its wares into the schools.

- Tandy Corporation has contributed $1 million worth of free computer courses to teachers since 1982 and has also awarded $500,000 in hard- and software to non-profits and others.
- IBM has contributed $12 million worth of school equipment to twenty-six school districts nationwide, benefiting more than 200,000 teachers and students.
- Xerox Corp. has contributed $5 million worth of computers to some forty inner-city neighborhoods.

Fighting Illiteracy Corporate Style

The U.S. Department of Education estimates there are 25 million illiterate Americans—those who cannot read or write a simple sentence. Millions more—some say as many as 60 million—are functionally illiterate, unable to read above fifth-grade level.

Each year the ranks of the illiterate swell with 1 million teenage dropouts and about 1.3 million non-English-speaking immigrants. Immigrants who are literate in their native tongue usually learn English—the rest do not.

You will not find many business leaders to dispute the Education Department's estimates. They know.

"The issue of functional illiteracy lies coiled at the center of our unemployment problems," says Robert W. Feagles, senior vice-president of Travelers Insurance Company.

Illiteracy costs the U.S. billions in welfare and unemployment benefits. And illiteracy is a contributing factor to the multibillion-dollar cost of keeping people in prisons. Half the prison population is illiterate, according to Diane Vines, director of the Education Department's National Adult Literacy Initiative.

"I am trying to remind people that there's a direct correlation between crime and illiteracy, between illiteracy and unemployment," says Barbara Bush, wife of the vice-president and longtime literacy activist.

But no one has to remind corporate America about the cost of illiteracy:

- At one New York insurance company, 70 percent of dictated correspondence must be redone at least once because of errors.
- A clerk at another insurance firm reimbursed a $22 dental claim with a check for $22,000. The clerk did not understand decimals.
- One medium-sized manufacturing company estimates it loses $250,000 per year because of mistakes by poorly educated, illiterate people.

If you think the solution is simply not to hire illiterates, think again. Remember the labor shortages of the late 1980s and 1990s, also known as the coming seller's market, that powerful trend compelling us to re-invent the corporation?

That same trend will soon make it increasingly impossible for companies to screen out illiterates. They simply will not be in a position to be that selective. Besides, they realize we cannot afford the future cost.

That is an important part of the reason that so many companies are joining the fight against illiteracy now. Aetna Life & Casualty and Gannett Foundation Co. contribute regularly to literacy programs, while Gulf & Western, J. C. Penney, and Citibank furnish space for tutoring sessions.

But the leading corporate literacy activist is probably B. Dalton Bookseller, which will contribute $3 million over a four-year period to combating illiteracy. Its goal is to recruit 50,000 volunteer tutors by 1986, a 150-percent increase over 1984.

B. Dalton of Minneapolis joined with ten other organizations including the American Library Association and the American Association of Advertising Agencies to form the Coalition for Literacy. The group's major activity is a national advertising campaign put together by New York's Benton & Bowles to recruit tutors and inform people about free teaching programs in their communities. The Business Council for Effective Literacy will pay $300,000 of the advertising company's costs.

Clearly, it is in the interest of business to have literate employees, but doesn't it go further than that?

Says Gloria Lanza, vice-president of the American Association of Advertising Agencies, "If we don't have people out there who can read, how can they read our ads?"

Closing the Math/Science Gap

There is another form of illiteracy threatening the booming information age.

Though we live in a high-tech society, the majority of us are becoming scientific and technical illiterates.

During the 1970s, scientific achievement tests declined steadily, and remedial mathematics courses in public colleges increased 72 percent.

This troubling lack of math and science skills handicaps the United States in a world where there is still economic competition from other technically competent countries—especially from Japan.

In a standard math test for thirteen-year-olds, Americans ranked eighth behind Japanese, Belgian, Dutch, Australian, British, Scottish, and French students.

And comparing the scientific and technical competence of American and Soviet students is a simple farce. Even if U.S. standards were substantially upgraded, American students would still lag behind their Russian counterparts: College-bound or not, Soviet students must take two years of calculus, four years of chemistry, five years of physics, and six years of biology!

This is disturbing, yet a deeper, more intractable problem is the critical lack of qualified math and science teachers:

- The National Science Teachers Association estimates that 60,000 of the nation's 200,000 science and math teachers are not qualified.
- Between 1972 and 1982, the pool of new science and math teachers declined 65 and 77 percent respectively.
- At least forty states cannot find enough math and science teachers.
- In Iowa, for example, the number of math education graduates dropped from 234 in 1970 to 38 in 1981.

It is clear that even if this society were determined to break out of its scientific and technological stupor, we could not do so—at least not by using conventional education resources. We simply do not have enough qualified teachers.

But American *corporations* do possess the valuable resource that could make all the difference. Within our high-tech companies are the world's most innovative scientific and technical minds—some of whom would have been gifted teachers but chose business over teaching young people for reasons that are not the least bit mysterious.

Beginning teachers average $14,278, for example, while accountants start out at $19,915, according to the Bureau of Labor Statistics, and systems analysts at between $22,500 and $28,500.

But business holds other, equally compelling attractions—the intellectually stimulating environment, the camaraderie of colleagues, the opportunity to grow and develop personal skills. Of course, the schools are supposed to offer these, too, but in the minds of many, they clearly do not.

Even if schools could afford to increase salaries enough to compete with business, the other amenities of the business world would persist.

For most local communities, the only way to close the math/science gap and upgrade science and math courses is by working out innovative ways to tap into the scientific and mathematical resources of American business.

And that is what is happening. All across America, business is responding enthusiastically to the schools and growing increasingly committed to closing the math/science gap.

In Chicago, for example, engineers from companies such as Ford Motor Co., Interlake, Inc., and Argonne National Laboratory teach 100 students from five suburban high schools a special course on how "book math" and science are applied in industry. Any student who has taken geometry or algebra—college-bound or not—can take the course. Those who pass a proficiency exam can get college credit.

North Carolina companies support the North Carolina School for Science and Mathematics, a residential school for gifted students.

In Georgia, Scientific-Atlanta, Inc., a satellite-communications equipment maker, invites students to visit its labs. "By providing role models, we can make it easier for them to decide to become engineers," says program coordinator Jesus Leon.

General Motors is investing $1 million a year in programs aimed at encouraging minority students to study math, science, and technology.

Dallas's SEED Program

In Dallas, nine Texas Instruments engineers serve as instructors in an extraordinary program in which disadvantaged students in twelve elementary schools are doing *college-level* algebra. It is a model for innovative excellence which would not be possible without the help of a committed local corporation.

The Dallas program is called Special Elementary Education for the Disadvantaged (SEED). It is an important model which demonstrates the connection between math, clear thinking, and self-confidence. According to SEED director Hamid Ebrahimi, its main objective is not math at all, but to increase self-esteem by showing students they can excel beyond their imagination.

"Math is the great equalizer," he says. "High and low achievers can sit around doing complex problems and their success will carry over into other parts of their lives."

"Add the numbers from 1 to 100 in seven seconds," the teacher might ask. Without calculators, even pencil and paper, they learn how to figure out the answers in their heads, a seemingly lost art in these high-tech days.

SEED instructors use the Socratic method, and students answer questions in unison. Randomly, the instructor picks individuals to prove their answers. There is not much emphasis on whether an answer is right or wrong, the idea being that the main way a student learns is by reasoning out how he or she arrived at the answer. The students are expected to help the person in the mathematical hot seat by silently waving their hands in agreement or disagreement with the proposed mathematical solution.

Classroom teachers believe these new skills spill over into other subjects. One fourth-grade teacher who had misgivings at first now endorses the program heartily. "Their thinking skills and listening skills have improved," he says.

Project SEED has been adapted to other communities with help from companies such as Bell Labs and IBM.

Connecting Company and Classroom

The key to closing the math/science gap is to replicate these school/business models so that engineers, computer scientists, and other technical people who want to teach some of the time can move more easily between the worlds of business and education.

All sorts of cooperative exchanges are possible.

Businesses can lend their science/math specialists to local schools for a semester of teaching or for a few classes each week, as in the Chicago and Dallas examples above. Kaiser Aluminum and ARCO grant employees paid leave to volunteer as teachers. Employees could coteach a course with a full-time professional teacher.

Businesses can hire science and math teachers to work part-time in business, supplementing their incomes while keeping up with state-of-the-art technology:

- Honeywell in Minneapolis recently started a summer jobs program for local math and science teachers.

- IBM operates a summer computer literacy program to teach teachers how to use the computers IBM has contributed to their schools.
- A summer jobs program for Cleveland teachers worked so well that one sponsor, Standard Oil of Ohio, plans to increase its participation from 25 to 100 teachers by summer 1985.
- A joint program between Digital Equipment Corporation (DEC) and the University of Massachusetts aims to attract science and math teachers by combining a fourteen-month master's degree program with a guarantee of three years of summer employment at DEC.

Virginia's High-Tech High School

The lack of science and math teachers is a challenge, but it is also an opportunity that could create new models of effective cooperation that could be used in many different areas.

In Fairfax County, Virginia, school/business cooperation has taken a different turn. Twenty-five local businesses have raised nearly $1 million in cash and equipment for a new college prep school of science and technology.

National companies with local branches such as AT&T, Mobil, Boeing, Honeywell, and Exxon have joined forces with local companies such as BDM Corporation, the county medical society, law and real estate companies, and public utilities to open the new facility at Thomas Jefferson High School in Annandale, Virginia, in fall 1985.

"We can't attract people for our business without an outstanding school for them to send their kids to," says Earle Williams, president of BDM International and a member of the county school superintendent's business advisory board.

Thomas Jefferson High School will be a jewel of a resource that should more than meet the goal of attracting job executive talent to Fairfax County. The science-and-math-minded kids who will attend will surely pronounce it "awesome":

- A $600,000 telecommunications lab will include a television studio and control room, a radio station, a weather station, and a satellite earth station.
- The biotech lab will be equipped for genetic engineering experiments in cloning and cell fusion.
- There will also be labs for energy, computers, and materials science.

"Business is committed to upgrading the overall quality of education in Fairfax County," says Mel Perkins, general manager of engineering at AT&T Communications Corp. and chairman of the superintendent's business advisory board. "We all live in this community, all our employees live here, and many have children going to the local schools. We want a quality environment."

The Boston Compact

"Give us literate, skilled graduates and we'll give them jobs." That is the deal some 200 Boston-area businesses have struck with the Boston Public School System.

It is revolutionary; it is risky and it is called the Boston Compact. But it is a new model of school/business cooperation that exemplifies the commonsense approach that people and institutions should stick to what they do best—that the schools stick to education and that business stick to business.

It is remarkable that the compact came together in Boston. The Boston school system has had a reputation for patronage and corruption, and there are many scars still remaining from a rough, at times violent, desegregation struggle that caused white enrollment to drop from 64 percent to 30 percent from 1970 to 1980.

All the while, the Boston schools must confront all the other typical problems facing urban education: illiteracy, an astronomical dropout rate (only half of Boston's ninth graders finish high school), budget cuts, and a cadre of teachers including some of the best and worst in the nation.

Given all the above, is the Boston Compact just another idealistic and unworkable scheme?

We think the Boston Compact will not only survive but evolve into a major educational model because it possesses these three factors: (1) an enthusiastic group of businesses that are motivated by economic necessity, (2) a very tough new breed of superintendent, and (3) a detailed plan spelling out precise, reasonable goals for both the schools and the businesses.

But it will not be easy. It will take the combined thrust of these three elements to break the powerful logic that breeds dropouts and unemployment: "Why should I study hard and graduate? There are no jobs out there for me anyhow."

The Boston Compact aims to break that vicious circle with this declaration: By 1986, every Boston high school graduate with minimum competency in reading and math will be guaranteed a job with a Boston area employer.

Unlike many public/private partnerships which overlook the nitty-gritty in favor of a declaration of "spiritual cooperation," the 106-page Boston Compact document lists identifiable, verifiable interim goals to be reached between the Compact's inception in September 1982 and the target date of 1986:

• The school system will reduce dropouts by 5 percent each year.

- Each year there will be 5 percent more graduates placed in either full-time jobs or higher education.
- Businesses will hire 400 graduates in 1983; 600 to 700 in 1984.
- Business will recruit other businesses to subscribe to the plan, which began under the auspices of "the Vault," a group of Boston's twenty-five leading CEOs. (They got this name because they once met in a vault.)

How did the Boston Compact rally so much business support? Undoubtedly, the Vault's prestige has helped. Companies like AA Glassmobile, Hub Mail Advertising Service, Inc., and Houlihan's Restaurant must enjoy seeing their names listed alongside Prudential, John Hancock, First National Bank, and Digital Equipment Corp. But the primary motivation—especially for the larger companies—is economic.

Initially, though, Boston's business community had the impression that school administrators did not welcome their involvement.

That was before the advent of "Six Gun" Spillane, the *Boston Globe's* name for Robert Spillane, the professional school superintendent hired in 1981. Shortly after Spillane took over, he fired eight of the system's seventeen high school headmasters (principals) and four tenured teachers for incompetence.

Business leaders respected Spillane's toughness and discovered that he wanted their support.

When William Edgerly, president of the State Street Bank and very active in Boston's local Private Industry Council (PIC), outlined the compact idea to Spillane, the Boston Compact was born.

Greater Boston, perhaps more than any place in America, has weathered—and weathered beautifully—the transition from the industrial to the information economy. Boston's old established economy already felt the impact of that mighty megashift in the early to mid-seventies—before the rest of the country.

Now Boston's information economy is well entrenched, and local employers are worried about getting the labor they will need to bring the new economy up to full speed.

"We already have a hard time filling jobs," says John P. LaWare, chairman of the Shawmut Bank of Boston. "There are a large number of kids who are totally unemployable."

How well is the Boston Compact doing? In 1984, 607 Boston high school graduates were placed in entry-level jobs with 220 employers. That meant the Compact met its goals of placing 600 graduates, 200 higher than the previous year's objective.

Graduates of seventeen public high schools and several alternative programs started with an average salary of $4.06 per hour, 36 cents per hour more than the previous year's average.

Not surprisingly, the graduates got jobs in Boston's booming information economy: 42 percent in banking, financial services, or insurance; 14 percent in health and hospitals; and 7 percent in retail food services. The rest of the jobs were in a variety of different areas, primarily information.

Boston has become a bellwether city for the coming seller's market. Corporations there are already facing the problems the rest of the country will confront in the late 1980s and into the 1990s. The Boston Compact is a daring solution. That is what makes it such an important new model.

Vouchers

Say the word *voucher* to someone from the American Federation of Teachers, the National Education Association, or the national PTA and you will have an argument on your hands.

Advocate the idea to one of these antivoucher groups and you will be lucky to get out alive. People who are against vouchers are similar to people who are against abortion—serious. Educational vouchers *are* an extremely radical idea. Vouchers would:

- take the government's education budget out of the schools and put it into the hands of parents;
- introduce free-market principles into a system where heretofore teachers and administrators enjoyed a monopoly and had too few incentives to excel;
- reward the best schools and let the worst die a natural death.

But the voucher idea has its supporters, too. We have endorsed the idea in many speeches. Nobel laureate economist Milton Friedman has championed the idea since 1962.

Now an increasing number of Americans are coming out for vouchers.

For the first time, more parents favor than oppose vouchers. A 1983 Gallup poll showed 51 percent in favor, 38 percent opposed, and 11 percent undecided. Only two years before, supporters and opponents were equally divided. During the 1970s, opponents had been in the clear majority.

Vouchers are beginning to sound like an idea whose time has come.

How would a voucher system work? Suppose it costs $2,500 per year to educate a child in public school. Under a voucher plan, the local government would give a voucher worth that much to the parents of every child. Parents could "spend" it at the school of their choice. Schools would compete for the vouchers on the basis of quality and subject emphasis and cash in their vouchers with state and/or local authorities.

The Anti-Voucher Argument

Competing for the best students and the most vouchers, schools would have to improve or expire.

It is controversial and radical.

Opponents believe vouchers would bring disaster, confusion, and disarray. They would encourage religious and racial prejudice, creating Nazi and KKK schools. Vouchers, they charge, are a form of subsidizing church-sponsored schools—which is unconstitutional.

"The adoption of vouchers would be the death knell of public schools," says Albert Shanker, president of the American Federation of Teachers and chief spokesperson in the anti-voucher camp.

"Instead of witnessing improvements under a voucher system, we would see our schools thrown into a supermarketlike atmosphere," concludes Shanker.

Ironically, voucher advocates use the supermarket analogy to demonstrate how much better off we would be if the schools were run more like free-market supermarkets offering new, improved educational products—schools!

Until now, the strength of the education establishment's rhetorical prediction that vouchers would "destroy the public schools"—as well as the lack of adequate experimental programs—has prevented educational innovators from giving the voucher system a serious try.

But as the demand for quality education grows, so does the willingness to consider educational vouchers.

Voucher Action in the States

In the bellwether state of California, law professors John Coons and Stephen Sugarman of the University of California at Berkeley tried but failed to get a school voucher initiative on the November 1984 California ballot. Coons and Sugarman became known in education circles for successfully suing the state government for failure to provide a minimum level of education for a California student in the famous Serrano-Priest case.

California's School Voucher Initiative would have created two new types of schools: Private Voucher Schools—that is, private schools entitled to redeem state educational vouchers—and Public Voucher Schools, public corporations organized by school districts, community colleges, or public universities. Existing private schools could have elected to qualify as Private Voucher Schools.

The plan would have disqualified vouchers to schools or people that advocate unlawful behavior, provide false or misleading information about the school, or advocate the inferiority of either sex or of any race.

Two other states, Texas and Colorado, have shown interest in the voucher system, according to the Education Voucher Institute.

Meanwhile, in Minnesota, Governor Rudy Perpich has proposed a voucher system within the public schools limited to students in their junior and senior years. Although the plan would benefit young people by allowing them to choose the schools that best fit their needs, part of the incentive is financial—it will save money if schools can specialize instead of having to offer all subjects.

In Louisiana, which already has an education tax credit, a group of business people, the Louisiana Association of Business and Industry, has developed a plan to see if vouchers are feasible in their state school system.

An interesting footnote: in some rural parts of New Hampshire where there are no high schools, parents already receive vouchers and can choose between public and private schools elsewhere in the state.

We often forget that the most successful education experiment in recent American history was a voucher system—the G.I. Bill. After World War II (and since), colleges, universities, and trade schools—private, public, and even church affiliated—competed to attract veterans to spend their educational chit at their schools.

Milton Friedman points out that veterans using the G.I. Bill attended Catholic and other religiously affiliated colleges without any significant challenge to the First amendment.

In response to those who predict that vouchers signal "the end of public education," advocates concede that a market-based system would indeed weed out the undesirable schools—but add that it would be a good thing.

The American public is saying, "If the public school system as we know it has to 'die' to get our kids quality education, it is a price we may have to pay."

The Business Connection: What Is Appropriate?

American corporations are in a position to make enormous contributions to the nation's schools. And there has probably never been a greater need for businesses to participate in the education process.

At the same time, it is extremely important that business contributes to the schools in a manner that is both sensitive and appropriate. Unfortunately, that is not always the case.

Some businesses have written curriculum materials that push their own viewpoint on young people.

In Des Moines, Iowa, for example, a statewide energy curriculum was criticized as "utility propaganda." The energy materials had been drawn up in part with a $70,000 grant from local utilities.

The kind of exploitation that represents the nadir of school/business is not always a case of outright propaganda. Sometimes it is simply overzealousness.

Ernest Boyer recalls that at one school adopted by an advertising agency, the entire curriculum was built around the advertising industry.

"In time, English literature or medieval history could get sloughed off because it did not fit into the containers called 'the advertising school,'" warns Mr. Boyer. "If an industry wants to use a school in this narrow sense to advance its ends, then we will have an unholy alliance."

Any corporation that steps into the education arena with its narrow self-interest in mind is simply asking for the criticism it rightly deserves.

Right on the edge of what is appropriate and what is not are the programs that aim to "explain free-market economy to young people," economic education kits, and the like, sometimes backed by local Chambers of Commerce. This is one kind of "probusiness propaganda" that business does not really need.

One reason this issue is so important: Industry materials are already a large part of today's curriculum. The current business/education partnership can only make them more common.

The Corporation as University

Universities are becoming more like businesses, and corporations are becoming more like universities of life-long learning.

The recognition that people are a company's critical resource—and its greatest storehouse of knowledge—is creating a boom in corporate training and education. Corporations are finally willing to invest in people and their skills through training and education to the degree that they have always invested in equipment.

When Don Burr of People Express talks about his company's hard assets, he is not talking about airplanes but people (the planes, he says, are the soft assets).

In the words of Robert Galvin, chairman of Motorola, we are thinking of people as "the ultimate high technology."

Now a benchmark report by the Carnegie Foundation for the Advancement of Teaching confirms what we have long suspected:

Training and education programs within American business are so vast, so extensive, that they represent in effect an alternative system to the nation's public and private schools, colleges and universities.

"There are sophisticated and growing alternative systems of education with roots firmly planted in the American business community and branches spreading to countries around the world," said Dr. Nell Eurich, author of the 240-page Carnegie report entitled "Corporate Classrooms: the Learning Business."

Corporations spend nearly $60 billion a year on education and training, according to the report, about the same amount spent on education in the nation's four-year colleges and universities. About 8 million people are learning within corporations—about the same number as are enrolled in institutions of higher learning.

The combined total spent by both private and public employers has been estimated at as high as $100 billion annually, a figure which Dr. Eurich considers too high.

Corporate programs were established because corporations were dissatisfied with traditional education systems, says Dr. Eurich. But now, because of the profit motive, corporate education *is often more efficient* than traditional education in trying new approaches—especially with computers and other technology, according to the Carnegie report.

The Carnegie report documents the transformation of corporations into institutions of lifelong learning:

- At least eighteen corporations and associations award academic degrees. Eight more will do so by 1988.
- Wang; Northrop Corporation; Arthur Andersen, the accounting firm; and Humana, the for-profit health chain, grant master's degrees, while the Rand Corporation offers a Ph.D.—not just for employees, but for the public.
- There are more than 400 campuses and buildings for education owned by companies such as Xerox, IBM, Pfizer, and Control Data.
- IBM, an educational giant, spends about $700 million a year in employee education.

What else do we know about education within the corporation?

Here is a thumbnail sketch of what is happening in corporate training, put together by the American Society for Training and Development:

- Information companies tend to do more training, with people in finance, insurance, and professional services getting the most training.
- Most training is offered in business-related subjects.
- Virtually all large companies have full-time educators on staff, as do three-fourths of all financial, communication, and transportation firms.
- Three-fourths of training goes to white-collar workers in most companies.
- Most training goes to people between the ages of twenty-five and thirty-four.
- People who possess the most initiative get the most training, since in most corporate situations you have to request training to receive it.

Sometimes in-house business education is a curious form of deprogramming newly recruited MBAs. Today's MBAs are "numbers crunchers," some companies complain, whereas what they need are "people managers." Corporations like Tandem, Bank of America, and CBS put newly hired business school graduates through training in interpersonal skills.

"We just hope the B-schools haven't screwed [them] up too much," says Robert N. Mills, General Electric's professional recruitment manager. MBAs will have to forget much of what they were taught in business school to fit in at GE, he adds.

"The future of business education may be headed toward the corporation," concludes William Hamilton, director of Pennsylvania's Management and Technology program.

Corporate education comes in a variety of different packages: evening classes, learning on company time, company-sponsored sabbaticals:

- Kansas City Power and Light has an evening education program where employees can study subjects ranging from electronics and computers to reading, writing, and stress management.
- More than 30 percent of Polaroid's work force take tuition-free personal development courses on company time, ranging from Spoken English I & II to Vibrational Analysis and the Process of Aging: Myths of Productivity.
- Each year Monsanto sends twenty of its best chemical engineers to Washington University in St. Louis, Missouri, for an intensive year-long update on current developments in the field, from computer applications to problem-solving techniques. More than 90 percent complete the program and go on to better positions with the company.

Monsanto's successful model illustrates the link that must be forged between high-technology businesses and institutions of higher learning, if technical experts are to achieve the lifelong learning they require.

That is also the idea behind Lifelong Cooperative Education, a concept put forth in fall 1982 by four professors at Massachusetts Institute of Technology.

MIT's Lifelong Learning

High-technology companies and universities must forge a close partnership to keep engineers up-to-date on state-of-the-art developments.

The need is obvious. By the time a student graduates from engineering school, his or her knowledge is already getting out of date.

How might such a continuing education program work? The MIT group is advocating tutored video instruction (TVI), an approach that just might have the right balance of high tech/high touch.

TVI combines the technology of videotaped lectures with the high touch of small groups and a tutor who can stop the video anytime (as can the participants), answer questions, and get a discussion going. Stanford University has pioneered TVI with engineers at Hewlett-Packard Co.

Clearly, the MIT people struck a chord with high-tech companies. A follow-up meeting held in spring 1983 attracted top executives from America's leading technology firms, including Frank Cary, chairman of IBM's executive committee, Frank Heffron, executive vice-president at Bell Labs, and Edson W. Spenser, Honeywell Information Systems chairman.

One of the program's main attractions, though, is its proposed modest cost, which, it is hoped, will appeal to smaller high-tech firms.

New Training Models for Small Business

Small business and self-employed people have to engage in
lifelong learning, too, but how can they compete with an
IBM that spends hundreds of millions on education? Help
comes in large part from state and community colleges and
from professional associations:

- The American Institute of Architects offers more than
  sixty courses and seminars annually.
- The American Management Association is in a class by
  itself, offering 3,200 programs with more than 100,000
  enrollments annually.
- The American Society of Mechanical Engineers offers
  some 100 courses.
- The National Association of Home Builders offers more
  than 200 courses, including a 2½-week course in brick
  technology considered a must for anyone new to the
  industry. The seminars are always filled even before
  officially announced.

Even without the resources of large companies, small
businesses and divisions of larger corporations are contracting
directly with colleges, universities, and community colleges. In some cases, they are transforming their offices and
plants into classrooms.

For the person balancing work, family, and continuing
education, it is a godsend. Businesses can meet specialized
needs through these unique business/education arrangements:

- Digital Equipment Corp.'s Burlington, Vermont, plant
  brought in teachers from the town's Johnson State
  College to teach production line workers business management. Digital supplemented the courses with—what
  else?—individualized computer instruction.
- Tugboat dispatchers studied marketing, customer relations, scheduling, and problem-solving in a program at

Seattle's Foss Launch and Tug Company taught by instructors from Seattle Central Community College.
• Technicians at Tektronix, Inc., in Beaverton, Oregon, can earn engineering degrees without ever leaving work. The University of Portland has teamed up with the computer manufacturer to design this prototype program which involved 200 technicians in 1983.

Cooperative education programs like these have grown tremendously since the University of Cincinnati started the first such program in 1906. Now there are more than 1,200 according to the College Board.

The Community College: A Special Role

In this new information society where human resources are the company's competitive edge, small businesses, such as retail stores, are turning to community colleges for help in education and training.

Henry Ford Community College in Dearborn, Michigan, for example, established its Center for New Directions to serve the needs of small-business people like the merchants at Fairlane Town Center.

The store managers at the Dearborn shopping mall had been promoted from sales jobs and had no formal management experience. Small-shop owners had a problem: how to train their managers without cutting into store hours.

The Center for New Directions responded with Sunrise Seminars—informal breakfast meetings in a mall restaurant where managers could discuss their needs and problems in a nonthreatening environment and learn management techniques—all before the stores opened.

The Dearborn mall's seminars cut costs, increased profits, created a network among store managers and increased community involvement. So successful was this model program that it has already been replicated at more than twenty malls throughout the country. More than eighteen colleges and 3,200 retail stores have participated.

In Search of a National Strategy

Despite the corporate training boom, no one is arguing that this fast-paced information society is blessed with all the training it needs. Millions of workers are out of a job today because they were not adequately trained or retrained.

Should the government enact public policies to encourage training?

One proposal, the Individual Training Account (ITA), developed by Pat Choate of TRW and popularized by Sen. Gary Hart (D-Colo.), is designed to anticipate the need for people to be trained and retrained throughout their lives.

Under the ITA proposal, companies and their employees would contribute equally to a tax-exempt training fund of up to $4,000. The money could be used for retraining programs already approved by state education agencies, apprenticeship programs, private industry organizations, national accrediting, and agencies which receive funding through the Job Partnership Training Act.

The strength of the ITA idea is the way it promotes training and retraining as lifelong processes.

Once a company has contributed to an ITA, it has an incentive to retrain people instead of just laying them off. That, in the long run, can help the company as well as the individual.

Motorola's Training Account Model

One major company has already created its own innovative approach to training—one which other corporations might consider adapting to their own needs. Motorola's individual training account set up in 1983 is showing managers how training can cut costs and increase profits and productivity.

"We were more interested in the cost of maintenance of capital equipment than in putting money where the greatest opportunity for improvement was—in our people," recalls Ed Bales, who with director of training Bill Wiggenhorn is responsible for Motorola's innovative training arrangement.

As of 1984, the company required each division to set aside a minimum of 1.5 percent of each employee's salary to be used for training that year. By 1986, the goal will be a minimum of 2.5 percent and, depending on the division's needs, may go as high as 10 percent.

"This is not a negotiable item," says Bales. "The initial funds come out of profits. This is never seen as an expense."

The program is structured to be used. Any division that does not spend its training budget must return it to the corporate treasury.

"Managers did not see [training] as a solution to their business problem," says Bales. "Now they are forced to try the new change."

"The only way to get the money," Wiggenhorn echoes, "will be to get people trained."

Three recent experiences at Motorola have given Wiggenhorn and Bales the ammunition they need to convince skeptical managers that training cuts costs and increases profits:

1. A group of engineers who took a four-hour-per-day sixteen-week course in problem-solving were subsequently responsible for an unusually high level of cost-saving measures. "Even allowing for total training costs . . . we saved about $2 million just through utilization [of the new skills]," says Bales.

2. Motorola measured the effectiveness of people who

took a three-month course in sales techniques against the performance of a control group. Over the course of a year, a $35,000 training investment produced well over $1 million in revenue over and above the sales of the control group.

3. To maintain newly automated factories, Motorola had been using mechanics with no formal training in electronics. The average downtime on machines needing repair was four days, so long that Motorola figured it would have to hire new mechanics with electronics backgrounds.

But instead, they decided to experiment. The mechanics were offered an electronics course taught on an interactive PLATO computer system which enabled them to learn at their own pace, taking an hour each of personal and company time for learning. Although the older mechanics balked at the idea at first—they thought admitting they needed training would be a blot on their records—most agreed to take the course.

The results were amazing. Within fourteen weeks, they had reduced downtime from four days to four hours.

Successes like these change managers' attitudes toward training. "Training becomes integrated into managers' thought processes when they think of solutions to problems," says Bales. "Before it was just add people, or capital. . . . Now they are thinking, 'Train people better.' "

Motorola's training model introduces a whole new perspective into the shift to corporation as university.

In an information society, education is no mere amenity; it is the prime tool for growing people and profits.

The University as Corporation

As corporations like Motorola evolve into institutions for training and higher learning, universities are seeking to become more businesslike.

They have to be. The combined forces of higher costs, less federal assistance, and increased competition for fewer students mean the colleges and universities have to think in terms of specialization, market niche, and strategic planning— just as businesses do.

Not the least of those problems is that there are fewer customers. The baby bust generation, whose small numbers will create the seller's market over the next few years, is already reshaping the college and university system. For the first time in U.S. history, there is a decrease in high school graduates—and it will continue for most of the next decade. In 1977, the peak year, 3.15 million people graduated from high school. In 1993, only about 2.3 million are projected to graduate.

Pittsburgh's Carnegie-Mellon University succeeded at beating the collegiate competition for these fewer students by analyzing which academic programs are strongest and concentrating on achieving a "comparative advantage" in its best areas. A 1981 plan to carry out that strategy achieved remarkable results:

- The school's cognitive psychology department moved from thirty-fifth to the nation's top-ranked program.
- Its computer science program is now tied with MIT and Stanford for first place, according to the National Academy of Sciences.
- And its applications are up 15 percent.

"Competition and the marketplace were unheard-of in college decision-making until the last year or two," says George Keller, senior vice-president at Barton-Gillet Co., a Baltimore consulting group and an authority on strategic planning for universities.

Strategic planning can mean eliminating programs, too. The University of Miami, for example, is eliminating its undergraduate education program because it would take too much money to improve it enough to compete with programs elsewhere.

Another sign of the colleges-as-corporation trend: Colleges and universities are now more likely to seek a president with a business background. Writes the *Charlotte* (N.C.) *Observer,* "The Ph.D. is no longer an ironclad requirement, and a business background is becoming increasingly important." David McLaughlin, president of Dartmouth College, was formerly president of Toro Co.

University President as CEO

Ronald Calgaard, president of Trinity University in San Antonio, is an excellent example of the new breed of business-oriented college president.

Calgaard's strategy, glowingly reported in *Forbes* magazine, is to " 'buy market share' of students, faculty and national attention."

For example, Trinity has an extremely high percentage of National Merit finalists—almost one-fifth of the freshman class entering in fall 1984. That means that Trinity, which neither of us had even heard of before coming across the *Forbes* article, would rank tenth in the nation in National Merit finalists, in the company of schools such as Harvard, Yale, Princeton, and Stanford.

How do they do it? Simple. Trinity offers a $5,000-a-year scholarship to any National Merit finalist. That is called buying market share. Similarly, the salaries of the school's faculty have been upgraded more than 60 percent in the past five years.

How does Trinity pay for all this market share? The school's $150-million endowment helps, of course, but more important, Calgaard continues to court wealthy contributors with the successful strategy of buying market share—in this instance, market share of prestige.

Trinity spends some $200,000 per year to bring the country's most prestigious (and most expensive) public speakers to the campus. At intimate dinner parties, potential donors sit next to speakers like Henry Kissinger, Alexander Haig, Ted Koppel, or Gerald Ford.

President Calgaard's marketing efforts are paying off. A survey of 662 college presidents conducted by *U.S. News & World Report* rated Trinity the second-best regional liberal arts college west of the Mississippi (St. Olaf's in Minnesota was first). "You're not going to attract students and faculty who never heard of you," says Calgaard.

Colleges That Grow Companies

In the process of becoming more businesslike, some colleges and universities are showing they recognize the importance of entrepreneurship. Yale, Brooklyn College, Rensselaer Polytechnic Institute and many other institutions of higher learning have created "entrepreneurial incubators," which offer inexpensive rental space and business services to hundreds of prospective new businesses, along with the opportunity to collaborate with other entrepreneurs.

As colleges become more like corporations, and companies evolve into lifelong universities, the two institutions are also growing more interdependent.

Business and Education: The Growing Intimacy

Cornell University is trying to create one of the country's closest working relationships between a major university and high-technology companies with more than $70 million in government and corporate support for a new supercomputer center. Most of the equipment ($30 million) is being supplied by IBM and Floating Point Systems. Cornell is negotiating with a score of other companies for funds and equipment.

Cornell, one of the top engineering schools in the country, has long had a measure of corporate support, but nothing like the scale envisioned now. Financial aid from corporations paid for about 10 percent of research projects during the 1970s. By 1984 it had reached 45 percent—and climbing. Of this growing university reliance on corporate support, Louis Robinson, IBM's university relations director, says, "The intimacy between American education and American industry is getting bigger and bigger all the time."

But this new alliance is not entirely noncontroversial. It has sparked a lively debate within the academic community. After business's $1-billion contribution, some educators question whether higher education can remain free from the taint of commercialism.

Some of the fears:

Will universities and professors with close business ties lose their credibility as "impartial observers"?

Will professors on the corporate dole be inhibited about—or prohibited from—discussing ideas with colleagues?

Will commercial ties divert university laboratories from basic research into commercial product development?

Will industry have too much control, by retaining patent rights, for example?

(No one seems worried about whether universities will taint corporations.)

In response to these uncomfortable issues, the editors of *The New England Journal of Medicine* now ask authors to disclose all business ties related to their research.

"Disclosure, we believe, is in everyone's best interest," wrote Dr. Arnold Relman in a May 1984 editorial.

The prestigious *Journal* is the first publication of its kind to require authors to disclose all ties, including part-time consulting, stock ownership or equity, and patent licensing arrangements. Editors at *Science* magazine are considering following the *Journal*'s lead.

To help sort out the issues, there have been widespread calls for uniform guidelines for business/university transactions.

But it sounds awfully top down to us—and ponderous. We think it is more likely each relationship will be worked out individually, perhaps through an independent outside review board of academics and businesspeople to oversee the business/university relationship.

Yes, the university will face the issue of commercial contamination. But with that first taint, the benefits will have far exceeded the cost.

We are impressed: Corporations appear to be taking to their new role as education activists with imagination and real verve.

High-tech companies, in particular, have found their market niche, so to speak, with the issues of science, math, and technology—areas where corporations clearly know something and feel confident about making a real contribution. Efforts like Texas Instruments' SEED project, the huge computer contributions of Apple and other industry leaders, and the willingness of companies like Digital and Honeywell to hire science and math teachers in summer jobs stand out as the best models to emulate.

The Ambience Factor

When corporations contribute to local education, they are investing in one of the ten considerations for re-inventing the corporation, the shift from infrastructure to quality of life. A good local education system is one of the prime assets in that increasingly valuable element—ambience. Good schools are often the key factor in recruiting the most creative, talented people to your company.

That ambience factor means there will be increasing

competition for the most effective school administrators, especially those with a track record for working with local businesses. As we were completing this chapter, a headline in the *Washington Post* took us by surprise. Robert Spillane, the Boston school superintendent who forged the Boston Contract, had been hired away by the Fairfax (Virginia) County school system, home of Thomas Jefferson High. That is the new science/technology school built with millions of dollars in corporate contributions. The best-quality-of-life cities and towns where corporations want to make a difference in education will all be in the market for this new breed of school administrator who is equally at home in the classroom and the boardroom.

Corporations did not embrace their new role as educator in order to compete with the schools, only to compete with one another. As Motorola's training account model shows, a $35,000 training investment paid off in $1 million in revenue. Once businesses entered this arena, the results-oriented spirit reigned and corporate training and education achieved a level of real quality. As the Carnegie report cited in this chapter acknowledges, corporate education is sometimes more efficient than in the traditional school system. In the foreword to that report, written by former U.S. Commissioner of Education Ernest Boyer, we find this statement:

It would be ironic if significant new insights about how we learn would come, not from the academy, but from industry and business.

It gives one pause. Furthermore, what if a corporation like IBM started awarding Ph.D.s just as the Rand Corporation already does? It would certainly give Harvard, Stanford, and MIT some pretty good competition.

6

Health and the Corporation

Even in the industrial society, when capital was the strategic resource, it made good business sense to keep your labor force in healthy shape. And corporations began offering health insurance as an employee benefit.

But now people are a company's *competitive edge*. It is more important than ever before that the people in companies be healthy.

But as health costs skyrocket, providing health care is becoming one of the highest costs of doing business. The annual corporate health bill has reached $100 billion.

"Our largest single supplier today is not a steel company as you might suppose, but rather Blue Cross–Blue Shield of Michigan," said chairman Roger Smith of General Motors.

"When you look at all our expenses, health care jumps right out of the stack," says Robert E. Mercer, chairman of Goodyear. "It's the one that has increased most dramatically." Goodyear estimates that health care accounts for $2 of the cost of a $57 tire.

Mercer speaks for virtually every corporate CEO and small business owner in America.

Not even the successful new information companies are exempt from the burdensome costs of health care. At Hewlett-Packard, annual health care bills have tripled from $500 per employee to $1,500 in only a decade.

The question is this: How can companies cut health costs while maintaining people assets in prime condition?

The companies that are successfully re-inventing the corporate role in health are pursuing a kind of high-tech/high-touch approach. The hard-nosed, high-tech part is the way corporations are finally applying their business acumen to health care costs. For example, they are putting an arsenal of information technology to use in auditing medical bills. The high-touch part is the accelerating corporate interest in prevention and wellness, a proven, people-oriented way to cut health care costs.

The Health Cost Spiral

Few of us notice how much money corporations spend on health care (though the awakening comes if you are unemployed). We consider health insurance a standard employee benefit, nothing remarkable. But part of self-management, part of taking responsibility for the whole of our companies, is recognizing the high cost of items like health care. That way we can share in the creation of win/win arrangements that promote individual health and wellness while cutting costs and increasing options.

Take the example of flexible benefits, discussed in a previous chapter, for instance. It makes no sense for companies to duplicate expensive insurance coverage in the 50 million two-career families. It is often cheaper for companies and better for people to give employees the option of choosing other, often less expensive benefits.

This brief summary is a reminder of the high cost of the health benefits we so often take for granted:

- In 1983, the United States spent 11 percent of the GNP on health care, versus 5.3 percent in 1960.
- . . . By 2000, though, we could spend 15 percent of GNP on health care.
- From 1960 to 1983, annual health care costs in the United States soared from $27 billion to $360 billion.

Your company's costs might be higher than a competitor's simply because of where its facilities are located. McDonnell Douglas in St. Louis must pay twice the cost of hospital rooms as Boeing in Seattle.

The Accountability Factor

Until recently, there has been little incentive for companies and the people in them to fight the health care cost spiral.

When people needed medical treatment, they got it, and third-party insurance reimbursed the doctor or hospital. No questions asked. Some policies required the consumer to pay a small deductible. But once that was paid, people had no incentive to think twice about the cost of a procedure, or to shop around for the cheapest place to go when their child broke an arm.

Similarly, hospitals and doctors had no reason to watch costs. Insurance companies gave them carte blanche, rarely auditing their bills item by item.

"There were no real controls within the system," says Donald Melville, president of Norton Company of Worcester, Massachusetts. "We wrote a ticket to provide free health care without any limits."

The anonymity of third-party payment created a built-in lack of accountability. The sad result was that most of us were buying health care the way the Pentagon bought spare parts. And corporate America (along with the government through Medicare and Medicaid) was picking up the tab.

An orgy of wasteful health care consumption makes health the most inflationary factor in the economy. Health care costs generally have raged ahead of inflation. Though inflation had been cut to below 4 percent overall in 1984, it was still more than 10 percent for health care costs.

"We appear to have turned the corner on most of inflation, but health care costs have shown little sign of improvement," said Federal Reserve chairman Paul Volcker.

The Government as Activist

The inflationary tide turned on health costs, however, in 1983, when the government—not the private sector—took the initiative that sparked a revolution in the way corporations purchase health care.

The government blew the whistle by announcing it would limit the amount of money Medicare would reimburse for various procedures. If you went to the hospital for an appendectomy, for example, and there were no complications, Medicare would reimburse the hospital only $3,700, the specified amount thought to be a fair, average, and just price for that operation. (Of course, a number of factors such as geographic region and the patient's age vary the figure at different hospitals.)

The government spelled out exactly how much it would pay for 468 conditions or diagnosis-related groups. Hence the popular name for the new policy, DRGs.

DRGs announced the beginning of a new ball game. Now an insurer was demanding that the health care deliverer control costs.

"We're watching the start of an economic transformation of the American health care system," said Dr. Paul Ellwood,

Jr., president of InterStudy, a health care research firm in Excelsior, Minnesota. "What's striking is how rapidly it is accelerating."

Much of that acceleration happened because of businesses. Although the government took the lead, corporations were already trying out a whole range of new ways to control health costs.

Again, there is a dual approach: cutting costs and preventing them through wellness and fitness programs. We present this chapter in the form of a checklist of options for corporate health activism. We encourage you to look at a variety of schemes, trying out some, while rejecting others, changing some, while blending others.

1. Move from being an anonymous insurer to being an activist health care consumer by auditing your health costs.

The Employee Benefits Research Institute estimates that up to 15 percent of the $100 billion spent annually on employee health insurance is fraudulent.

Now many companies are going after their chunk of that fraud by auditing medical bills. It might sound tedious and expensive, but it is neither: Most companies hire a specialist and still come out ahead.

A. S. Hansen, Inc., a Chicago benefits consulting firm, estimates you can save up to $3 for every $1 invested in hospital bill audits. That is not surprising considering that one auditing firm reported that 90 percent of all hospital bills contained errors. Connecticut General Life Insurance Co. saved $2.50 for each $1 spent on audit fees in 1984. One New York insurance firm saved $1.88 for each $1 paid in audit fees.

Audit firms like Medical Advisory Services and Equifax Services will perform audits for your company. In 1982, Equifax saved its clients $1.91 for every $1 paid in audit fees. Medical Advisory Services also will provide referral services such as second opinions and preadmissions testing (which shortens a hospital stay and is cheaper than getting tests done after a patient enters the hospital).

A growing number of companies audit their own bills. Auditing makes sense. Equifax Services found errors in 98 percent of the bills it audited in 1984. Lockheed scrutinizes 80 percent of all submitted claims and manages to get most reduced anywhere from $2 to 30 percent of the total bill. Hewitt Associates found that, of the employees it surveyed, the percentage auditing hospital bills increased from 39 percent in 1982 to 68 percent in 1984.

2. Hire medical experts to monitor treatment.

How can corporate managers be expected to control health costs? They aren't doctors.

An increasing number of corporations and their insurance companies are getting outside help—independent health professionals who serve as a sort of peer review board to monitor health care costs. That might mean reviewing a proposed treatment before hospitalization, or during treatment, or examining a claim afterward. The results can be startling, as these examples demonstrate:

- If an employee of Motorola, Inc., of Arizona or an employee dependent must be hospitalized, the company's inside review board must okay the admission. After the patient goes home, a review board of peer physicians checks out further treatment. This and similar procedures have saved the company at least 15 percent in annual hospitalization costs.
- In the first quarter of 1983, Pacific Mutual Life Insurance Company's review program saved $3.36 for every $1 invested.

- Since 1983, an inside medical staff at Zenith Radio Corporation has advised people before and after surgery about treatment alternatives. In the program's first quarter alone, it saved Zenith $53,000.
- Since 1983, Chrysler Corporation has prescreened foot surgery—and has saved an extraordinary $1 million a year while reducing the cost of podiatry services 30 percent.

These are just a sampling of the remarkable results companies all across America are achieving simply by paying the same attention to health costs as they would to any business cost.

But the best programs do even more. They give people incentives in monitoring their own health care costs—the ones they would have mindlessly passed on to the corporation.

Uniroyal, Inc., of Connecticut gets people to audit their own health bills. If they find errors, they split the overcharge with the company and pocket half themselves. A number of companies have similar programs—Pillsbury, Illinois Central Gulf Railroad, and Carson Pirie Scott and Company. But United Technologies boasts the most generous program. The people who find mistakes get to keep 80 percent.

3. *Put together a local coalition of corporate cost busters.*

Some 130 local business groups have joined together in the past three years to counter the high cost of health care. One of their main objectives is to pool their collective information about local health care costs. And computers are helping them become more conscientious health care consumers.

How else but with computers could nine major Cleveland companies screen 80,000 employees and dependents to find the most cost-effective hospitals? Stouffer, General Electric, Lubrizol, Standard Oil (Ohio), Sherwin-Williams, Parker-Hannifin, Eaton, and TRW are sharing their claims files to reduce their $40-million annual health care costs.

- In Omaha, seventeen employers formed the Employers Health Care Cost Containment Committee of Omaha to investigate local health costs and figure out how to cut them.
- Ten Maryland companies—including three large Baltimore banks—have put together a program to review hospital admissions for nonemergency cases. It is similar to the state's Medicaid procedures which have saved the state more than $10 million.
- Twenty of St. Louis's largest corporations are taking on the local health establishment to cut costs, which are a staggering 30 percent above the national average (both admission rates and hospital stays are abnormally high there).

Companies that compare notes with fellow health consumers are getting critical information: Who charges what for whom? Is anyone price gouging? How much have costs gone up recently? And perhaps most important, can we get a group discount?

A Florida case shows how powerful cost containment coalitions can be. Tampa's Cost Containment Board identified the city's Women's Hospital as "high-priced." The board could not cut the hospital's prices, of course, but it did pressure Women's Hospital to reduce its budget $1.7 million, saving the average patient $40 per day.

4. Take matters into your own hands: build your own clinic.

After Goodyear Tire and Rubber failed to negotiate what it considered reasonable rates with health care providers near its plant in Lawton, Oklahoma, the company took decisive action. It built its own $180,000 medical facility on-site—X-ray machines, lab, pharmacy, and all. Too expensive? Goodyear figures it costs them half the price of local care.

5. *Self-insure your company.*

The other way of taking matters into your own hands is for your company to sock away all those expensive health insurance premiums and pay health claims itself. It is financially viable and, in this information society, the computer makes it technically possible. One individual with a personal computer can process the same amount of claims as half an office did ten years ago.

It is a trend that must have insurance companies worried. For example, of 268 companies surveyed by The Wyatt Co. in 1984, 57 percent in some way self-funded their medical plans. The same year Coopers & Lybrand found 62 percent of mid-sized and large firms were self-funded.

The worst part, from the insurance company's viewpoint, is how much money it saves. A recent survey by Temple, Barket and Sloane determined that it can cut claims-processing costs in half.

But isn't it risky? Not really. Most companies hedge their bets with a comparatively inexpensive stop loss insurance, essentially a policy with a huge deductible.

And it need not be tedious. The premiums go into an insurance account and most companies hire a third-party administrator to disburse funds in payment of claims. You can also contract with a large insurance company to process claims.

Another advantage: Self-insuring means you can customize insurance. A Minnesota company, for example, wrote a special provision into its own insurance policy. It requires all employees to wear helmets when riding snowmobiles—a rule the state does not enforce. Not surprisingly, the rate of serious accidents decreased after this clause was added.

6. Take another look at HMOs—better yet, create your own.

The Health Maintenance Organization (HMO) is a proven price buster. You and/or your company pays the HMO a flat monthly fee that ranges from 10 to 40 percent less than a full option health insurance premium. In return, you get unlimited care ranging from flu shots to brain surgery.

No surprise costs. No bills to audit. No building your own clinic.

And they make money while saving you money. For-profit HMOs have become hot stocks on Wall Street. Philadelphia-based U.S. Health Care Systems went public and raised $44 million.

How do HMOs cut costs and make money? By stressing preventive care, outpatient treatment, and other cost containment methods. In most HMOs, the medical staff is on salary so they have no incentive to overtreat. Another cost-cutting incentive: The staff shares profits at the end of the year.

Though it is not a new approach, it is one which may have appeared too experimental when your company last considered it. But now that HMOs have established a track record, they warrant another look—on the other hand, some innovative companies are starting their own.

HMOs have saved corporations—as well as individuals—a lot of money.

Some 13.6 million people belong to health maintenance organizations. But there are indications that the figure is about to increase dramatically. Blue Cross–Blue Shield, which had the foresight to ask what business it was really in and created fifty-seven of its own HMOs, reports its HMO enrollments increased 32 percent during the first half of 1984. It is not surprising, then, that by 1990, 40 million people could belong to HMOs, according to a study by the InterStudy research group.

What is behind the growing popularity of the HMO, which is flourishing despite what many feel is a distinct disadvantage about the structure—that you cannot see "your own doctor"?

Quite simply, its cost. Not a little bit of savings, a lot.

For example, the state of Wisconsin projected a health care budget of $13 million for its employees. After just 5 percent of them joined HMOs only $8 million had been spent by year end 1984. United Technologies, which offers seven HMOs, used by only 1,000 of its 50,000 employees, saved $200,000 in 1984. And FMC, a Chicago-based company with 30,000 employees, saves $1.3 million a year using HMOs.

And the results of that survey track with the experience of others in the field. Bradley Arms, senior vice-president and chief financial officer of CIGNA Healthplans, Inc., of Dallas, says, "Hospital use for our HMO members is 333 days per 1,000 members and that's about half the rate under the typical indemnity plan."

Cost savings under HMOs are widespread and consistent: TRW, Inc., the Dallas-based aerospace contractor, saved more than $1 million in a year by using an HMO. In 1983, Ford Motor Company's HMO use saved the company $7 million.

And there is a trend in the HMO business that is making it easier to realize savings like those. The nation's 290 local and regional HMOs are coming together into national networks. That means that if your company has facilities scattered all over the country, you do not have to deal with thirty-seven different local HMOs.

- The Kaiser Foundation Health Plan, based in Oakland, California, grew from 3.5 million members in 1978 to 4.6 million in 1985 and from operating in six states to thirteen states in 1985.
- Blue Cross has HMOs in twenty-six states.
- Prudential Health Care Plan, an aggressive industry leader, has mushroomed from operating in just one state in 1978 to eleven in 1984. The number of corporations participating in Prudential's program increased 30 percent in both 1983 and 1984.

"It is absolutely clear to most people in the industry that the national HMO networks are the wave of the future," says Robert Ditmore, president of Share Development Corp., a Minneapolis stock offering group that watches the HMO market carefully. "We'll probably end up with ten to fifteen that dominate the industry."

But your company need not wait for an HMO to set up shop in your area. In North Carolina, a group of cost-conscious businesses asked local hospitals and doctors to form an HMO. But no one showed any interest.

"There was no competition here," recalls James Bernstein, director of the North Carolina Foundation for Alternative Health Programs.

So the business group successfully recruited several HMOs to come to them. (Then, of course, the locals responded by setting up their own HMO.)

7. Join a Preferred Provider Organization (PPO).

PPOs link people and companies who want lower health care costs with doctors and hospitals who want more patients. If your company refers people to these health care providers, they reward you with cost efficiency (i.e., discounts, usually). Your company in turn gives people incentives to choose the PPO, offering, for example, to cover a larger percentage of the bill than other, presumably more expensive doctors or hospitals.

Security Pacific Bank has saved two dollars for every one dollar invested in its PPO, Med Network. Alan Jeffery, employee benefits vice-president, reports that employees are pleased with the service.

In Dade County, Florida, the PPO that school district employees use is credited with cutting the rise in health care bills in half.

8. Send your minor emergencies to a Freestanding Emergency Center.

Emergicenters are small, conveniently located clinics designed to treat walk-in patients more quickly, efficiently, and cheaply than hospital emergency rooms. While you would still want to send people to hospitals for major emergencies, emergicenters are an excellent choice for minor ailments or accidents on the job.

Some 2,300 emergicenters have cropped up all along highways and in shopping malls during the past dozen years. By the end of 1985, there will be 3,500. Their growth seems to have no end in sight. By the end of 1985, they will have received 45 million visits.

"I'm absolutely convinced that this type of health care will be typical in the next two decades," says Randy Brown, vice-president of Humana, a hospital management chain which owns fifty-seven MedFirst urgent care centers.

What is the thrust behind the growth of emergicenters? One factor is clearly the old real estate adage "Location, location, location."

St. Louis's MedStop is in a shopping center between a

drapery shop and a Chinese restaurant (perfect if you are allergic to MSG).

Like supermarkets, emergicenters draw from a five-mile radius. With the growth of the suburbs, what sense does it make for a suburbanite with a broken arm to go to a downtown hospital emergency room? Says one entrepreneur, "Our new center will make getting five stitches as easy as going out for a cup of coffee."

But the convenience that emergicenters offer means more than location. Most centers are open from twelve to sixteen hours a day 365 days a year. Some never close.

Your minor emergency is treated in forty-five minutes or less. Forget the long waits in the office of a doctor who acts as if your time is worth nothing.

Says the owner of one emergicenter in Austin, "Consumers want rapid, courteous, competent medical care. People want to see a doctor but they don't care who he or she is."

"I think it's great," says Marilyn Shanahan, who took her eleven-year-old into the Convenient Medical Care Center in a Washington, D.C., suburb. "I didn't have to wait."

Because of their prime locations and emphasis on quick efficient service (exactly what the public wants), the medical establishment has called emergicenters "Medical McDonald's," "7-11 Medicine," "Doc-in-a-Box," or "Kentucky Fried Medicine." Perhaps an attempt to discredit what they realize is serious competition.

"There's no question about it," says American Academy of Family Physicians spokesperson William DeLay. "It does offer a serious competitive challenge to traditional medical practices."

Pricewise, how much competition does it actually amount to? Companies that send people to emergicenters instead of emergency rooms realize immediate cash savings:

• In St. Louis, treatment for a sprained ankle at MedStop

will cost half as much as the St. Louis hospital emergency room.

- In Alexandria, Virginia, the Old Towne Walk-in Medical Center will dress a burn for between $4 and $15, versus a minimum charge of $50 just to get inside a hospital emergency room.
- A typical hospital emergency room will charge $136 to treat bronchitis compared with $34 at the average emergicenter, according to the National Association for Ambulatory Care.

In the long run, however, the greatest impact these new medical models will have is on the overall cost of medical services. As doctors and hospitals recover from and respond to the challenge (some say threat) of emergicenters, we, the consumers, are the ultimate beneficiaries. The emergicenter alternative is one example of reducing costs while improving service.

Hospitals are now setting up their own version of the emergicenter:

- In Pensacola, Florida, University Hospital has established a Unicare Center for minor emergencies. It treats about 85 percent of the cases that used to go to the emergency room.
- Phoenix's Memorial Hospital rearranged its emergency fee schedule to cut costs for minor emergencies (and stem the flow to Medical McDonald's).

And doctors are experimenting with all sorts of new ideas to become more like the convenient alternative. Many are expanding their hours by joining with others on rotating shifts. In New York City, for example, at least four "house call pools" offer patients twenty-four-hour-a-day house calls for slightly more than an office visit.

Here's the bottom line: Insurance will cover most proce-

dures performed at emergicenters. The federal government
has approved Medicare payments to the centers. Blue Cross–
Blue Shield will reimburse you for more than 700 procedures done at an emergicenter.

With these two giants accepting the idea, it is safe to say
that emergicenters are a medical mainstay.

9. Encourage your people to use ambulatory surgicenters.

More than 60 percent of corporate health care costs go
toward hospital bills. So when people need minor surgery, it
makes sense to consider doing it outside a hospital.

That is the rationale behind freestanding surgery centers
or surgicenters. Since 1970, more than 300 surgicenters
have grown up all across America. By 1988, almost 600
will be doing a $1-billion business—and saving almost half
again that much in hospital costs.

Still, is it safe to risk any kind of surgery outside a
hospital? Surgicenters provide care "comparable to that of
hospitals," says David Ehrenfried of Blue Cross–Blue Shield
Association. One reason for this excellent safety record is
that they avoid all risky operations.

Surgicenters offer advantages for both individuals and
doctors (who are paid the same whether they operate in a
hospital or surgicenter). Psychologically, it is comforting to
know that after surgery, you can be back at home with
friends and family. Like emergicenters, they are conveniently
located and, because patients recuperate at home, surgicenters
are by definition cheaper. Doctors gain because they can
schedule operations closer together. Both doctor and patient
avoid the nuisance of being "bumped" by emergency surgery, since it is not performed at most surgicenters.

Corporations, insurance companies, and HMOs are jumping
on the surgicenter bandwagon for reasons of safety, service,
and, above all, cost.

Uniroyal, Inc., of Middlebury, Connecticut, gives employees a $50 bonus if they choose ambulatory surgery (when appropriate) instead of checking into the hospital. In so doing, Uniroyal believes it saves between one-third and one-half of the total cost.

General Medical Centers, a Health Maintenance Organization in Anaheim, California, has built its own ambulatory center. During its first twelve months of operation, it saved nearly $300,000, or about $430 per procedure on some 700 non-emergency operations.

These examples show how cutting out the hospital stay for minor surgery saves money. But a study by Pacific Mutual Life Insurance Company goes further—establishing that it is cheaper to have same-day surgery in a surgicenter than in a hospital. Overnight surgery is 122 percent more expensive than outpatient surgery. Yet same-day surgery in a hospital is 54 percent more expensive than at a surgicenter.

So although hospitals are clearly in the ambulatory business—70 percent have remodeled to do same-day surgery more cheaply—they cannot beat the low overhead advantage of surgicenters.

On the other hand, surgicenters cannot compete with the high-tech advantages of large facilities in the case of major surgery. In the mundane sector of nonemergency minor procedures, though, where cost is an important consideration, corporations can recommend surgicenters with confidence.

10. Consider creating a smoke-free workplace.

"We view smoking as the principal health hazard of the company," says Dr. Loring Wood, medical director for research and development of New York Telephone Company.

Everywhere in America, people who work together are confronting head-on the issue of smoking on the job. But now companies from Boeing in Seattle to the *Salina* (Kansas) *Journal* to Campbell Soup are taking action to eliminate smoking and create a cleaner, more attractive work environment.

There are a number of reasons behind this trend toward banning or at least restricting smoking in the workplace.

Smokers Are the Minority

Nonsmokers now are clearly the majority. Two out of three adult Americans do not smoke. It is more popular to consider their desires rather than tolerate what is now minority behavior.

"You don't want to tell your majority, 'Well, to heck with you,'" says Robert Beck, executive vice-president of Bank of America, which recently separated its smokers and nonsmokers.

Though the debate rages on about the harmful effects of "passive smoking"—that is, the smoke nonsmokers inhale just from being around smokers—there is no question about the annoyance and extreme irritation smoking causes nonsmokers, nor about the way smoking changes, actually pollutes, the workplace.

No one can smoke in the computer room—don't people deserve the same protection?

More and more companies think so.

"It is the responsibility of management in any company to provide the cleanest, safest, and most healthful environment for its employees," says Mal Stamper, president of The Boeing Co., which is gradually instituting a smoke-free workplace. "When we provide a better operating atmosphere for our high-tech machinery than we do for the people who operate them, then it's time to reassess policies and that's what's been done."

Responsibility

Holding off, for a moment, on the overwhelming consideration of cost, is it a company's *responsibility* to tolerate and pay for smokers who are engaged in self-inflicted injury?

Public safety employees such as police and fire fighters cannot smoke on duty or off in Alexandria, Virginia, Wichita, Kansas, and Shaker Heights, Ohio. They are required to sign a pledge not to smoke, because if they develop heart or respiratory disease or high blood pressure, they are eligible for death and disability benefits. These counties are not about to pay people for harming themselves.

But isn't that what every company that hires smokers is doing?

Cost

Clearly, it costs more to employ smokers. When they become ill and/or die prematurely, company-paid health benefits pay the cost. But smokers are also responsible for higher rates of absenteeism, tardiness, accidents, fires, and other property damage. And there is more.

Smokers are simply less productive due to the simple act of smoking. Ninety-two nonsmokers can do the work of 100 smokers. And they increase a company's cleaning bill. Unigard Insurance in Seattle got $6,000 lobbed off its maintenance contract by a grateful cleaning service when it went smoke-free. Finally, smokers have twice as many workplace accidents as nonsmokers, according to the National Institute for Occupational Safety and Health.

Does it make sense to tolerate smoking in your workplace?

That is the question that Dennis Burns, owner and president of Pro-tec, a sports equipment manufacturer, asked himself. Now Pro-tec refuses to hire smokers.

"In the beginning, I hired smokers with the agreement

that they didn't smoke at work. In every case, it didn't work,'' says Burns. Smokers, he learned, would sneak cigarettes in the bathroom and just outside the company gate.

Finally, one day Burns drove up to the gate with an important client to find two employees smoking and ''cigarette butts everywhere.'' That day he stopped hiring smokers.

What about the potential talent he's lost? Burns shakes his head, ''How smart can they be if knowing what we know about the medical hazards, they're still smoking?''

What exactly are those hazards? This quick review of the evidence against smoking should refresh our memories:

- Smoking *causes* 350,000 deaths per year. (Unbelievable— we personally had actually forgotten this massive indictment.)
- Lung cancer is 700 times more common in smokers than in nonsmokers.
- One-fourth of all heart disease is the result of smoking.
- Seventy-five percent of chronic bronchitis and 80 percent of emphysema (major causes for disability retirements) are caused by smoking.

Does that make you feel a little less fascist for wanting to mandate a smoke-free workplace?

How does a company go about doing that? How will smokers react? What about a more conservative move, separating smokers and nonsmokers?

The experience of Fred Vandegrift, who took the draconian measure of creating a smoke-free environment at the *Salina* (Kansas) *Journal,* shows the transition need not be confrontational or dramatic.

Vandegrift created a clean and airy environment in (of all places) a newspaper office by giving people an incentive—a $500 bonus for quitting smoking. Those who kept puffing after three months would have an economic incentive, too. They could start looking for another job.

"We thought about the possibility of having some area in the plant to let the [smokers] smoke, but because we were such a small plant and we wander around, we felt that wasn't feasible," says Vandegrift. "So we said, 'No, if we are going to bite the bullet, we are just going to bite it.' "

What were Vandegrift's results? "We went smoke-free from the day I announced the ban," he says. There were thirty-one smokers. The majority, twenty-four, quit cigarettes and collected their $500, four still smoke off the job, and three left (for reasons unrelated to smoking, Vandegrift claims).

How did smokers react?

"The only problem I had was with the nonsmokers. They felt that they were being discriminated against because they didn't have the opportunity to get a $500 bonus. I told them their reward was the opportunity to work in a smoke-free environment," says Vandegrift.

Vandegrift raises an important point. Many companies shy away from antismoking policies because they expect vocal, even violent reactions from smokers who believe it is their right to smoke. But the companies that enact smoking policies find a fair amount of support among smokers.

Pacific Bell, for example, has a complicated smoking policy, the bottom line of which is that nonsmokers have the right to a clean, smoke-free environment.

But before the policy went into effect, Michael Eriksen, manager of preventive medicine and health education, surveyed 103,000 Bell employees on their attitudes toward smoking. Almost three-fourths of the people, including smokers, favored establishing a smoking policy. The majority favored separating smokers and nonsmokers.

Similarly, a Gallup poll commissioned by the American Lung Association found that 55 percent of smokers and 82 percent of nonsmokers favored separate smoking/nonsmoking areas.

The Boeing Company is in the process of going completely smoke-free. Since April 1984, smoking has been banned in most common areas: hallways, classrooms, meeting rooms. The company informs all new hires that it intends to create a smoke-free workplace in the near future.

MSI insurance of Arden Hills, Minnesota, since January 1, 1985, has banned smoking through its 700-employee office.

The Minnesota Medical Association has organized a co-alition to end smoking in Minnesota by the year 2000. They hope to do that by educating the public on the hazards of smoking and by gradually increasing the number of smoke-free workplaces and public places.

"In the health care industry, we have to set an example," says Dr. A. Stuart Hanson, leader of the movement. "It doesn't help you if you advise a patient to quit and then he sees a doctor in a white coat smoking in the doctor's cafeteria." The official name for the effort is the Minnesota Coalition for a Smoke-Free Society 2000.

11. Re-invent your company into a wellness workplace.

The most effective way to cut health care costs is to prevent hospital and doctor bills by promoting health, wellness, and well-being among the people in your company.

Wellness programs are not just trendy anymore; they are a proven way to cut health costs:

• New York Telephone Company saves at least $2.7 million annually from wellness programs.
• After instituting a wellness program, Toronto's Canada Life Assurance recouped $37,000 in direct savings, and

noted a turnover decrease that saved $231,000 and a 22-percent reduction in absenteeism.

- Lockheed estimates $1 million annual savings on life insurance premiums alone thanks to its wellness program.

But you cannot save that kind of money simply by being pro-exercise.

"There is more to wellness than physical fitness," says Ann Kieshaver, wellness manager for the Washington Business Group on Health. "Companies are looking at environmental changes. No-smoking-on-the-job policies, for example. We're also seeing a big rise in stress management programs."

The best results come from a multifaceted, holistic approach to health, incorporating a variety of components, from creating a smoke-free workplace to screening for high blood pressure to serving healthy food in the company cafeteria to teaching meditation and other relaxation techniques to reduce stress.

"Changing corporate culture can be as simple as changing the vending machine foods to healthy snacks," observes Rebecca Parkinson, director of health education and promotion for AT&T. "It's sending a message to employees that the company supports better habits."

Virtually every aspect of corporate life sends some sort of message about a company's health values:

- PepsiCo supplies a Sony Walkman and library of tapes at every workout station.
- New York Telephone taught employees meditation to reduce stress—and saved the company $268,000.
- The Los Angeles fire department teaches trainees to enter the "alpha state" for improved mental functioning through meditation techniques.
- Johnson & Johnson and IBM have instituted comprehensive programs of health checkups, exercise, and

"lifestyle" classes for smoking cessation and stress management.

Having said that fitness is only one part of a total wellness program, we must acknowledge that it is an important part and that corporations can act in many specific ways to foster fitness consciousness:

- General Electric gives people the hint by providing laundry service, towels, T-shirts, and shorts at no cost to employees who exercise at the company's Fairfield, Connecticut, headquarters. "We give them everything so they don't have any excuse not to work out," says Haiti Pieters, director of corporate fitness. It seems to have convinced half of GE's 650 employees at headquarters to exercise regularly.
- Rodale Press, publisher of health-conscious publications such as *Prevention* magazine, holds exercise breaks instead of coffee breaks. Almost half of the 800 employees at Emmaus, Pennsylvania, spend part of their workday jogging, swimming, or dancing.
- Hospital Corporation of America believes in paying people to exercise: 96 cents for every mile you swim in the company pool (7½ miles per month minimum), 24 cents for every mile jogged or walked (30 miles per month minimum), 6 cents a mile for bikers (120 miles a month minimum).
- At PepsiCo headquarters in Purchase, New York, "everybody exercises, from the porter to Donald M. Kendall, the chief executive officer," according to Dennis Colacino, PepsiCo's fitness director.

Dr. Kenneth Cooper's Aerobics Center in Dallas is a focal point for corporate physical fitness programs. Sixty corporations are members, and there is a waiting list of twenty-two or more.

One of those members is Overhead Door Corp., located only half a mile from the Aerobics Center. All corporate officers work out at the center—almost every morning—running, playing basketball or racquetball, lifting weights, or swimming.

When Jeff Miller joined Overhead Door as vice-president for manufacturing, he said that he couldn't say that the center was the deciding factor, but it definitely was a factor.

"I was impressed both by the Aerobics Center and by Overhead Door's commitment to fitness. It showed they care about their employees," he said.

Overhead Door's CEO, Bob Haugh, a great fitness buff, insists that joining the center's program is not a requirement for advancement. "But there's no doubt that it's catching on," he says. "And it should be. Business needs to display this kind of concern for their employees. It's just good business."

Texas Instruments in Dallas has one of the city's most extensive fitness facilities. T.I.'s fitness programs are run by an employee organization called the Texins Association. Of its 20,000 employees in the Dallas area, an extraordinary 11,000 belong to the Texins Association, each paying a $50 annual dues that covers the whole family. Impressively, 80 percent of T.I.'s new college hires join immediately.

Betty Jones, a thirty-one-year-old secretary and nine-year T.I. veteran, started a fitness program two years ago. She now takes a fitness class after work three times a week and runs thirty miles a week. "The fact that the facility is here, that I don't have to go somewhere to work out, really helps," she says. "If I had to go to some health club somewhere, I probably wouldn't do it because it would be too much of a hassle."

A tip-of-the-iceberg manifestation of the emphasis in corporate America is the Manufacturers Hanover Corporate Challenge held in New York City each November, involving corporate teams from around the country competing in a

3.5-mile race. Winners are determined by the finishing times of the top three members of each team. There is also a winner's category for the top male and top female chief executive officer.

Corporate-sponsored diet programs are one of the fastest-growing employee benefits, according to *The Wall Street Journal*. Some of these programs are run by in-house staffs, but many companies hire diet-control specialists. Diet Workshop of Brookline, Massachusetts, and Weight Watchers International, based in Manhasset, New York, dominate the corporate market so far. One innovative new model is Vienna, Virginia's Creative Wellness program which fuses a diet program with stress management and color therapy.

Companies believe that weight control programs help increase productivity, reduce health care cost, and improve employee morale. According to George Masteralexis, senior administrator of Polaroid Corp.'s recreational service department, "When a person starts losing weight, he or she starts dressing better, looking better, and feeling better. Absenteeism decreases, and productivity increases. This is what we are shooting for."

About 30 percent of 1,185 companies surveyed by *U.S.A. Today* provide education on nutrition and helping workers lose weight; another 23 percent are considering it.

In the spring of 1984, Hub Mail Advertising in Boston provided nutrition seminars for its employees resulting in a 45-percent decrease in cholesterol in their diets and a 34-percent drop in sugar. The cafeteria menu was redesigned to complement the emphasis on nutritious food.

A model wellness program, however, would incorporate fitness and go on to stress management, health screening, weight control, and nutrition. These are some of the elements in Sentry Life Insurance's comprehensive wellness program, which has been running for more than eight years.

Sentry has an on-site fitness center with a twenty-five-meter pool, gymnasium, racquetball and handball courts, an indoor golf driving range, a weight training room. The program centers on individualized fitness goals for company people and their families.

But Sentry also offers early glaucoma screening, low-back clinics, hypertension screening, a program on dental health, and classes on healthful cooking.

Sentry uses health professionals for weight control and nutritional counseling and fitness experts to teach skiing, slimnastics, first aid, self-defense, and cardiovascular fitness.

The most interesting part of Sentry's wellness program, though, is its "quiet room." It is designed for people who want to take a relaxation break instead of a coffee break. Sentry teaches stress reduction and relaxation techniques and offers the "quiet room" in which to practice them. Imagine if every company in America provided this kind of a sanctuary from day-to-day stress.

Comprehensive wellness programs like these are becoming an established, cost-effective alternative to the exorbitant health costs. Control Data's Stay Well program is in its sixth year and showing positive results. Johnson & Johnson's markets its own in-house health care program. At Tenneco, Inc., the people in the wellness program are turning in higher performance ratings. And at Lockheed, employees taught how to lower blood pressure have succeeded in almost every case.

How does the high touch of a wellness program compare with the other sensible business-oriented approaches to saving money suggested in this chapter—auditing bills, joining HMOs, using emergicenters, and similar suggestions?

The whole purpose of a wellness program is to change people's entire lifestyles. Our lifestyles, not some strange diseases, are killing us. When our habits make us sick and kill us, our companies pick up the bill. It is as simple as that.

When you teach people to quit smoking, lower their blood pressure, relax, eat and drink healthfully, you are acting out one of the major themes of this book: Reinventing the corporation must be a win/win proposition for both the company and the people in it. Nothing illustrates that principle better than promoting total health on the job.

There are three compelling reasons for corporations to promote ambitious wellness and fitness programs.

The first is the necessary concern about their human capital, the health and well-being of their competitive edge. It will be very important that companies communicate through such efforts concerns about the well-being of their people. As Jeff Miller of Overhead Door said about the Aerobics Center, "It showed they care about their employees."

Second is the overwhelming consideration of cost. Wellness, health, and fitness programs are the preventive approach that keeps health costs to a minimum. It is really shocking; companies that consider themselves cost effective and profit conscious somehow allow themselves to run up exorbitant health care costs. The aim of this chapter has been to demonstrate some of the most innovative ways companies are cutting costs dramatically simply by taking a businesslike approach to health care costs—something they should have been doing all along.

Third, those entering the work force for the balance of the century will be attracted to corporations that have fitness facilities, nutritious cafeteria menus, and smoke-free workplaces—all complementary to their lifestyles.

All of this will be very important in a strong seller's market. Joe Zimmerman, head of the Texas Instruments' Texins Association, says, "We hire a tremendous number of professionals and the fact that we have such a program is a very big consideration in whether they choose our firm over somebody else's."

7

Women and the Corporation

Women are flooding into the job market, boosting economic growth, and helping to reshape the economy dramatically. Women have seized two-thirds of the jobs created in the past decade. And they have been the linchpin in the shift toward service and away from manufacturing.

Because a rapidly expanding labor force is a principal element in propelling an economy into a fast-growth track, the influx of women into the job market *may be the major reason that the U.S. has emerged so much healthier than other countries from the economic shock of the 1970s* [emphasis added].

That is *Business Week*'s description of the crucial role women are playing in the thriving U.S. economy, what *Business Week* calls "The great American job machine... the eighth wonder of the world." In fact, 1984's economic growth in the United States—at nearly 7 percent—was the highest since 1951.

The acknowledgment of women's contribution to America's extraordinary economic well-being is a long time coming, but as we become more fully entrenched in the information economy, it is becoming clearer that, if industrial America was a man's world, the new information economy is an era when women's economic achievements can be showcased.

The impact of working women is behind many of the important new models for re-inventing the corporation, from increased interest in flexible work schedules and benefit plans to the new respectability of intuition.

As women earn respect and power in the marketplace, they are forcing companies to recognize their legitimate needs.

Day care, for example, is finally being viewed not as a woman's problem, but as a work issue. As members of two-career families, women are compelling companies to question relocation policies that uproot families and leave spouses unemployed, to grant both maternity and paternity leave, and to question rules against employing spouses at the same firm.

As women with established careers become first-time mothers, some are gradually succeeding in negotiating part-time or contract arrangements in order to keep up their careers while their children are young.

By their sheer numbers, women are changing the world of work for other women, as understanding bosses who themselves had to take sick leave to care for a child, and as entrepreneurs who, like Mary Kay of Mary Kay Cosmetics, have the vision of creating a company where women can be mothers and millionaires.

Working women are demanding a whole range of new goods and services. And from businesslike maternity clothes to expensive, well-trained nannies, their needs are being met by—who else?—women entrepreneurs.

But despite gains in the workplace, women have come face-to-face with a single intractable problem—the continuing wage gap between male and female workers.

Whether executives or clerk-typists, women earn consistently less than men with the same education and experience. Women managers earn just half as much as their male counterparts. Among college graduates, women earn a paltry 55 percent of what men with the same schooling earn, according to a recent Conference Board report.

But even on this disheartening front, there has been some cause of late for optimism: The most recent data show that women's wages are finally inching up against men's. And as we move toward the seller's market of the late 1980s, those wages will rise still further.

Traditionally, women have earned only about sixty cents for every dollar men earn. In fact, in the 1970s, after millions of women entered the labor force, that percentage actually fell to only fifty-seven cents. But now women's wages are starting to move upward from sixty cents in 1980 to sixty-four cents in 1984. We believe that percentage will continue to rise.

Women's wages will reach 74 percent of men's by the year 2000, says James Smith, the coauthor of a Rand Corp. study of women's earnings in the workplace.

Smith's projection makes sense. For one thing, corporations have grown used to being able to choose from a large pool of well-educated female job seekers, the women of the baby boom. These women, in their twenties and thirties, who are as likely to work as men, are the demographic group responsible for the working women's revolution.

But for the most part, this group has already been absorbed into the economy and is being replaced by the less populated generation that followed them, the baby bust. As a result, the number of entry-level workers in traditionally

female occupations—clerks, financial service and retail
workers, for example—will be sharply reduced. And that
will drive up wages in some pink-collar jobs—that is,
traditional low-paying women's work.

Although Smith's forecast would represent a sizable economic leap for women, seventy-four cents to the dollar does
not represent pay equity.

**In our hearts, we all know that what we pay women is
not fair.**

Even the most hardened free-market businessman knows
that it is unfair to pay women less than they are worth, less
than they contribute to an enterprise.

Today, women all across the country are raising the issue
of comparable worth—which is so basic to any discussion
of women and the corporation.

To attract competent women workers, companies will
have to go beyond comparable worth, not just paying
women what they are worth, but also subsidizing day care.
Some corporations will operate their own day-care facilities.
The sight of mothers and kids lunching together at the
company cafeteria will be a new one in corporate America.

As companies anticipate the labor shortages of the late
1980s and the 1990s, and discover the wisdom of developing
reputations as "great places to work," as companies acknowledge the key role women are playing in the extraordinary economic vitality of the United States today, they must
increasingly seek to become great places for *women* to
work. A company does not earn such a reputation by paying
women less than they are worth, by letting women fend for
themselves about day care, by forcing young mothers to
choose between a full-time career or none at all, or by
keeping women out of the male managerial club—a club
which can learn so much from women about the manager's
new role as coach, teacher, facilitator.

The Androgynous Manager

Clearly, though, the corporate world is still a man's world. As the Conference Board study showed, 10 percent of college-educated women hold management jobs compared with 25 percent of comparably educated men.

But under this male-bastion model, corporations, for a number of reasons, are losing out as much as women. Every corporation wants the most competent people working on their side. But companies which permit themselves the luxury of unconsciously sexist attitudes lose out on a wealth of talent which resides equally in men and women. That is simply bad for business.

When women and men are segregated in the workplace, formulating stereotypes of each other's behavior, they can become blind to genuine abilities each possesses. Women, for example, are rarely considered great deal-makers, but a recent study demonstrates that they are. Dartmouth College's Amos Tuck School of Business Administration videotaped 41 men and 23 women students in simulated negotiation sessions.

According to Leonard Greenhalgh, the study's coauthor, women are more flexible, less deceptive, more emphatic, and more likely to reach agreement, while men were just the opposite.

"When a man visualizes a negotiating situation, he sees it as a one-shot deal to win or lose, like a sport or a game. A woman sees it as part of a long-term relationship," says Greenhalgh. Since most business situations involve long-term relationships, the female approach is more productive, he concludes.

But now in the information society, as the manager's role shifts to that of the teacher, mentor, and nurturer of human potential, there is even more reason for corporations to take advantage of women's managerial abilities, because these people-oriented traits are the ones women are socialized to possess.

The problem is that most women feel that they must be more like men if they are to succeed in a male-dominated corporate environment and that is a mistake both for women and for companies, according to Alice Sargent, author of *The Androgynous Manager*.

"The appropriate style for the manager of the '80s is an androgynous blend, one that combines the best of traditional male and female traits," says Sargent.

Alice Sargent's message is this: Men and women should learn from one another without abandoning successful traits they already possess. Men can learn to be more collaborative and intuitive, yet remain result oriented. Women need not give up being nurturing in order to learn to be comfortable with power and conflict.

We are re-inventing the corporation into a place where intuition is respected and where the leader's role is that of a facilitator, teacher, and nurturer of human potential. That means that women can transform the workplace by expressing, not by giving up their personal values.

Working Women: The Numbers

Despite a lot of media publicity, we have not yet grasped the simple truth about working women: We are moving to a time when virtually all women will work at paying jobs.

Now nearly 55 percent of women work—compared with only 38 percent in 1960 and only 27 percent in 1940. That is dramatic change. But statistics do not tell the whole story. Nor do they foretell the future of working women. For many categories and types of women, especially younger women, the percentage is substantially higher:

- Seventy percent of all college-educated women work.
- Virtually all women in their twenties and thirties work unless they have small children, and even then ...
- Half the women with children under six years work.

That day when almost all women will have paying jobs is getting closer and closer. Among younger women it is already here. In the last half of the 1980s and throughout the 1990s, today's 54-percent figure will move up into the 60 percentile and higher. The Bureau of Labor Statistics estimates that in 1995, 60 percent of women will work. We think that figure quite conservative.

Slowly but surely, women's labor force participation (as labor economists call it) will move toward matching that of men, about 75 percent. We often mistakenly think that all men work, not realizing that some 25 percent are disabled, unemployed, in prisons, or part of the underground economy.

Today as many women in their twenties and thirties work as men in their twenties and thirties.

There are really only two large groups of nonworking women: (1) women over forty-five who never rejoined the work force after their children were grown and (2) about half of the women with very young children.

As older women move demographically into retirement age, the work force participation will match that of men, and may exceed it.

A powerful impetus behind the growing percentage of working women is the coming seller's market. Those labor shortages of the 1990s that will force us to re-invent the corporation will ensure that women will continue working.

New Work Patterns

In the space of a generation, women's work patterns have
undergone a complete metamorphosis. The mothers of the
1950s led completely different work lives than their daughters are experiencing today.

The women who mothered the baby boom generation
worked briefly, then retired to suburbia to raise children.
Twenty years later, once their children left for college, the
baby boom mothers went back to work—maybe.

But millions of their daughters—today's baby boom
women—*will never miss a day of work because of child
rearing*, because they will have no children. By the time the
first wave of the baby boom enters menopause, more than
20 percent will have had no children. That contrasts with
about 10 percent three decades ago.

The majority will have children. But unlike their mothers,
today's women are working right up until their delivery,
taking between a few weeks and a few years off to have
one, or occasionally two, children and then heading right
back to work.

Today's most dedicated working mothers stay home only
until their children reach preschool or school age. Once
their youngest child enters school, mothers look for work in
droves. Mothers with preschool children—56 percent of
whom worked in 1982—are the fastest growing segment of
the labor force.

Working women are creating the phenomenon of two-
career couples—the numbers of which doubled during the
1970s. Once a sociological oddity, two-career couples are
now the norm. There are now some 34 million dual-earner
couples.

"We've seen a revolutionary change in the last fifteen or
twenty years, and I don't think we realize how significant it
is because we're living it," says Leon Bouvier, a demogra-

pher with the Washington, D.C.–based Population Reference Bureau. "More and more women are working at meaningful jobs because they want to."

Mr. Bouvier's sentiments were echoed in a *New York Times* poll taken in late 1983, showing that women found work and independence as satisfying as home and children. These new values contrasted sharply with opinions expressed in a 1970 poll asking the same questions.

Erma Bombeck notwithstanding, the popularity of motherhood has clearly declined in a short thirteen years. In 1970, 53 percent of the women said motherhood was one of the best parts of being a woman. By 1983, fewer than half as many, 26 percent, agreed with that statement.

Love of work is on the upswing. In 1970, a mere 9 percent of women listed work outside the home as enjoyable. By 1983, that percentage nearly tripled to 26 percent.

The Two-Career Couple

How has the two-career couple influenced corporate relocation policies? To answer that question, the New York–based research firm Catalyst has studied both couples and companies. Not surprisingly, most couples said they would be reluctant to move unless both could pursue their careers and gain financially through the move. "This reluctance translates into an executive refusal rate of 25 percent," the study reported.

"Relocation is the issue that has really brought the two-career family into corporate focus," says Catalyst's Felice Schwartz. Companies are often failing to notice the human factors behind relocation, Catalyst believes.

But companies are beginning to respond to the needs of two-career couples involved in relocating:

- New York's Union Pacific Corp. offers informal assistance to help spouses find new jobs.

- AT&T's employee relations director recommended that spouses be paid a month's salary to tide them over while looking for a new job.
- When both spouses are employed by IBM, the company will "make every effort" to get the spouse a job in the new area.

General Electric noticed, for example, that its on-campus recruiters are constantly asked about corporate policy toward two-career couples.

"Changes in values, especially among younger employees, have made career advancement and financial gain alone less persuasive inducements to relocate. Today's employees are giving more weight to family and financial considerations and are sharing household and parenting responsibilities," the Catalyst study concludes.

No wonder people are reluctant to move. The paychecks of women workers are making Americans far more affluent.

According to a Conference Board study, high-income households tend to include working women. Two-thirds of the households with incomes between $30,000 and $35,000 include working women. Among households earning between $40,000 and $50,000, more than 70 percent of the women work.

A sign of the times: Retailers must open Sundays to get a crack at the working woman's new money. She often has no other time to shop.

The New Mother: Older and Working

For the first time in American history, large numbers of women in their thirties and even forties with established careers are having their first baby. It seems they are determined to avoid their mothers' job history, that is, of reentering the job market around age forty or forty-five, self-confidence bruised after years of child rearing. Instead, the baby boom women have delayed having babies until achieving some level of worldly success.

Today's mini baby boom is being born to the generation of delaying mothers who "should" have had their firstborn ten years ago when they were, say, between twenty-two and twenty-four. Instead, the stork is visiting these women in their thirties.

There was an 83-percent increase in the number of first births to women thirty to thirty-four between 1972 and 1980, from 7 births per 1,000 women to 12.8 births. But by 1982 it had increased again to 14.6 percent. For women between thirty-five and thirty-nine, the first-births rate rose by 57 percent between 1970 and 1982. So even during the baby bust of the 1970s, the trend toward older mothers was getting established.

Through the strength of their numbers, career women and mature mothers have re-invented motherhood and women's work patterns and are slowly forcing institutions to re-invent the workplace to respond to their needs.

Time for Mothering

How are today's mothers and the companies where they work managing the issue of maternity leave? The answer is indeed slowly and not at all well. Corporate maternity-leave policies, for the most part, seem to be a throwback to the days when women's careers lasted a few years instead of several decades. This is one area where re-inventing the corporation is desperately lagging.

In a 1984 survey of Fortune 1500 companies about maternity-leave policies, Catalyst found that only about half offered unpaid leave and that only 7.4 percent had paid leave. The majority—95 percent—offered disability only. The Pregnancy Disability Act of 1978 requires that leaves related to pregnancy be treated like any other disability.

The study also discovered that the amount of leave most working women took—whether they were managers or not—was three months.

Given today's small families of one or perhaps two children, that translates to between three and six months out of a work life that might span forty or fifty years. Even if women took off more time, say six months as Dr. Edward Zigler, an expert on child care, recommends, we are still talking about a maximum of about one year over the course of an entire career!

Is that too much to ask in order to reproduce the species? Most companies seem to think so. Despite the multibillion-dollar contributions women make to corporations and society at large, they are nickeled and dimed when it comes to taking a few years off to participate in the miracle of having a baby.

"Unlike 75 other countries including Canada, France, and West Germany, the United States has no provision guaranteeing women the right to leave work for a specified period to care for a baby, and no job protection or cash benefit to compensate for not working because of pregnancy or childbirth," writes Georgia Dullea in *The New York Times,* citing studies by Dr. Alfred Kahn and Dr. Sheila Kammerman of Columbia University. Dullea was covering a conference sponsored by the Junior League, which favors a national policy giving working parents the right to take leave to care for infants without losing job security.

Does the government have to step in to guarantee women the right to have babies without losing their jobs? Or will companies change to accommodate the new, increasingly female worker?

"The corporate motivation is there," believes Catalyst's Phyllis Silverman, who reports that companies are studying leave policies and asking her organization for information and guidance. "As one company representative told me, 'Now that we've put all this money into recruiting women, we had better find a policy that's going to help keep them.'"

Alternative Schedules

Successful women combining careers and motherhood need alternative work schedules for the years following childbirth. Although some of the new middle-aged mothers want to be back at work full-time as soon as possible, the majority want options—a part-time professional job with benefits, job sharing, flextime, consulting jobs, professional work on a temporary basis.

Like all pioneers, the mothers with careers are achieving mixed results. Some are forging creative solutions with their employers; others are forced to choose full-time career, motherhood, and total exhaustion.

"The price is very high," says Charlene Barshefsky, thirty-five, the mother of a two-year-old daughter and a partner in one of Washington, D.C.'s most prestigious law firms. "The emotional turmoil, the exhaustion, the frustration of having too many things to do and not enough time."

For some women, like Janine Harris, also a Washington lawyer, that price was too high. She gave up a lucrative partnership after the lawyers in her firm refused her proposal to work part-time.

"People in law firms aren't very flexible," says Harris. Yet the feminization of the legal profession could transform the legal profession's stodgy old image into that of a bellwether in women's issues. In the mid-1970s, women made up only 5 percent of the legal profession; now they number 15 percent. For some years now, women have made up between one-third and one-half of most law schools. By

the year 2000 women will make up about one-third of the
legal profession.

But whether in law, business, or other professions, mothers
with careers are running headlong into the same problem:

**Work patterns and career ladders are based on male
standards—since those are the only standards that have
applied until now.**

And some male executives, like the personnel manager at
a large industrial company who turned down a woman's
request for part-time work, are intent on keeping things
exactly as they are: "If we give it to her, we'll have to give
it to everyone. Who doesn't want to work part-time?"

Besides, he adds angrily, "I don't get to see my son
much, either. If women want the rewards of top jobs, the
money and prestige, they've got to be prepared to make
sacrifices."

These are the hardened, even mean-spirited attitudes
working mothers are sometimes up against. Nevertheless,
there is one key factor that is enabling them to break
through to the new work patterns they want—their own
experience, ability, and the investment the firm has made in
them.

When a woman makes herself so valuable that the organization would rather have her part-time than not at all, she
gets the work schedule she wants.

"The reality is that women who are considered valuable
are having flexible options. The vast number of women are
not," says Dana Friedman of New York's Conference Board.

True, but these pioneering women are creating the new
models that will gain growing acceptance and become tomorrow's norms.

Insurance companies, banks, and other information companies are leading the way. A *Business Week* story entitled
"Companies Start to Meet Executive Mothers Half-Way"

cited examples of executive women who worked out part-time arrangements at CIGNA Corp., First National Bank of Atlanta, Control Data, Cleveland's AmeriTrust Corp., United Bank of Denver, First National Bank of Chicago, and First International Bank of California.

New Businesses for Working Women

Working women in two-career families have higher incomes, but their lives are not all glamour. Even allowing for the husband who "helps out around the house," most working women hold the equivalent of a second full-time job keeping house, cooking, and caring for children. It does not take much imagination to see that the hours spent at these tasks can easily add up to thirty or forty per week.

The National Commission on Working Women interviewed many working women to see how they cope with their demanding schedules. Half the working women they interviewed said they have no leisure time whatsoever.

The situation literally begs for new services and new models and offers enormous opportunities for entrepreneurs who understand the needs of working women. Who is better equipped to fill that need than other women who work for themselves?

A recent article in the *Washington Post* about affluent working mothers notes that Washington, D.C.'s K Street Corridor, the fancy downtown area favored by lawyers, lobbyists, and expensive restaurants, is reflecting the boom in working mothers.

Within about six months, women entrepreneurs started three new businesses catering to the yuppie mothers. Mother's Work, a maternity boutique selling dress-for-success business clothes with names like "The Conservative," "The Barrister," and "The Executive," opened in June 1984. About two months later, another woman entrepreneur opened Child's Play, one of the first downtown day-care centers. "The cure for the ten-hour guilt complex," its founders suggest. The annual fee is $5,000 (that ought to ease your guilt complex).

The third new business is Lawyer's Lawyer, "a kind of Kelly Girl for attorneys," says its founder. It places attorneys—mostly women with small children who cannot work full-time—in temporary jobs at area law firms. The lawyers earn $25 per hour, half what Lawyer's Lawyer charges the client.

Lawyer's Lawyer fills the need for professional women to work part-time during prime childbearing years, while building on the trend of contracting out. It also illustrates the opportunities for women entrepreneurs to sense new business possibilities that men could easily ignore.

Well-to-do dual-career families have crated an enormous demand for full-time or live-in housekeepers and child-care workers—again a great opportunity for women to open businesses that place these workers.

"We get at least 100 new calls per week," says Bonnie Gillespie, corporate manager of Mother's Work, an Arlington, Virginia, agency that places live-in help.

The need for skilled professional child care in the home is causing a revival of the old model of the English nannie, American style.

Terri Eurich, thirty-four, was eager to get back to her personnel management job in Denver after her daughter's birth. But day-care centers there had a waiting list nineteen months long for infants.

Her response was to start National Academy for Nannies, NANI for short. There has been no need to advertise.

"We've received calls from California, Utah, New York, New Orleans, and Florida, and we aren't even in the phone book," says Terri.

Entrepreneurs are starting nannie schools all across America. Milwaukee has Nannys, Ltd., and the American Nannie Plan course is based in Claremont, California.

Nannies—some college graduates, others experienced child-care workers—earn between $600 and $800 per month, plus room, board, and benefits—a figure well-to-do two-career couples are willing to pay for professional individualized child care in their home. Some parents even pay for the nannie course—$2,000 at NANI. At Nannys, Ltd., students do not pay tuition for the sixty-hour course. Instead, a placement fee is deducted from their wages.

Nannie schools are still another case of the female entrepreneur taking advantage of the tremendous business opportunities of the working women/two-career couple revolution.

Day Care

The need for day care is at the core of the new relationship between the corporation and the family.

It is the fourth largest item in many family budgets, after taxes, housing, and food.

For the parents of the 8 million children who need it, it is one big constant worry.

Yet, when it is good, it consistently increases the productivity of millions of working parents.

Day care. Adequate, reliable, moderately priced day care. The issue has been around for as long as women have worked.

During the 1970s, when huge numbers of women joined the labor force, enrollment in nursery schools shot up 71 percent. The 1970s also saw the traditional sources for day care—grandmothers, aunts, and trusted family friends—decline. Either they were too far away or they had to work as well.

Although some 8 million children need day care, there is space for only 2 million children in child-care centers. The need for day care shows no signs of slowing down. And it is estimated that the number of children needing day care will increase to 10.5 million by 1990.

But only now—because of the huge number of working women and the beginning of a seller's market—are corporations embarking on re-inventing day care from a woman's problem to a work issue.

The National Employer Supported Child Care Project in Pasadena, California, estimated that there were some 415 employer-sponsored child-care programs in 1982, compared with 105 in 1978. But by October 1984, the Pasadena group counted some 3,000 companies that had made some change in policy or services to accommodate the needs of working parents. A 1978 General Mills/Lou Harris study of human resources executives found that 67 percent expected to provide child-care benefits within the next five years.

It appears the human resource people were right about the trend toward more child care: In fall 1984, *Newsweek* counted some 1,500 organizations involved with day care, compared with only 100 six years earlier.

Equally noteworthy, corporations are learning that child-care programs increase productivity and morale and reduce absenteeism and turnover. So day care is another example of a win/win arrangement: Working parents gain—and so do companies.

If you're a working parent with young children, go to work for a high-technology company with a young president or a family-owned or family-related business.

That is the advice of Dr. Dana Friedman, a specialist in early child-care education and author of a day-care study funded by the Carnegie Foundation.

The Carnegie study identified 600 companies that provide day care or day-care benefits. Most fit the above description, according to Dr. Friedman, who believes that corporations will increasingly have to take a leadership role in providing day care. As *Newsweek*'s estimate shows, that is already happening.

According to Dr. Friedman's study, parents actually do *not* favor companies building an on-site day-care facility. What they want instead are child-care options. They want to choose where to place their children and therefore would prefer a voucher system. Polaroid Corp. has a voucher system. Vouchers save corporations the significant cost of building and outfitting a day-care center while increasing parental options.

Once a company decides to become involved with day care, there are many possibilities:

- Businesses and community groups in Miami, Boston, and San Francisco are creating centrally located day-care centers.
- Hewlett-Packard and TRW together finance about 15 percent of the costs of Child Care Service Center. In return, employees whose children attend the center get as much as a 20 percent discount and are put atop waiting lists.
- Seven Long Island businesses have contributed about $12,000 to open a new day-care center.
- Some employers contract with independent day-care centers to save a given number of slots for employees.
- Many companies, including Honeywell, 3M, and Steelcase, the office furniture maker, operate information and referral services to help their people find dependable day care.

But for some corporations the best way to offer day-care benefits is as part of a "cafeteria of benefits" package.

For example, Chemical Bank, the nation's sixth largest bank, introduced in January 1983 a flexible benefits program which includes day care as one possible benefit.

Procter & Gamble claims to be the first large company in

the United States to offer day-care benefits as part of its flexible benefits plan, called Flexcomp.

The main advantage: All employees select from the same menu of benefits. So those who pick child care are not favored over others.

Phyllis Silverman, corporate child-care manager for New York–based Catalyst, which studies issues related to work and women, says, "A company wouldn't necessarily want to favor an employee with children by putting up a day-care center and not providing special money for an employee who has, for example, aging dependent parents."

The need for day care is encouraging a number of inspiring, innovative models outside the corporate sphere which nevertheless offer ideas to both parents and their companies.

One of our favorites is a joint day-care/nursing home in Steamboat Springs, Colorado. Grandkids Day Care Center is operated by the Routt Memorial Extended Care Center, a nursing home for about forty senior citizens. Although children spend most of their time learning and playing with teachers, young and old get together for exercise, field trips, and arts and crafts.

Rent-A-Mom, a Denver-based, nationally franchised, twenty-four-hour-a-day domestic referral service, claims to offer everything a Mom can do.

The *Seattle Times* wrote: "Rent-A-Mom will pick up a sick kid, take him home, tuck him into bed and care for him until Working Mom comes home. She'll greet him after school, help with homework, prepare meals, balance check-books, shop and tutor in subjects as diverse as computer training and papier mâché. One Rent-A-Mom service even helped to deliver puppies."

Because they must recruit nurses in a tight labor market, hospitals have become leaders in providing day-care benefits. For example, St. Anthony's Hospital in Denver runs a center for 138 children of nurses and doctors. Its hours: 6:00

A.M. to midnight. With the coming labor shortages, corporations will follow the hospitals' lead, competing for women workers by offering day care.

There is a growing body of evidence that company-sponsored day care pays off in increased productivity, decreased absenteeism, and better employee morale.

A study at Texas Women's University showed that a $50,000 investment in a day-care program can save some $3 million in employee turnover, training, and lost work time.

In Freeport, Texas, a heart pacemaker manufacturer, Intermedics, Inc., has operated a day-care center since 1979, including a night-care service for employees on the 4:00 to 11:00 P.M. shift. Though the center technically operates at a loss, the company has reaped an important benefit: a 9-percent drop in absenteeism among its 1,000 (mostly female) workers. That amounts to a $2-million savings in reduced turnover costs since the center opened.

At Dallas's Zale Corporation, parents can eat lunch with their children at the firm's on-site center for seventy children. A company spokesperson says employees no longer rush away from their desks at five to pick up their children at suburban centers that close at six. The increased productivity, he says, is well worth the effort invested.

Valerie Riefenstahl, a senior financial analyst at Zale Corp., was offered a job when her baby was only three months old. "It was about $2,000 less than I wanted," she said. "But because of the child-care center, I came to work here."

Nyloncraft, Inc., a 450-employee company in Mishawaka, Indiana, created the state's first twenty-four-hour day-care center. About 85 percent of the employees were women, many single parents with young children. Like the other firms cited here, the company realized improved morale.

Absenteeism declined to an extremely low 3 percent and turnover was substantially reduced.

"We were an employer of 250 people, and at the end of 1978, we wrote 900-plus W-2s, which means we turned every job in the plant over three times," says Nyloncraft's Bob Tennyson. Two years after the day-care facility was opened, Nyloncraft, with some 200 more employees, wrote only 26 more W-2s than the number of jobs.

But Nyloncraft discovered its child-care center produced still another, unexpected, benefit—it helped sell the company to potential customers.

"It wasn't intended, but you bring somebody to the learning center and their whole attitude toward us is, if this company is this progressive, then they must be somebody I want to do business with," says Nyloncraft president Jim Wyllie.

Says Nyloncraft customer Tom Murphy, vice-president of manufacturing at Fellowes Manufacturing Co., in Itasca, Illinois, "I think I was probably more impressed with the day-care center than I was with the plant—and it's a great plant."

Comparable Worth

Comparable worth is the women's economic issue that asks the question, "Why should a truck driver be paid more than a secretary?"

The simplified answer is that (until recently) men have always been truck drivers and women have always been secretaries and men have decided.

The aim of comparable worth is to change all that.

Women are making great gains in the world of work, but not in the economic rewards that accompany work. Between 1960 and the mid-1980s, the percentage of women who work has increased from about 38 percent to 55 percent, yet working women still earn only about sixty-four cents for every dollar a male worker earns. According to a study by *Working Women* magazine, however, professional women are now making steady gains, earning seventy-five cents for each dollar a man earns, compared with only seventy-one cents in 1983.

Equal pay for equal work—which became the law of the land through the Equal Pay Act of 1963—has not helped the overall wage gap, though, because men and women are segregated into sex-specific jobs.

The comparable worth debate picks up where equal pay left off. Comparable worth advocates argue that traditional women's work has been substantially undervalued because it was once considered only an adjunct to the family income, whereas traditional men's work may have been overvalued because in society's eyes, that income went to support a wife and children.

The idea is that women should get equal pay for work of comparable value.

In other words, if the skills and responsibilities of a secretary are comparable to those of a truck driver, they should make about the same salary. They do not. Secretaries earn an average of $12,000 (in 1982, according to BLS), while truck drivers, heretofore primarily male, earn an average of $16,300 per year. (Many would argue that being a secretary requires considerably *more* skill than being a truck driver.) Similarly, why should household workers (mostly female) earn only $5,600, while mostly male janitors earn $11,400?

Comparable worth advocates believe organizations should analyze the skills, effort, education, responsibility, and working conditions each job requires and pay people accordingly. That way women's economic contribution will be matched in their paychecks.

To us, it sounds pretty difficult to argue against, but arguments against comparable worth have been loudly raised.

Critics of the comparable worth theory say it is illogical and unworkable. Economists have warned it would be highly inflationary. The U.S. Chamber of Commerce estimates it would cost the U.S. economy $300 billion. Some have even argued it would be contradictory to women's interests.

But the most outrageous reaction against the simple fairness of comparable worth came from a most unexpected quarter—the U.S. Civil Rights Commission. Its chairman, Clarence Pendleton, called comparable worth "probably the looniest idea since 'Looney Tunes' came on the screen."

It is difficult to imagine how Pendleton could have insulted women more or been more out of touch with the times.

Because despite the many arguments against comparable worth, there are many indications that it is an idea whose time has come. Courts, state and local governments, unions, and individual corporations have already analyzed pay structures and begun to correct inequalities against women:

- New York will review all state job salaries for sex bias.
- Minnesota has begun a $42-million four-year comparable worth plan for state employees. Now women in traditionally female occupations are receiving special raises to bring their salaries up to par.
- In late 1984, Virginia completed a study which concluded that a wage gap between male and female salaries exists in nearly all private and public organizations.
- New Mexico has allocated $3 million to close the sex-biased wage gap there.
- Iowa has allocated $10 million to institute a comparable worth system and will invest between $30 million and $50 million to reshape its pay system.
- The General Accounting Office is studying how it might do a full-scale comparable worth study on the more than 360,000 federal employees in the Washington, D.C., area.
- In May 1985 the city of Los Angeles agreed to give $12

million in raises to 3,900 clerks and librarians, mostly women, to bring their salaries into line with manual labor jobs held by men.

"The federal government should serve as a model employer and should lead the nation in identifying and eliminating that part of the wage gap which is attributable to discrimination," said Rep. Patricia Schroeder (D-Colo.), one of the measure's main sponsors.

Comparable worth advocates won their most important court case to date in the bellwether state of Washington, where a judge ordered the state government to pay its women workers what is estimated at between $300 and $850 million in salary increases and back pay. "You can't legally balance the budget on the backs of women," ruled U.S. District Judge Jack E. Turner.

Though that ruling has been appealed, the state legislature enacted a bill requiring Washington State to eliminate the wage gap by 1994.

The key in the Washington case was that the state had previously conducted a study that documented widespread discrimination on the basis of sex—and then did nothing to rectify the situation. That is important because many more state and local governments and private companies are concerned enough about comparable worth to enact similar studies.

All totaled, at least thirty states and scores of localities have introduced legislation to study comparable worth and consider changing pay systems.

Bottom up in the states and localities, comparable worth— that loony idea—is becoming the accepted standard of fairness. But some women's groups want more—they want the federal government to enforce comparable worth standards on private corporations.

Although that sort of government regulation of business is completely against the current mood of the country, the growing political power of women is not to be ignored. So long as women vote, comparable worth will have advocates who want it to become law.

Women's increased political power is raising everyone's consciousness about comparable worth, and that is positive. Corporations should be analyzing their pay scales (which they do periodically anyway) and paying people what they are worth to the company. That is simply good business.

But the real boost for comparable worth is coming with the seller's market.

To attract the best women and the best men (who want to work for a fair company), companies will want to earn a reputation as a comparable worth employer—and maybe even advertise themselves as such.

What have model corporations done with comparable worth?

A few companies, like AT&T, have conducted their own job evaluations to ferret out sex bias. The AT&T scheme involved fourteen factors—for example, "communication skills." It measured jobs in many different categories, taking into account both physical and mental stress. AT&T claims the study showed little discrimination, but should a comparable worth case be filed against the company, it now has a body of evidence to support its innocence.

Other corporations, including Westinghouse and General Electric, settled comparable worth cases out of court with the International Union of Electricians. The IUE claims there have been more than a dozen such cases. The unions involved with comparable worth *are* re-inventing themselves as champions of the new worker—women.

Private corporations ignore the comparable worth issue at great risk. Although most of the action on comparable worth is happening in the public sector, some state legislatures are trying to force private industry to act.

- Hawaii, for example, passed a nonbinding law asking private employers to set up comparable worth standards.
- Pennsylvania is considering mandatory comparable worth standards, which could be in effect by 1986.

In 1978, Eleanor Holmes Norton, then head of the Equal Employment Opportunity Commission, predicted that comparable worth would be "the women's issue of the 1980s." That prediction appears to have come to pass.

Companies have a choice. Either they can sit tight, do as little thinking as possible about comparable worth, and hope it will go away, or they can decide to use it as an opportunity to prepare for the seller's market. The companies that get serious about being fair in compensating women will become known in the marketplace as comparable worth employers and will attract the best people, especially the best women.

A company does not have to answer every complicated question raised by comparable worth. It need only analyze its pay system fairly and honestly. That is the bottom line of comparable worth.

Few things in this century are as important to social and economic change in America as the extraordinary increase of women in the work force. But in the buyer's market of the last two decades, corporations have been slow to accommodate to this changing work force. The seller's market, just getting under way, will change that. Market forces will do what habit, tradition, and mind-set have not done: acknowledge and reward women for their contribution to the enterprise.

Women under forty now are as likely to work as men, but the mentality of corporations has not changed substantively from what it was thirty years ago when the mothers of these

women worked a few years and then retired to the suburbs
to raise families.

In the corporate mind-set, management is still a man's
world. And that is why there is so much scoffing at such
notions as comparable worth. Deep down, industrial America
does not allow that women should be seriously considered
for the ranks of upper management.

We have spoken to the top management groups of many
of the largest corporations in this country. And whether the
top of the management pyramid is 35 people or 135 people,
we know before we enter the room that there will not be one
woman in the audience, and if there is, she will be the
assistant treasurer.

**The Chinese say, "Women hold up half of the sky."
There are as many women coming into the work force
today as men. And the corporations that acknowledge
women for contributing equally to the company's future
will attract not only the best women but also the men
who have a well-developed egalitarian sense of the new
world.**

Politics is beginning to show the way. A record number of
women were elected to state legislatures in the November
1984 elections. There are now 1,067 women in state legislatures, 14 percent of the total number of the fifty states. That
is triple the 350 female legislators in 1971. While in most
states women make up about 10 percent of the legislatures,
they have a greater percentage in the bellwether states (those
states that are trendsetters): California, 12.5 percent, Florida, 19, Connecticut, 21, Washington, 24, and Colorado,
25. This strongly suggests that women's legislative gains
will continue, and this at a time when state legislatures are
having a greater impact on people's lives than the U.S.
Congress has.

In corporate America, men decide. At the polling booth, both men and women decide.

Geraldine Ferraro's vice-presidential candidacy opened the way for women from both parties to run for president. And here is something to think about:

For decades, our most enterprising men have found better things to do than run for president. But for America's women, it is now easier to be elected president of the United States than to become chairman of IBM.

Some very competent women can now run for president against a field of mediocre men. This could lead to a string of women U.S. presidents.

Let us put the question this way: Which will come first, a woman president or a woman as CEO of one of the Fortune 100 companies? Tells you something, doesn't it?

8

Re-inventing the Corporation in Japan

To one degree or another, the trends discussed throughout this book are forcing all industrialized countries to re-invent the corporation. Even in Japan, with its paternalistic approach to workers and its lifelong employment practices, we are seeing the beginnings of profound change, the beginnings of the re-invention of their corporations. We wanted to look at the corporation in Japan for two key reasons. First, if it can happen there it can happen anywhere. That is to say, some elements of Japan's culture—the emphasis on tradition and uniformity, for example—seem to contradict the need for individuality and entrepreneurship which has characterized re-inventing the corporation in the United States. Nevertheless, as we will demonstrate in this chapter, the Japanese *are* synthesizing cultural values and the need to re-invent the corporation. The second important reason is this: What is happening in Japan is fundamentally important to developments in the United States.

The interplay of economic developments in and between Japan and the United States is not only basic to the well-being of those two nations but is creating a degree of mutual economic cooperation and development unparalleled in world history.

We agree with Masaya Miyoshi, who is the senior managing director of the Japan Federation of Economic Organizations. After saying that the common need for business of the United States and Japan was to seek mutual capital and technological interchange, Miyoshi, in a speech before the Asia Society in Washington in April 1984, said he saw the two countries increasing cooperation by studying and playing to their respective strengths. "It is expected that after a long-term process of such dynamic intermingling, the industries of the two nations will eventually converge."

Eventually people will come to speak of "U.S.A.–Japan, Inc."

Japanese corporations are restructuring themselves and are beginning to re-invent their people practices. *The Japan Economic Journal (JEJ)* in 1984 ran a two-month-long series on "The Remaking of Japan's Major Corporations." In its introduction to the series, *JEJ* said, "Waves of rapidly developing high technologies are now willy-nilly forcing Japanese corporations to make swift and bold adjustments for survival." Much of this chapter is drawn from that series.

Japan's key materials industries—iron, steel, textiles— have been steadily diversifying their product lines, mostly in the direction of high-value-added "downstream" areas, ever since the business slump touched off by the 1973 oil crisis.

Toray Industries, which made its name in rayon, was one of the first of these basic industries to undergo a structural change. For several years, it has pushed a new image-building program under the slogan "A New and Another Toray," and highlighted nontextile sections, carbon fiber, and biotechnology. But it is still uncertain which precise direction it will follow.

"In the high-growth period when synthetic fibers were in their spectacular ascendancy, we knew perfectly where we were headed," says Osamu Sato, a member of the company's management planning office. "From now on, however, we have to grope for our new destinations." To which *The Japan Economic Journal* adds, "Now that many of the nation's mainstay industries, such as iron and steel, automobiles, home electric appliances and foodstuffs, have entered a period of maturity, a great many of the nation's leading companies find themselves in predicaments similar to Toray's."

Toray's new products include soft contact lenses, reverse osmosis membranes, artificial kidneys, and various electronic materials. There is a big question as to whether any of the new business can ever replace the past successes Toray had with rayon and nylon.

"Biotechnological products will certainly come in bloom in the twenty-first century," a Toray executive projected. But "the problem is how to earn our way through the remainder of this century."

In response to in-company criticism of Toray's lack of a clear-cut strategy for new business lines, president Yoshikazu Ito says, "You are the ones to foster new business. If you truly believe in your ideas, don't hesitate to translate them into reality."

Toray has now embarked upon an ambitious "perception revolution" program in search of a new and powerful corporate identity.

They are doing something else, too.

Toray is now engaged in creating a new comprehensive technological headquarters in Shiga Prefecture, the company's birthplace, where it will employ up to 3,000 researchers and technological experts. The idea is to have Toray's "technological brains," including those on the company's board of directors, housed together in a single place some 240 miles away from the company's head office in Tokyo. "No other company," comments *The Japan Economic Journal*, "not only among Toray's fellow textile companies but also among companies in all other business lines, has ever dared to take such a bold managerial step."

"Toray is now placing extra emphasis on two subjects," explains managing director Saihei Nomura, chief of the company's production headquarters. "One is to bolster its cost competitiveness in the textile sectors and the other is to consolidate its production systems for many new nontextile fields, such as pharmaceuticals. In order to make a success of these pursuits, technological experts in research, development, production, and engineering are required to organically pool their resources in many common projects. Because of the wide dispersal of technological experts throughout the country, Toray has so far been unable to employ swift, companywide technological strategies."

From Toasters to Semiconductors

The giant Matsushita Electric Industrial, has been single-mindedly devoted to the production of home electric appliances since 1918. Now, however, Matsushita is completely restructuring itself for forced entry into the field of electronics. It is now throwing all funds and resources into semiconductors, telecommunications, and information-related equipment. "We are planning to outgrow the image of a home appliances manufacturer by the end of 1986," says Matsushita's president, Toshihiko Yamashita.

In 1984, Matsushita Electric Industrial dramatically announced that it had decided to depreciate its semiconductor manufacturing equipment and facilities in a single year rather than in the five years the Japanese government allows. Matsushita is scrapping its equipment each year, so that it will be able to always use the newest and most advanced machines and equipment. That's very expensive—including high tax penalties. It is an extraordinary strategy. Matsushita's executive director in charge of finances, Hajime Suzuki, says, "Lose some to win big is what I say to everybody. Being a latecomer in the semiconductor field, we won't be able to catch up with the front-runners if we stick to conventional ways."

Soichiro Suenaga, president of another Japanese company, Mitsubishi Heavy Industries, Japan's biggest manufacturer of heavy machinery and industrial plants, expresses the same sentiment more bluntly: "Dinosaurs and mammoths died out simply because they were unable to cope with the changes in environments. No one can say that our company, a true mammoth, will not follow their footsteps to extinction unless each of us succeeds in earning his own way."

Re-inventing the Japanese Steel Industry

Nippon Steel Corp., by far the largest steel maker in the world, is now undergoing drastic change. It, like other steel companies, got caught between new competitors in South Korea (and Brazil and other newly industrialized nations) and the advent of plastics.

As *The Japan Economic Journal* put it in April 1984, "The swiftly evolving high-tech age is strongly pressuring Nippon Steel Corp., one of the most representative big businesses in Japan, to totally revamp its organization, corporate strategy, production systems, labor-management relations, etc."

Sounds like re-inventing the corporation.

During 1984, there was a striking symbolic change in the leadership of Japanese industry: For the first time in history, electronic machinery surpassed iron and steel in equipment investments.

Nippon Steel, Japan's leading company for the last eighty

years, is now trying to turn itself into an integrated manufacturer of key nonsteel industrial materials: ceramics, semiconductor and compound materials.

For a long time, the Seiko group ran after expansion under the slogan of "catching up with and overtaking our Swiss competitors." (It sounds a little snappier in Japanese.) In the late 1960s, members of the Seiko group, fiercely competing among themselves, successfully developed quartz timepieces which catapulted Seiko into a long lead over its Swiss competitors—who adamantly stuck to their mechanical timepieces. (Switzerland's share of the total world timepiece market plunged from 41 percent in 1971 to a mere 8.5 percent in 1982.)

Now, however, there are warning signs that the timepiece industry has reached maturity and is losing earnings capacity. Seiko is responding by re-inventing itself through long-term development programs running to 1990.

The overriding corporate strategy for the Seiko group of companies is "from Seiko of timepiece fame to Seiko of information-related equipment, including timepieces." And the shift has been remarkable for this enormously successful company. In 1970, watches accounted for 100 percent of the combined sales of Seiko Instruments & Electronics and Suwa Seikosha Co., another core of the group. By 1982, watches accounted for only 40 percent of the sales of these units. In 1983, printers and parts for computers had greater sales than watches, the first time in the history of the company that another product outsold watches.

Seiko is still the world's largest timepiece manufacturer, and huge profits of today and yesterday are being used to fund the future, a future in which that 40 percent will continue to recede.

Even given this history, "We are simply surprised at the swiftness with which corporations rise and fall," says chairman Kentaro Hattori of Hattori Seiko.

Regrouping for the Age of Galloping High Technologies

Hitachi, Ltd., has more than 10,000 research and development experts, spends more on R&D than any other Japanese company, has seven major research institutes, and in 1984 announced that it will establish still another research institute to engage in basic studies—projects aimed ten to twenty years from now.

Because of the rapid progress in the microelectronic revolution, Hitachi's research laboratories have been so swamped with applied research there has been no time to do basic research. So Hitachi has created a new basic research institute, which opened in April 1985.

"We will boost the share of R&D outlay to 8 percent of our total sales by fiscal 1988, and more than 60 percent of the entire outlay will go to semiconductors, information disposal systems, and other high-tech sectors," according to Hiroshi Watanabe, executive director in charge of R&D.

Hitachi's R&D expenditure will grow to around $1.3 billion in fiscal 1988. Although Hitachi is by far the biggest R&D spender among Japanese corporations, it still compares poorly with its Western counterparts, Siemans, IBM, and GE. *The Japan Economic Journal* says that although many Japanese businessmen often speak of the necessity of expanding outlays for basic research "in order to promote originality and creativity among Japanese R&D experts, they are unfortunately not as swift in their action as with their words."

One of the most important problems now facing Japanese corporations—as well as American corporations—is to create a system designed to foster creativity and originality among R&D personnel by fully acknowledging and rewarding important breakthroughs. The formulation of a new evaluation system for R&D achievements is an important part of the creation of the new long-term basic research institute at Hitachi.

It has been reported that there is an unwritten law at Hitachi that R&D people have to come up with at least some concrete results within five years of the start of their research projects if they work at the Central Research Laboratories and within two years if they work at other institutes. Even Hitachi does not deny that this unwritten law has resulted in Hitachi R&D people gravitating to easy-to-complete projects.

The primary objective of the new basic research institute is to develop more long-term projects, technologies which will come into being in the rapidly approaching twenty-first century. "If R&D personnel remain bound by the ongoing myopic evaluation system, there will be no meaning to creating a new basic research institute," said *The Japan Economic Journal*. "It is true that, unlike universities, private corporations are not in a position to devote their R&D personnel to purely scientific projects. If they seek immediate results only as they did in the past, however, they may very well write themselves off in the present age of galloping high technologies."

Global Counterpurchases

Japan's massive trading companies—the *sogo sosha*—are facing a new problem which is surfacing as part of the shift to a truly global economy: demands for *counterpurchases*.

Counterpurchases are a form of barter trade recently and increasingly employed by developing countries. Many developing countries will now import plants and equipment from industrial nations only if the seller will purchase primary products from the developing country up to a certain percentage of initial sale. The giant trading company C. Itoh & Co. set out to arrange the sale of a large oil refining plant totaling $1 billion to Indonesia. After much back-and-forth, Indonesia's final condition was that 40 per-

cent of the purchase price had to be in Indonesian-made
commodities exclusive of highly marketable crude oil and
natural gas, commodities such as lumber, tuna, prawns, and
palm oil. C. Itoh would then have to find ready markets to sell
these products. Reluctantly, C. Itoh finally decided to make
the deal. This was some time ago. Today, the share of this
form of barter trade has grown from around 3 percent in the
1970s to more than 30 percent of all trade today. Some
claim it is as high as 40 percent. And it is spreading rapidly.

**If you are not willing to participate in the practice of
counterpurchases, you are severely limiting your trading
prospects.**

The Ford Motor Co. of the United States had to accept
huge amounts of sheepskin in exchange for its automobile
exports in Uruguay. China paid in raw silk for consulting
services offered by Pierre Cardin of France. General Electric
has fifty counterpurchase specialists in its trading division,
probably the most sophisticated in the United States. Another form of counterpurchase involves taking payment for
the construction of an industrial plant in the goods eventually produced by that plant.

The barter trade experts—the so-called switchers—in such
European centers as Vienna and Zurich have been at it for
years and have worldwide networks, but their activity has
always been on a limited scale. The new counterpurchase
practice is on an immense scale and is contributing as much
as anything to moving us to a single, unitary, global economy.

Inside-the-Company Ventures

There is a lot of talk in Japan today about "big business
disease," the slow decision-making and stagnation that
seem to be inevitable in large, bureaucratic organizations.

One approach to outwitting slow-moving bureaucracies sounds a lot like the intrapreneurship we discussed in Chapter 2, "Ten Considerations in Re-inventing the Corporation."

At Hitachi, for example, an "inside-the-company venture" was established in the spring of 1983. Earlier in that year, Hitachi's president, Katsushige Mita, was approached by managing director Mansanori Ozeki and was asked to create a special plant for office automation equipment "in order to make up for the company's serious delay in the field." In response, Mita might have said, "We won't be able to make any profits out of such a new plant." Rather, he said, "Why don't you build a small shed and start from there as our predecessors did when they founded our company?" It sounds remarkably like what IBM's Don Estridge said when given the challenge to build a personal computer to compete with Apple's PC: "If you're competing against people who started in a garage, you have to start in a garage."

Ozeki took Mita literally and established a small working place not very different from the shed Mita spoke of. The young venture now turns out a product, a secondary graph disposal device utilizing a computer. The system is currently shipped at a monthly rate of about seventy sets, a good figure for such specialized equipment, although the operation is still running a deficit—as are many start-up businesses. "If we are afraid of running red ink, then we shouldn't have started an intracompany start-up venture in the first place," according to Yasuo Miyauchi, executive director in charge of accounting.

President Mita says, "We'll take full advantage of this kind of venture in order to develop new high-tech products and foster them into big sellers."

As *The Japan Economic Journal* points out in its coverage on the trend in Japan toward what we would call intrapreneurship, it takes from thirty to forty minutes for a

mammoth tanker weighing 300,000 tons to change its course.
And likewise, a big corporation with tens of thousands of
employees finds it very difficult to adapt swiftly to sudden
changes in the business environment. "In the present age of
high technology, when whirlwind innovations and the result-
ant drastic changes in industrial structures are the order of
the day, a mammoth and rigid structure can easily cost a
company its life."

While not nearly as in vogue as in the United States,
intrapreneurial units are beginning to pop up in companies
throughout Japan. Norio Ohga, president of Sony Corp., is
enthusiastic about such ventures. "I'll try to create as many
within-the-company new ventures as possible," he says.
Bridgestone Tire Co.'s president, Kunio Hattori, says that
"we are trying to turn existing organizations into new-
ventures units."

Sharp Corp. has applied some entrepreneurial notions to
its R&D efforts. The Osaka-based electric-electronic machinery manufacturer, employing 5,000 engineers, now has
a special group of about 300 select researchers divided into
subgroups of 10 members, each having a specific research
theme. The leader of each subgroup can freely handpick its
members. Even board members and heads of business
departments cannot refuse requests from the leader of a
subgroup. The idea is for the subgroup, virtually spearheading
the company's high-tech efforts, to take full advantage of
the company's human, as well as all the other, resources.

**In order to overcome the "big business disease" and
revitalize a huge corporation, it is necessary, according to
a growing sentiment in Japan, to form and take full
advantage of many small "within-the-company" organizations.**

Professor Shumpei Kumon of the University of Tokyo
says, "Large corporations have begun losing their effectiveness

as management systems, and corporate leadership initiative is coming increasingly from the ranks of smaller venture enterprises.''

In this same spirit, Japanese companies are pushing the development of smaller, more independent units. "The best corporate structure today comprises a small strategic center supported by many front-line outfits," says Isamu Yamashita, chairman of Mitsui Engineering & Shipping Co. Yamashita believes that a small and highly maneuverable outfit is far better in today's high-tech age than the kind of mammoth organization which enjoyed spectacular economics of scale in its heyday.

Kawasaki Heavy Industries, Ltd., a leading heavy machinery maker, in the summer of 1984 launched a new organization-revitalization project called "Challenge 100." Under the new program the Kobe-based company has granted increased autonomy to its fifteen business departments formed along product lines. The head of each business department is fully responsible for production, purchasing, sales, and R&D. The head office takes care of only personnel and financing.

"The head of each department is something like the president of a small company," says Kanehiro Hasegawa, president of Kawasaki. "If a certain department fails to put in a good performance in a certain period of time, it is destined for scrapping." If the head of each business department is provided with enough authority and responsibility, he will not act dependently on others, says Hasegawa.

High-tech start-up ventures are now mushrooming in Japan, creating the so-called venture business boom. And "the boom seems likely to last. The possibility is strong that they will play a vital role in changing the basic foundation of Japan's industrial structure," according to *JEJ*.

Japan has its Steve Jobs, too. Japan Soft Bank, the nation's largest distributor of computer software, is headed by founder-chairman twenty-six-year-old Jung-eui Son.

Yutaka Usui, president of Cosmos 80 Co., said that the rigid organizational setup of a big business could not be well suited to the coming highly advanced information society.

Professor Hideichiro Nakamura at Senshu University, managing director of the Japan Economic Policy Association, believes start-up ventures offer an important avenue of self-expression: "In Japanese industrial society thus far, art and academia are the only areas where the intelligence and sensitivity of the younger generation have been allowed to flower. Today, however, self-realization both for managers and for employees is becoming possible in venture business. That is why I wager that new ventures will continue their steady growth."

Re-inventing Ringi

One of the striking things about re-inventing the corporation in Japan is that *ringi,* or consensus-building, a unique and heralded feature of Japanese-style management, is finally beginning to be cumbersome in the present age of high technology. The process precludes snap decisions and dilutes responsibilities.

"If it were possible, we would like to completely eliminate the consensus-building processes," says Takeshi Miyazaki, director in charge of personnel affairs at Nippon Steel Corp. "As it is, we are now undertaking a thorough overhauling of the processes." It is not at all rare, adds *The Japan Economic Journal,* in the course of the consensus-building processes "that excellent proposals and ideas submitted by front-line workers lose their freshness and viability."

Niigata Engineering Co., an integrated machinery producer, has greatly simplified the consensus-building processes. Only a single *ringi-sho*—a request for decision—is now prepared at Niigata Engineering, and the number of people who see the request paper is limited to only four or five absolutely vital persons. In the past, some twenty people would have to see and give consent to the request paper before the proposals were authorized.

Vision 2000

Toa Nenryo Kogyo, K.K., an oil refiner 50 percent owned by Esso Eastern and Mobil Petroleum, and about the only high-profit oil company in Japan, in July 1984 formed a special study team of young "cadets" who have spent from five to ten years with the company. Known as the "Vision 2000 Group," the fifteen young up-and-comers meet for lunch each day. It is a fairly informal group, with a large assignment. The group's duty is to make a set of proposals, by spring 1986, for "management in the forthcoming twenty-first century."

"The young men who are now in their fifth to tenth years of work with us will be in the top executive positions in the twenty-first century," says vice-president Nobuyuki Nakahara. "It will be to their immense advantage at this moment to dabble in strategic thinking by trying to formulate bold visions for the future of the company." Members of the Vision 2000 Group are free to break off from their regular tasks to go out for lectures, information gathering, and other activities if they think it necessary for their vision-creating work.

The Junior Board System and the Outsiders System

Kibun Co., a leading food maker, has a junior board system. Once every month, fifteen young board members selected from the company's various departments and subsidiaries attend a "board meeting" presided over by the company's president and study the company's development strategies, organizational problems, and other vital topics. The tenure of the board members is one year, and their

records are taken into consideration when they are up for
promotion. Now five years after the start of the system,
those who have worked "on the board" are clear leaders in
the company's promotion sweepstakes.

Showa Musen Kogyo, an electronic parts manufacturer, is
trying to revitalize its organization in very un-Japanese
fashion by inviting able personnel from outside to join
them. All the board members, from president on down,
joined the company in their midcareers, a very unusual
group in Japanese business society. "In the rapidly evolving
high-tech age," says Showa Musen's Akitaka Ideda, "it is
absolutely necessary to invite able personnel from outside
to prevent the entire corporate organization from going
stale."

The Worker Exchange System

Also very un-Japanese is what Chiyoji Misawa, the president of Misawa Homes Co., a leading home builder widely
known for its managerial strategies, is planning. Misawa is
creating a worker exchange system with companies in completely different industries. Behind this unique system is
Misawa's belief that the twenty-first century will be an age
of interdisciplinary activities. Misawa's final objective is to
form a group of 100 corporations in widely different industrial sectors in which worker exchanges are conducted
freely.

Jiro Tokuyama, president of Nomura Management School,
endorses worker exchange systems and introduction of able
personnel from outside. "Educating future executives with
no outside experience can be likened to judoists practicing
only with their colleagues," says Tokuyama. "The word
'interdisciplinary' is just as important in business as in
academia."

Subsidiary Strategy

Many Japanese companies are turning to what they call the "subsidiary strategy," which involves entrusting the future of new enterprises to new independent units. It is a strong trend that is growing. Only a few years ago, subsidiaries were used as dumping places for excess staff or to keep unprofitable divisions at arm's length. Now the meaning of subsidiaries has been completely turned around. Strategic subsidiaries are now units that pioneer products and services that are expected to become the mainstays of the future.

In June 1984, Hitachi established Hitachi VLSI Engineering to specialize in the development of VLSI (very large scale integrated circuits) applications. In January of the same year, Canon, Inc., founded Canon Components to make integrated circuit peripherals and printed circuit boards for use with office automation equipment. Canon's president, Ryuzaburo Kaku, sees the new subsidiary as a "venture business for opening up advanced technological fields." Canon plans to spin off many more such subsidiaries in the future.

Another aspect of this strategy is to turn R&D divisions into subsidiaries so that it won't "take forever to get to the production state." Akebono Brake Industry Co. set up a new subsidiary, Akebono Research and Development Center, in April 1984 for just that reason. The company thinks that turning existing R&D divisions into subsidiaries fosters an "entrepreneurial spirit" among the researchers.

Japanese-style management, characterized by lifetime employment, seniority-based promotion systems, and companywide unions, is now being called into serious question.

Noting that group orientation, high adjustability, and diligence have long been the special characteristics of Japanese workers, and that these characteristics have been instrumental in bringing about spectacular successes to conveyor belt–based production systems, *The Japan Economic Journal* sounded a warning to its readers in the summer of 1984. "Recently," *JEJ* said, "an increasing number of blue collars are finding their *raison d'être* outside the plants. They do not hesitate to emphasize their individuality and refuse to work as mere cogs in corporate machinery. The time may soon come when Japanese corporations willy-nilly will have to come up with new production systems designed to contribute to harmonious co-existence between worker and machine." This is not some bleeding-heart do-gooder talking. This is the fabled *Japan Economic Journal* addressing Japanese businessmen.

Long-Hour Shift System

The Japanese are now accommodating to differing work styles.

At 7:30 in the evening when most workers prepare to leave for home, four young workers arrive at an old music box assembly plant located on Lake Suwa in Nagano Prefecture. Tomomitsu and three other skilled workers work only on the night shift. These are the "owl troops," who work in an otherwise almost vacant plant. They continue to work eleven hours and thirty minutes until 7:00 the next morning.

This music box assembly plant is part of Sankyo Seiki Mfg. Co., the world's largest music box manufacturer, accounting for 75 percent of the market. Within the company, the Lake Suwa plant has a unique work schedule. Like the "owl troops," the daytime counterparts work for eleven hours and thirty minutes, from 8:00 A.M. to 7:30 P.M. Both shifts work three consecutive days, regardless of the days of the week, and take three consecutive days off. Three on, three off. At other plants, workers put in the normal eight-hour workdays in two shifts.

The Lake Suwa long-shift employees work their long shifts for less than half a year. Their pay levels, however, are 25 percent higher for day shift workers and 45 percent higher for "owl troops," compared with those of regular workers putting in eight-hour workdays. Sankyo Seiki is planning to fully automate its music box production by 1988 and put all of its 400 workers on the long shifts by that time. Long shifts are not everyone's cup of tea, but evidently there are plenty of workers who are attracted to three days on/three days off to staff the plants.

Growing automation in the music box assembly plant has turned the production process largely into one of inspection and scrutiny with minimum manual labor. Sankyo Seiki says an eight-hour workday system simply does not blend in with the type of work involved. This, plus a growing number of young workers in their teens and twenties who like to collect holidays, has given birth to the long-shift work system. "The system has its merits both for workers and the company," according to Susumu Morikawa, director and manager of the company's music box division. "The long-shift system is the best solution now available."

"Because of the long-hour shift system, I am now able to enjoy surfing to my heart's content on Pacific beaches in Shizuoka," says Tomomitsu Murata with satisfaction.

At least two other companies adopted similar long-hour work systems this year, Rhythm Watch Co. and Seiko Electronics Industry Co. It reportedly has been very successful at both companies. When a corporation wants to recruit young blue-collar workers in the Tokyo metropolitan area, it has to put want ads in newspapers at least several times. When Rhythm Watch published ads for the long-shift system, it was flooded with applicants. Female applicants for day shifts ran up to four times the number required. "We never dreamed that the system would be so popular," said Shinidii Sato, Rhythm's director of personnel.

Five-Day Workweek

There is a big push in Japan for a five-day workweek, knocking off Saturday from the work schedule, something the United States did many years ago. Reduced work hours is the most important demand put forth by Japanese labor in recent years.

In the fall of 1984, however, a private advisory panel to the country's Labor Minister, the Labor Standards Law Study group, expressed its belief that a forty-hour workweek was "premature" for Japan. In its interim report it called for a statutory nine-hour, five-day workweek to replace the current eight-hour, six-day workweek.

Panelists from seven Western countries participating in an International Symposium on Shorter Working Hours, held early in 1985 in Tokyo, uniformly criticized Japan for its long working hours. The symposium was sponsored by the Japanese Confederation of Labor (Domei), which planned to use the criticism in negotiating for shorter working hours. Some attending the symposium claimed that Japan's practice of long working hours actually prevented other countries from further shortening their own working hours. While Western countries are extending worker holiday periods, panelists pointed out that the workaholic Japanese take only 57.6 percent of the vacation days coming to them. But this is clearly changing among younger workers, and in time, the five-day workweek seems inevitable. Quite apart from government guidelines, the number of five-day-workweek companies is growing every day.

Japanese corporations are also rapidly extending mandatory retirement beyond the traditional age of fifty-five. Almost half the companies with more than thirty workers are now using sixty as their cutoff age, according to Japan's Labor Ministry, which has encouraged the change. Many companies are now moving to the age sixty-five plateau.

Computers, Hidden Qualities, and Japanese Networks

Since the late 1960s, Japanese corporations have used computers in their personnel offices for computing wages and salaries and rudimental data on employees. Now they are being used in much more sophisticated ways, especially for "skill inventories" of all employees. The "use of computers is important, there is no doubt about that," says Hiroshi Sakuma, until recently vice-chief of personnel at Showa Denko, K.K., a major diversified chemical company. "But the true test of the personnel department from now on is how successfully it will pick up the hidden qualities and capacities of workers not revealed in various papers and printouts."

Ishikawajima-Harima Heavy Industry Co. (IHI) calls such skills and knowledge inventories its competitive "secret weapon." ("Please get a couple of employees who have strong connections with this client—it's simply imperative.")

Toyo Engineering Corp., a leading engineering firm, in 1983 launched a computerized program to relocate up-and-coming workers. Under the chairmanship of vice-president Masahiro Ohi, a "personnel rotation committee," an arm of the president, studies relocation of young employees with four, seven, and ten years with the company and formulates personnel relocation programs designed to foster capable personnel systematically.

The shift from one-man-style management to group and organizational management was played out in a public and symbolic way in mid-1984 when Noboru Goto—one of the most charismatic chief executives in Japan, and a prime example of the one-man boss—resigned as head of the Tokyu group to assume the presidency of the Japan Chamber of Commerce and Industry. The Tokyu group is huge, comprised of 288 companies at whose center is Tokyu Corp., Japan's most profitable railway operation. Among its companies are one of the nation's largest real estate devel-

opment firms, leading department store chains, a top advertising agency, and the largest hotel chain in the country. And
Goto ruled the empire with an iron hand. But in 1984, the
Tokyu group went through a profound transition, which
some say was orchestrated by Goto himself. Now the
company is run by a group "linked up horizontally and
organically," much like the networks described earlier in
this book. Goto and other top Tokyu executives firmly
believe that further advances in high technology in the
office, factory, and home will "usher in a bona fide age of
leisure," and that the new structure will allow Tokyu to take
full advantage of that new age. The group is now engaged in
nourishing three prospective new areas of business, which
they refer to as the three Cs. The three are cable television,
credit cards, and culture.

Women and the Japanese Corporation

**In Japan, the avenue for women into business manage-
ment appears to be computer software.**

The first female chief in a full-fledged department made
her debut at NEC on July 1, 1984. Mitsuyo Yoshimura's
official title is Manager of the Second Common-Software
Development Department of the Basic Software Development Department. "I have been constantly put through the
wringer from the very day I joined the company," says
Yoshimura. "Now I know how lucky I have been for having
been treated not as a woman but as one of the research
boys." She was recently promoted to the equivalent of
corporate vice-president in charge of basic software development for NEC.

Yoshimura graduated from the prestigious Ochanomizu
Women's College in 1962, majoring in mathematics. She
joined NEC that same year and began working as a member

of the technological development section in the computer plant at the company's electronic machinery division. Her section was involved in developing software for computers.

In those early days, computer hardware was very expensive and only a limited number of people had access to the machines. Yoshimura had a special disadvantage. As a woman, she was barred from doing night work because of the nation's labor laws. To get around this, Yoshimura often arrived very early to do "morning overtime" or worked on Saturday afternoons when most of her colleagues had begun to head for home. In time, Yoshimura acted as leader of a team devoted to developing a new assembler language. "I was so immersed in my work that I never noticed that many people had grave misgivings about my acting as a team leader because of my gender," she now says.

Yukio Mizuno, Yoshimura's former chief, says, "Software development is work of the brain through and through. Gender simply does not matter. That's the primary reason why Ms. Yoshimura has traveled successfully."

Sharply growing demands for software have created a new field of work where able individuals can take command regardless of their sex—even in Japan.

At Toshiba Corp., Kyoko Sawai is team leader in the computer and office automation systems division. Sawai is the only female team leader in the entire Toshiba organization. After graduating in 1968 from Tokyo Women's University, a top-rated school, Sawai spent seven years in developing programs and six years in supporting salesmen specializing in software marketing. Today, Sawai is responsible for all phases of product planning for both hardware and software of analyzer-processors.

"I don't believe that there is as yet complete gender equality even in the field of software," Sawai says with a smile. "But my secret belief is that the software business is better suited for women than men."

Yoshimura and Sawai are the first crop of female developers of computer software. But *The Japan Economic Journal* reports that now that computers are extensively used throughout industry and demands for software are sharply mounting, many computer makers and electric machinery manufacturers are annually employing new female university graduates "in the hundreds as software-related personnel." Although their immediate aim is to make up for the shortage of new male university graduates suitable for software work, it is by no means their only aim. According to *JEJ*, computer and electric machinery manufacturers are now quite serious about fostering new female recruits into true software specialists.

Health and Wellness

Contrary to the image most Americans have of Japanese corporations and health—born of the many times Americans have seen the exercise periods of Japanese workers on television—Japanese corporations have in the past handled health considerations defensively, not positively, just enough to get by the criteria set forth by the nation's labor laws. That is now changing.

Health and wellness programs are being pushed by Japanese corporations more than they ever have been in the past.

The Japan Economic Journal, in almost a paraphrase of our chapter on health, put it this way: "With the arrival of the high-tech age with all kinds of microelectronic gadgets and highly sophisticated information systems, corporations simply cannot turn their back on a sharply increasing number of stress-induced health troubles among their workers. Unless they solve this all-important problem and successfully revitalize their workers to face new challenges, they can very well lose out to their better-prepared competitors. Degrees of physical fitness of workers can actually decide the battle among competing companies.''

Tokyo Gas Co. set up a single health promotion office in 1981. Until then, the company's health maintenance programs had been conducted by several scattered offices. The health promotion office will unify and orchestrate all health-related efforts under a single umbrella and signal their increased importance to the company. All Tokyo Gas employees have company-sponsored health checkup sessions. Those judged overweight are channeled into special exercise classes. In 1984, the entire twenty-seventh floor of Tokyo Gas's headquarters building was transformed into a physical fitness center. Employees can drop in at the center and work out anytime they please.

Japan's largest shipping company, Nippon Yusen Kaisha (NYK), has a powerful Health Consulting System (known as HCON) for the health maintenance of its seaman workers. Using computers, the HCON system evaluates the fitness of seamen for on-board duty and schedules thorough medical checkups for them. The system now covers 2,000 seamen, and NYK is planning to expand it to cover all its employees.

NYK is now involved in re-inventing itself from a shipping company into a fully integrated distributor covering sea, land, and air transportation. The company sees physical fitness for all its employees as indispensable if it is to pull off its ambitious structural reform successfully. Thus the extraordinary emphasis on its HCON system. It embraces their office employees as well. ''We will make a thorough study of ills being caused by office automation and work out effective remedies,'' says Kiyoshi Goto, deputy chief of NYK's welfare department and a key figure in the HCON program.

Meditation Rooms and Culture Courses

Meditation rooms in Japanese companies are seen as places both to reduce stress and induce creative thinking. The meditation room at Minolta Camera's Senni Center, the company's R&D headquarters in Toyonaka City in Osaka Prefecture, is on the eleventh floor in a room whose door bears no identification. The room is divided into six compartments each measuring 27.5 square feet and each containing only a desk and a chair. On June 22, 1984, Yoji Hirata, chief of Minolta's electronic image technology department, ran out of that meditation room after sitting there for half an hour with his eyes fixed on the hills beyond the window. He ran out having come up with a good solution to a technical problem he had been facing for some time. Hirata visits the meditation room when he is bereft of good ideas. There he can enjoy his own time and space "without being bothered by anybody or anything."

Hirata says that he often uses the meditation room "to evaluate subordinates' work performances, to shake out obstinate hangovers, and sometimes to take a lazy nap." Managing director Ichiro Yoshiyama, vice-director of Minolta Camera's R&D division and creator of the meditation room, believes people should use the room as they see fit.

Yoshiyama says he has long been aware of the shortcomings as well as the merits of team activities. "When individualistic researchers form a team," he says, "they are liable to generate friction and stress—serious blocks to free flights of fancy and good ideas." This realization led to the creation of the meditation room, Yoshiyama says.

Japan Air Lines Co. is another company which goes to extra lengths to reduce stress and to help employees come up with good ideas. in May 1984, the company inaugurated four "cultural courses" for its employees—arts, go games, horticulture, and cooking. Once a week, all sorts of workers, including pilots, engineers, package tour planners, flight attendants, and accountants, get together for the courses.

The cultural courses are the company's attempt to foster

horizontal relationships among its workers, who are strictly vertical in their job classifications. The company hopes that by mingling workers it will be able to get flexible-thinking and better-performing workers.

Ever since the February 1982 crash of a DC-8 jetliner in the Bay of Tokyo, which killed twenty-four passengers, proved to have been caused by a mentally disturbed pilot, Japan Air Lines has been engrossed in firmly establishing a companywide health maintenance program. Creation of the cultural courses is part of the company's efforts to promote communications among its workers and reduce their job-related stress.

Hiring Foreign Employees

In this global economy, the Japanese are increasingly moving to a global recruiting of employees.

"Eight years of experiment have given us strong confidence in successfully using foreign employees," says Chiyuki Honda, managing director in charge of personnel headquarters of Kobe Steel, Ltd., Japan's fifth largest steelmaker. "By introducing foreign employees, we have succeeded in giving a healthy culture shock to their Japanese counterparts, forcing the latter to realize the importance of internationalization." And further, "From now on, we will try our hardest to turn foreign employees into an integral part of our operations."

Of Kobe Steel's twenty-eight foreign employees, whose nationalities include American, British, Canadian, Egyptian, Chilean, and New Zealander, thirteen are teachers of English, while the remaining fifteen occupy front-line positions in such sectors as overseas public relations, plant servicing, exports, and materials procurement. Kobe Steel sees the foreign employees as part of the "internationalization efforts of Japanese employees," and is now moving to greater use of foreign employees, taking full advantage of their special knowledge, experience, and personal ties as persons born and raised in foreign countries. "Our future foreign employees," says Honda, "will be either those who complement their Japanese counterparts in various special capacities or those who will bolster our overseas strategies."

Motomitsu Yamanoue is manager of international planning in Kobe Steel's personnel section. He has been taking care of foreign workers since 1976, when the company started employing non-Japanese workers. Yamanoue, forty-four, worked for a U.S. corporation before joining Kobe Steel in 1966 and is sensitive to how it feels to be a "foreign employee." He is now under "strong pressure" from the engineering and machinery divisions to recruit high-technology-related experts, especially in electronic/electric fields, who are now in short supply in Japan. He is told: "We don't care what nationality they are."

Employment of foreign workers in Japan is under some legal restrictions that have prevented most Japanese companies from employing foreign workers. Under the pressure of corporations which are striving to get superior talent wherever they can find it in order to "successfully cope with the inexorable advance of the high-tech age," these barriers are beginning to yield.

Well-known NEC Corp. started employing foreign workers in 1982. By mid-1984, it had on its payroll eight language instructors and eleven R&D experts in electronic fields. In obtaining the approval of the Ministry of Justice for employing foreign R&D personnel, NEC argued that employment of highly sophisticated R&D experts "is indispensable in the present age of breakneck technological development" and that there were not nearly enough of such personnel in Japan.

The global economy imperative will loosen all foreign employment restrictions in all countries around the world.

Some of these changes and new directions may seem small to some Americans, but most are extraordinary to the Japanese. And it is just the beginning. *JEJ* says approvingly, "Many informed parties are calling for an overall review of the important factors of corporations, including balance sheets, the present state of the stock company system and the idea of inside-the-company profit centers. They say that such reviewing is of the utmost urgency as the value system itself is now undergoing rapid changes."

The information age is highly suitable to Japan because of its low demands on energy, resources, and labor. And that realization is spreading across Japan like a contagious disease.

Professor Shumpei Kumon of the University of Tokyo pushes it all the way: "The final and greatest social impact of the information revolution will be a synthesis of Western and Eastern thought to form the guiding ideal for a new global social order."

Conclusion

None of us knows what the re-invented corporation will look like. Yet one thing is certain: The corporations described in this book are evolving in ways that are so exciting and so impressive that no organization can afford to ignore them.

Harvard Business School professor D. Daryl Wyckoff puts it this way: "Anyone who isn't studying People Express and the way they're managing people is out of their minds."

Similarly, new models like W. L. Gore's sponsor system, Motorola's training account, and Sentry Insurance's wellness program among others are significant corporate breakthroughs. They demonstrate how the information society is impelling us to cast off the old, industrial way of doing things and to re-invent the corporation.

"If I had to go way out on a limb, I would say that large corporations as we have known them will not exist in thirty years' time." That is the way Allan Kennedy, coauthor of *Corporate Cultures,* describes the direction in which we are headed. Kennedy, a former McKinsey consultant now running his own software applications firm, says companies will be unable to hold on to their people, because too many others will have gone out on their own and struck it rich.

Instead of thirty years, though, we think Kennedy's prediction will come true in half that time, by the year 2000. Here is Kennedy's scenario:

"If IBM wants to stay IBM in some fundamental way, it is going to have to change. . . . How can IBM hold on to its best group of microcomputer designers unless it is willing to spin off a subsidiary and let those guys take it public? Or why else would those guys design a machine for IBM? They've seen Don Massaro, say, leave Xerox [to start Metaphor Computer Systems, Inc.] and get $15 million in venture money. Don would have been crazy to stay at Xerox and do it for them.

"So if you are running IBM, and you recognize that you aren't going to be able to keep a good designer, you can contract the work out. Or you can set up a subsidiary and give the key people equity, with IBM providing the seed capital, the building, and the colleagues to talk to.

"You're going to end up with something like a holding company with a lot of these little subsidiaries."

Now, that's re-inventing the corporation.

And it is a continuous process that we are only just now beginning. We can fantasize about where it might lead. We can try to be corporate futurists about it all. But what finally happens will probably be even more radical and more exciting than we can now imagine.

Look at how far we have already come. The industrial society transformed workers into consumers; the information society is tranforming employees into capitalists. But remember this: Both capitalism and socialism were industrial systems. The information society will bring forth new structures. And the companies re-inventing themselves are already evolving toward that new reality.

The seller's market will be the impetus behind many of these changes. And it is good news for everyone to whom the corporation may have given short shrift in the past.

In the 1960s, socially responsible corporations dutifully studied their own prejudices—racism, sexism, and ageism. In the 1970s, individual women, blacks, and older people pioneered their way through the corporation and became role models for the millions of others who were shut out of that buyer's market.

In the seller's market of the 1980s and 1990s, though, companies will turn to these groups in need of their valuable labor. The best hope for unemployed, unskilled people is the combined impact of the booming information economy and the baby bust. Corporations will need people desperately, and on their way to mastering the education business, companies will know how to train them. Women and older people will profit, too.

Corporate policy toward older people will take a 180-degree turn. Instead of offering incentives to retire, companies will make it well worth their while to stick around.

Women's wages, especially in secretarial and clerical fields, will grow to reflect declining numbers of entry-level workers—and the increased options for women in other areas. Our most competent women used to become secretaries and teachers; now they are running their own businesses and will soon run for president. The people who want competent secretaries (and teachers) will have to pay them what they are worth.

Instead of expressing fear and ridicule toward comparable worth, corporations should turn it to their full advantage. The best approach is to preempt the market by jumping in and getting aggressive about comparable worth. There is much more to be gained in a seller's market from earning the reputation as a fair-pay employer than there is to lose by paying women what they are worth to the enterprise.

Women are moving to the center of the new work force.

And in the new workplace, the old, adversarial relationship that existed between unions and management is being replaced with win/win arrangements, such as job sharing, wellness programs, and flexible benefits plans. Virtually every successful new model for re-inventing the corporation was based on the mutual interest of corporations and the people within them.

One of the most fundamental shifts, of course, is the movement away from the authoritarian hierarchy—where everyone has a superior and everyone has an inferior—to the new lateral structures, lattices, networks, and small teams where people manage themselves.

Even the ideal of corporate social responsibility seems outdated now. Corporations could elect to be ''good citizens'' deigning to help the community, not harm the environment and be ''nice'' to people. It was all rather condescending. But now because of the increasing connectedness between the corporation and society, being responsible is part of the social and economic contract, the Boston Compact being an excellent example.

That interconnectedness between the corporation and the other aspects of life—education, health, the family, and the community—means a company cannot sit back and complain about the lousy school system, about the women's movement making it harder to transfer people, about the high cost of employee health bills. Corporations have to act and act on the basis of the interconnectedness between people and profit. That is better than social responsibility. It means that corporate interests and the interests of people and communities are increasingly the same.

As we travel around the country talking about TLC—thinking, learning, creating—some educators are asking what it means for their curriculum. Should they bring back the study of logic? Increase courses in study skills? What about all the arts programs cut back to make room for computers?

Now that we are putting more and more computers into the schools, the last thing we ought to be doing is eliminating the high touch of music, the arts, drama, and literature. Instead, we ought to be preparing to celebrate a renaissance in the arts in order to balance all the technology we have pumped into this society. It is through the arts that we explore our humanity, our spirituality—the counterballast to having to live with high technology.

The curious transformation of corporations into universities and universities into businesses is an analogue for what is going on throughout this society. We used to be able to divide our institutions into neat little boxes and say this is a bank, this is a retail store, this is a hospital, this is a business, and this is a school. But now we are erasing the lines that draw the boxes. You can walk into a K mart and open a money market account. You can walk into a freestanding emergicenter that is run like a business, get better service than you would at a nonprofit hospital—and pay less.

And health *is* increasingly a business matter. As a nation of farmers working in the fields all day and, later, as a nation of laborers also using our bodies to work, we had little need for or interest in going to a fitness boutique at the end of the workday. But now we are a nation of clerks; we use our heads all day, not our bodies. In that context, it is easy to see that fitness is not a fad and to see why it is appropriate that corporations become deeply involved in health and fitness.

If the Japanese were worthy rivals in the industrial era when autos and steel dominated the economy, they are even better suited to being our prime global competition in the information age. In the industrial society, the United States for a time held the advantage of lower energy costs than Japan. But the information society requires little in the way of energy and other natural resources. The Japanese are gearing up to take full advantage of their new opportunities in the information society.

Yet the Japanese have a long way to go before beating the United States in the information revolution. The Japanese have one culture, one history, and one race. Superb as they are, that is a limiting factor. They are very good at hardware, but the United States is better at software, at thoughtware.

That is because the United States has the richest mix of ethnic groups and races the world has ever known. The richer the mix, the more the creativity. It is not by chance that the United States has won 125 Nobel prizes and Japan has won only 2.

In the United States, we have not yet begun to develop the real potential of our fantastic mix of people, our real competitive edge in the global market.

To reach our full potential as individuals, as companies, as a country, though, we need a vision.

People want to make a commitment to a purpose, a goal, a vision that is bigger than themselves—big enough to make them stretch and grow until they assume personal responsibility for achieving it.

But suppose your company makes widgets. How do you create a vision that inspires personal responsibility? Maybe by taking such great pride in your widgets that your reject rate is 0.00 percent. Perhaps your vision is that you deliver new widgets to the customer anytime of the night in any weather. Or maybe it is that people—the customers and employees of Widget, Inc.—always come before the widgets.

Whatever your company's vision, you know it is effective when people in the company take personal responsibility for achieving it.

When we were in Japan to promote *Megatrends* in 1983, we were deeply impressed by the commitment of employees. Wherever we went—in taxis, hotels, restaurants, offices, factories—every person seemed to be taking personal responsibility for the success of whatever enterprise he or she was affiliated with.

Think about that.

Suppose every single person in your organization were taking personal responsibility for the success of the whole organization. That is what happened when Jan Carlzon turned the organization chart upside down.

People know.

People want to make a commitment.

One of the best-kept secrets in America is that people are aching to make a commitment—if they only had the freedom and environment in which to do so. As Bill Gore says, "It is commitment, not authority, that produces results."

The re-invented corporations will constitute a list of what we might call "the Fortunate 500," measured not by the numbers, but by quality of life.

The word will get around about which companies have nourishing environments for personal growth, and those will attract our very best and brightest, thus assuring their survival into the next century.

We hope you will work for and with Fortunate 500 companies, making money, having a good time—and doing business only with people who are pleasant.

Notes

Chapter 1 Re-inventing the Corporation

11   The information about Jan Carlzon within this chapter is based on a story in *International Management*, December 1982.

11-12 W. L. Gore & Associates is discussed at length in "The Un-Manager," an *Inc.* story which appeared August 1982.

12   Our knowledge of New Hope Communication is from personal experience and interviews with Doug Greene and his staff.

15   Steve Jobs is quoted in *Young, Gifted and Rich*, by Ralph Gardner, Jr. (New York: Simon & Schuster, 1984).

15-16 The numbers on the whittling away of middle management appeared in a story entitled "The Whittling Away of Middle Management," in *International Management*, November 1982, and in *Business Week*, April 25, 1983.

16   The use of computers at United Technologies and Firestone Tire & Rubber is discussed in "Computers Invade the Executive Suite," *International Management*, August 1983, as is the story about Ben Heineman.

17   The shrinking of middle management in West Germany and Japan is discussed in *International Management*, November 1982.

19   The figures on the baby boomers are from "Here Come the Baby-Boomers," *U.S. News & World Report*, November 5, 1984.

19   We stole this great aphorism on economists and entrepreneurs from George Gilder.

20   The decreasing number of teens in the work force and the contrast with the 1970s appeared in "Are Unemployment Forecasts Too Gloomy?" *Business Week*, April 23, 1984.

20-21 The figures on work-force growth in the 1970s, 1980s, and 1990s and on people age sixteen to twenty-four came from "Why Late Retirement Is Getting a Corporate Blessing," *Business Week*, January 16, 1984.

21   Information on the army's successful efforts in teaching illiterates is from *Unfit for Service*, by John Naisbitt.

22   "Why GM Isn't Satisfied with Being No. 1," *U.S. News & World Report*, March 11, 1985.

25   The story about Warren Bennis appears in *International Management*, October 1981.

25   We learned about Hanover Insurance Co. from Peter Senge.

26   *The Psychic Side of Sports*, by Michael Murphy and Rhea White (Addison-Wesley, 1978). The sports examples cited are also from that book.

27   The vision of Cray Research was supplied by Peter Senge.

28   What we interpret as Steve Jobs's vision is described in *The 100 Best Companies to Work for in America*, by Robert Levering, Milton Moskowitz, and Michael Katz (Addison-Wesley, 1984). The $10-billion vision is from *Inc.*, April 1984.

28   What we interpret as Kenneth Iverson's mission is also from the April 1984 *Inc.*

28   Control Data's mission is pretty well known. In *Esquire*'s March 1984 issue, we found a list of the various ways it has been realized.

28   Fred Smith's story is recounted in *Inc.*, April 1984.

29   Bill Gore's vision on creating his company and his quote on that subject appear in *Inc.*, August 1982.

30   Senge and Kiefer's description appears in "Metanoic Organizations: New Experiments in Organizational Design," an unpublished paper.

30-31   From *Second Wind: The Memoirs of an Opinionated Man*, by Bill Russell and Taylor Branch. Copyright © 1979 by William F. Russell. Reprinted by permission of Random House, Inc.

32   Senge and Kiefer's quote, the description of metanoic organizations, and the quote on tension resolution appear in "Metanoic Organizations," described above.

33-34   The material on Robinson Jewelers is based on "Rituals and Stories, Heroes and Priests," a story in *Inc.*, December 1982.

34   Through personal discussions we learned how Donald Burr and Bill Gore keep the vision alive.

34-35 For more on Carlzon, see *International Management,* December 1982.

35 Bill Gore on authoritarian organizations from a W. L. Gore & Associates company memo dated May 7, 1976.

37-47 It was our good fortune that *The 100 Best Companies to Work for in America* by Robert Levering, Milton Moskowitz, and Michael Katz (Addison-Wesley, 1984) was published just as we were researching examples of re-invented companies. *The 100 Best* rated companies on the basis of pay, benefits, job security, ambience, and opportunity for advancement. These are different criteria than what we are looking for in re-invented companies, that is, companies with vision and alignment, new corporate structures, new ways to reward people financially, and an environment for personal growth. We suspected, however, that many of the 100 best would also possess the characteristics of re-invented companies. Though many did, others did not. *The 100 Best* was our only source for these companies: Advanced Micro Devices, Trammel Crow, Hewitt Associates, Quad/Graphics, Analog Devices, Inc., Nordstorms', Olga, Electro-Scientific Industries, and Preston Trucking.

38 The *Fortune* story "Eight Big Masters of Innovation" appeared October 15, 1984.

39 The contest at Milbar Corp. is described in *Inc.*, May 1984.

39-40 The evolution of Kollmorgen Corp. is described in *Inc.*, April 1984.

39-40 Bob Swiggett's quote on autonomy is from Kollmorgen Corp.

42 The list of companies with parallel ladders and the description of the IBM program appear in "A Second Way to the Top," *The New York Times*, February 10, 1985.

43-45   The material on these pages about W. L. Gore & Associates draws from personal interviews with the Gores and from an internal company memo dated May 7, 1976.

45-46   The announcement of the new Kimberly-Clark management team appeared in *The New York Times*, November 12, 1984.

48-51   "The New Corporate Design" appeared in *Industrial Management Review*, MIT's Sloan School of Management, Fall 1965, Vol. 7, No. 1.

Chapter 2   Ten Considerations in Re-inventing the Corporation

54-62   We have drawn frequently from *The 100 Best Companies to Work for in America* for examples in these pages; we will cite other sources when used.

54-55   The quote from Lew Lehr is from a speech delivered February 28, 1984, at Florida A & M University.

56   The example about Molex, Inc., is from "Travel Broadens Shop-Floor Minds," *International Management*, November 1980.

57   The examples of corporate sabbaticals is from "Sabbaticals Spread from Campus to Business," *U. S. News & World Report*, January 28, 1985.

58-59   The material on Cleveland's TRW plant, the Chrysler plant in Indiana, the pay-for-knowledge program at General Motors, and the Illinois National Bank is from "A Work Revolution in U.S. Industry," *Business Week*, May 16, 1983. The example of Nissan's Smyrna plant is from a company spokesperson.

61   Bob Swiggett is quoted in *Inc.*, April 1984.

62   Changes at PepsiCo are described in *The Wall Street Journal*, October 23, 1984.

62-63   Jim Pinto is quoted in "A Call to Action," in the November 1983 issue of *Inc*.

63   The story about Robert Metcalfe's 3Com appeared in "Incentives for Growth," *Venture*, March 1983.

63   The Lotus example is from *Changing Times*, December 1984.

63-64   The figures from the National Center for Employee Ownership appeared in "The New Role for ESOPs, Warding Off Takeovers," *The New York Times*, January 2, 1985.

64   Jerry Knapp of CableData is quoted in the *Sacramento Bee*, July 30, 1984.

64   The information about Cummins Engine's profit-sharing plan was cited in "Profit-Sharing Plans Reward Productivity," *The Wall Street Journal*, November 5, 1984, which is also the source for the list of companies using cash profit sharing.

65   That people work only 50 percent of the time: *The Work Ethic* by D. J. Cherrington (Amacom, 1980).

65-67   All the bulleted examples from *The 100 Best Companies to Work for in America*, cited above.

66-67   The experience of Jim Dietz at Wilson Labs is from "In Search of the Retentive Incentive," *Inc.*, May 1984.

67   Linnton Plywood and Publix Super Market examples are from *The 100 Best Companies to Work for in America*, cited above.

67   Ripley Industries example is from the *St. Louis Post-Dispatch*, September 21, 1984.

67-68   The material on Fred Schmid Appliance & TV Co. is from the *Denver Post*, February 9, 1985.

68   "Business and the Law, Worker-Held Enterprises," from the April 17, 1984, issue of *The New York Times* is the source for the Mondragon, Spain–style worker co-ops. The same article produced the statistics from the Industrial Co-operative Association.

68   Our information on Weirton is from *U.S. News & World Report*, May 7, 1984; from the November 12, 1984, issue of *Business Week;* and from Weirton's public relations department.

64-72 Our sources for the section on contract staffing are *Nation's Business*, October 1984; *U.S. News & World Report*, August 27, 1984; the *Dallas Times Herald*, May 26, 1984; *Newsweek*, May 14, 1984; and interviews with Norrell Temporary Services.

73   Wilson Learning Corp. told us about their employee network.

73-74 For company clubs see *The New York Times*, August 6, 1982.

74-75 John Akers is quoted from his speech at European Management Forum, Davos, Switzerland, February 4, 1985.

75   3M's goal of 25 percent new products is from *In Search of Excellence* (New York: Harper & Row, 1982).

75-76 The material on intrapreneurship in airlines is from "Now Airlines Are Diversifying by Sticking to What They Know Best," *Business Week*, May 7, 1984.

76-77 The Terra Tek information is from "When the Employees Are the Entrepreneurs," *Venture*, June 1980.

77-78 Material about the Foresight Group is from personal interviews; from "Intrapreneurship: Holding On to People with Ideas," *International Management*, March 1982; and from "Rewiring Corporate Thinking," by Gustaf Delin, in *Public Relations Journal*, August 1983.

79   Entrepreneurship courses in business schools are from *Business Week,* March 5, 1984, and from University of Washington professor Karl Vesper.

80   Steve Arbeit is quoted from a personal interview.

80   Tom Peters's quote is from a privately circulated paper.

80-81   Paul Hawken, *The Next Economy* (New York: Random House, 1983).

81   McGill's Mintzbert is cited in Senge and Keifer's paper, "Metanoic Organizations," which is also the source for the material attributed to Senge and to David Mahoney.

82   Weston Agor, "Tomorrow's Intuitive Leaders," *The Futurist,* August 1983. This is also the source for the material on Newark College.

82-83   The story about People Express, "That Daring Young Man and His Flying Machines," appeared in *Inc.,* January 1984.

83   The John Kenneth Galbraith quote is from *Inc.,* April 1984.

84   *Forbes,* "The Up & Comer 300," November 5, 1984.

85   Don Estridge's quote on garages is from *Inc.,* April 1984, as are the other details about his Florida IBU.

85   Heavyweight/lightweight quote from IBM's *Think,* September/October 1982.

85   *The Soul of a New Machine,* by Tracy Kidder (Boston: Little, Brown and Company, 1981).

85-86   The material on NCR and Don Coleman is from *Inc.,* April 1984.

86   Xerox, Exxon, and Monsanto are mentioned as venture

companies in "Big Business Tries to Imitate the Entrepreneurial Spirit," in *Business Week*, April 18, 1983, as is
General Motors' investment in Biological Energy Company.

86   Standard Oil of Indiana is cited in "Mutual Benefits,"
Inc., June 1984.

86-87   The Wayland Hicks quote is from *Business Week*, April
18, 1983, as is the quote "these are brilliant, independent
individuals. . . ."

87   Information on the plants operated by W. L. Gore &
Associates is from personal interviews with Bill and Vieve
Gore.

87   Robert Swiggett quote is from Kollmorgen Corp.

89   Plans of the Massachusetts High Tech Council were reported
in "The New Agenda," *Boston Globe*, November 13,
1984.

89   Information about Portland is from "Why Oregon Sudden-
ly Looks Good to High-Tech Companies," *Business Week*,
November 5, 1984.

89-90   Examples of companies moving to quality-of-life locations
from "Hunting for Creative Minds," *The New York Times*,
February 10, 1985.

Chapter 3   Re-inventing Work

93   Stephen Zimney is quoted in "Computer People," *Business Week*, February 20, 1984.

94   "Shifts in Work Put White Men in the Minority,"
by William Serrin, *The New York Times*, July 31,
1984.

97   The material on the Fitzgerald, Georgia, GM plant is from
a company spokesperson.

97   James Renier's quote and actions from "A New Era for Management," *Business Week*, April 25, 1983.

97   John Welsh is quoted in "The Shrinking of Middle Management" from the same issue.

98   Bill Parzybok is quoted in the *Denver Post*, February 20, 1983.

98   Donald Burr is quoted in "That Daring Young Man and His Flying Machines," *Inc.*, January 1984.

99   The 1980 Gallup poll is reported in *Putting the Work Ethic to Work*, by Daniel Yankelovich and John Immerwahr for the Public Agenda Foundation (PAF), 1983. That report also listed the ten desirable qualities in a job.

101   Daniel Yankelovich, *New Rules: Searching for Self-Fulfillment in a World Turned Upside Down* (New York: Random House, 1981).

101   John Crystal is quoted in "Too Many People Trapped in Jobs: Consultant," the *Montreal Gazette*, June 8, 1984.

102   Buck Blessing is quoted in *Life Options*, Spring 1983.

102   "The Switch Is On," *Newsweek*, May 28, 1984. This is also the source for the estimate that one-third of Americans switch jobs, and for the quotation from Susan Manring.

103   *What Color Is Your Parachute?* by Richard Bolles (Ten Speed Press, 1972).

103   Much of our information on John Crystal, Richard Bolles, and the development of life/work planning is based on "Taking Charge on Campus: A Quick Guide to Life/Work Planning," by Penelope Garner.

103-   Information about Life Management Services from personal interviews with Hal and Marilyn Shook.
104

105- The National Commission on Employment Policy, *Ex-*
107 *changing Earnings for Leisure: Findings of an Exploratory National Survey on Worktime Preferences*, 1980.

107 The percentage of people on alternative schedules is from "Flexible Work Hours Gather Momentum," *U.S. News & World Report*, September 28, 1981, as is the Work in America projection.

106 Lennart Arvedson's "total employment society" is from *Work Times*, published by New Ways to Work, Summer 1983.

107- The source for this information on flextime is the Septem-
108 ber 28, 1981, *U.S. News & World Report* story, except for the following: Hewlett-Packard from *The 100 Best Companies to Work for in America*, and Meredith from personal interview.

108 Quad/Graphics information is from "Management by Walking Away," *Inc.*, October 1983.

108 Goodyear and Firestone material and Stanley Nollen's story are from the *U.S. News & World Report* story cited above.

109 "After Flexible Hours, Now It's Flexiyears," *International Management*, March 1982.

110 Part-time work at Control Data is described in the *National Newsletter* of the Association of Part-Time Professionals (APTP), Fall 1983.

110 List of part-time employers compiled through personal interviews.

110 Part-time work at Citibank described in "Child Care Concerns Are Changing the Workplace," *USA Today*, July 13, 1983.

111 Helen Axel is quoted in the Fall 1983 newsletter of the APTP cited above.

111   *The Job Sharing Handbook*, by Barney Olmsted and Suzanne Smith (Ten Speed Press, 1985).

111   The Atlantic Richfield information is from "Beyond the Fringes," by Kathryn Phillips, *New Age Journal*, December 1984.

111   Laurie Forster is quoted in "Job Sharing," *U.S. News & World Report*, August 23, 1982.

112   Job sharing examples are from the August 23, 1982, *U.S. News & World Report* story and from *The Job Sharing Handbook*, both cited above. Job sharing in education is from *The Job Sharing Handbook*.

112-
113   Information on Levi Strauss is from personal interviews.

115-
116   Clo Ross quoted in "Beyond the Fringes: How Smaller Companies are Profiting from Flexible-Benefits Plans," *Inc.*, March 1984.

115-
116   See "Cafeteria Plans to Make Employee Benefits Flexible," *USA Today*, July 6, 1983.

116   The American Can Company figures are cited in Hewitt Associates' *On Flexible Compensation*, July 1983.

117   "Twilight of the First-Line Supervisor?" by Peter Drucker, *The Wall Street Journal*, June 7, 1983.

117-
118   The Pratt & Whitney, John Deere, and Inland Steel examples are from "The Transformation of Basic Industry," *High Technology*, October 1984 (Special Report).

118   The Best Industries example and quote are from "Production Problems Become More Manageable," *Business Week*, April 25, 1983.

118   Northrop's Hawthorne plant and the Tandem example are cited in "The Revival of Productivity," *Business Week*, February 13, 1984.

119   *Putting the Work Ethic to Work,* published by the Public
          Agenda Foundation, 1983.

119   Dennis Wisnosky is quoted in "Robotics," *International
          Management,* March 1983.

119   Thomas Gilmore is quoted in "The Shrinking of Middle
          Management," *Business Week,* April 25, 1983.

119-   Ford's Edison plant is described in the April 25, 1983,
120   *Business Week.*

120   The information on GM's Orion plant is from a company
          spokesperson.

120   Warren Publishing Corp. is described in "A New Wrinkle
          in Retirement Policies," *Inc.,* November 1983.

121   Declining percentages of older workers are from *Statistical
          Abstracts of the United States 1984.*

121   The figures on the increasing numbers of older workers are
          from Lawrence Olson, Sage Associates.

121   Varian Associates is cited in "Why Late Retirement Is
          Getting a Corporate Blessing," *Business Week,* January 16,
          1984.

122   Percentage of the older Polaroid workers still on the job is
          from *Management and the Older Worker,* AMA Manage-
          ment Briefing, 1983.

122-   Examples on these pages are from AMA's *Management
123   and the Older Worker,* cited in the note above, and from
          personal interviews with the assistance of National Older
          Workers Information System, University of Michigan, Ann
          Arbor, Michigan.

124   Dun & Bradstreet figures and the number of self-employed people are cited in *Venture*, May 1984.

125   The material on Tom Schooler's Petmobile is from a personal interview.

125   Scott Alyn's greeting cards are described in *Venture*, September 1982.

125   Gary Gygax is described in ''The Psychic Rewards,'' *Venture*, February 1983.

125   Chipwich example is from *Newsweek*, July 12, 1982.

126   Venture capital figures are from a spokesperson at *Venture Capital Journal*, Wellesley Hills, Massachusetts.

126-   Hank Heeber and Betty Barkyaumb are described in ''In-
127   side the Entrepreneur,'' *Venture*, May 1984.

127   Joseph Mancuso and Philip Bredesen are cited in ''Being Your Own Boss,'' *Venture*, May 1984.

127   The psychological study is cited in ''Inside the Entrepreneur,'' *Venture*, May 1984.

127   *Running Your Own Business*, by Nancy Flexman and Thomas Scanlan (Argus Communications, 1982). Quote is from *Venture*, December 1982.

127   Robert Kuhn is quoted in ''The Psychic Rewards,'' *Venture*, February 1983.

128   Carl Hathaway is described in ''The Psychic Rewards,'' *Venture*, February 1983.

128   Information on Eliane Kesteloot is from personal interviews.

128-   Tricia Fox is described in "Being Your Own Boss in
129   America," *Venture*, May 1984.

129   Phyllis Gillis is quoted in *Newsweek*, January 9, 1984.
           Numbers of home-based businesses is from the *Venture*
           story, May 1984, cited above.

129   National Association of Home-Based Businesses is cited in
           the *Venture* story, May 1984, noted above.

129   Peggy Boston and Barbara Isenberg are described in
           "Worksteaders Clean Up," *Newsweek*, January 9, 1984.

131   Leon Danco is quoted from a personal interview.

131   Harry Levinson, "The Fifty Largest Private Industrial
           Companies," *Fortune*, May 31, 1982.

131-   Bullets on family business and the description of Stroh's
132   Brewing Co. are from "The Silent Strength of Family
           Business," *U.S. News & World Report*, April 25, 1983. Last
           bullet is from "The SOB's," *Across the Board*, May 1980.

132   Thirty-percent figure is from the *Across the Board* story
           cited in previous note.

133   Leon Danco is quoted in *CBR*, April 1979.

134   Allied Supply Co. from the *U.S. News & World Report*
           story, April 25, 1983, cited above.

134   The material on Gerald Slavin and SOB's is from the
           Across the Board story, May 1980, cited above.

134-   Danco on daughters is from the *U.S. News & World Report*
135   story, April 25, 1983, cited above.

134   The 500,000 figure is from "When a Daughter Takes Over
           the Family Business," *Business Week*, March 29, 1982.

135   The Johnson Publishing material is from the *U.S. News & World Report* story, April 25, 1983, cited above.

135   The Häagen-Dazs story and the Center for Family Business quote are from "Like Father, Like Daughter," *American Way*, January 1983.

136   "When Wives Run the Family Business," *Business Week*, January 17, 1983, is the source for information on this page.

Chapter 4   The Skills of the New Information Society
142   For a complete discussion of how trends in education seem to swing back and forth, see. "The Educational Pendulum," by Diane Ravitch, in *Psychology Today*, October 1983.

142   *An Open Letter to the American People: A Nation at Risk. The Imperative for Educational Reform. A Report to the Nation and the Secretary of Education by the National Commission on Excellence in Education*, April 1983.

144   Other important reports included Theodore Sizer's "A Study of High Schools," in *High School*, the Carnegie Foundation for the Advancement of Teaching study authored by Ernest Boyer (New York: Harper Colophon, 1983); "A Study of Schooling," by UCLA's John Goodlad; and *The National Task Force for Economic Growth*, put together by forty-one governors, corporate leaders, and others.

144   The *Newsweek* summary and the Boyer quote appeared in "Rx for High Schools," September 26, 1983.

145   The number of commissions and task forces is from "The Push Is On," *USA Today*, April 30, 1984, as is the number of states seeking better textbooks.

145   Number of states enacting reforms are from the U.S. Department of Education.

145   Bill Honig is quoted in "Back to School and Back to Basics" in *U.S. News & World Report,* September 19, 1983, and in "The Push Is On," *USA Today,* April 30, 1984.

146   George Gallup is quoted in "Poll Finds Rising Confidence in Schools," *The New York Times,* August 5, 1984, a story about the 1984 *Phi Delta Kappan* education poll; so too the findings that people are willing to pay more for education.

146   The figures on teacher pay and on increased taxes in half the states are from the *USA Today* story, April 30, 1984, cited above.

147   Figures on problem-solving and inferential reading ability from *"The New York Times* Education Survey," January 19, 1983.

147   Kuykendall is quoted in *USA Today,* "The Push Is On," April 30, 1984.

148-   The thinking quote is from *Learning-to-Think,* by Edward
149   de Bono and Michael de Saint-Arnaud (Capra/New, 1982), as is the other information about de Bono and his school.

149   See de Bono's "The Direct Teaching of Thinking as a Skill," *Phi Delta Kappan,* June 1983.

149   De Bono's words cited here as an aphorism are from his *Phi Delta Kappan* article, cited above.

149   The description of de Bono's curriculum and of PMI are from his *Learning-to-Think,* cited above.

150   Nat Giancola is quoted in "In Schools, a New Focus on Thinking," *USA Today,* January 17, 1984, as is the other information about the New Jersey program. However, we learned about Dr. Lipman from *"The New York Times* Education Survey," January 8, 1984. The fifth-grade class which increased scores 15 percent was on Long Island, according to the *Times* education survey.

151   The University/Urban Schools National Task Force material is from "*The New York Times* Education Survey," January 8, 1984.

151   The list of cities to be studied is from *USA Today*, January 17, 1984.

151   Xavier's successful thinking program is cited in "*The New York Times* Education Survey," January 9, 1983.

152   *On Writing Well*, by William Zinsser (New York: Harper & Row, 1980).

152   The survey was conducted by City University of New York in 1983 and reported in "*The New York Times* Education Survey," January 8, 1984.

153   This section about learning how to think by learning how to write is based on a *New York Times* education survey devoted to the subject—must reading for any school embarking on such a program. It appeared January 8, 1984.

157   The Doris Lessing quote is from "Learning How to Learn," *Asia*, July/August 1982. In that article she quotes Richard Burton.

160   Roger Von Oech's *A Whack on the Side of the Head* (New York: Warner Books, 1983). We also used "A Whack on the Side of the Head," a story in the *San Jose Mercury* of February 8, 1983, and personal interviews with Von Oech.

161   "How Imagineering Calms the Nerves" is from *International Management*, May 1982.

162   Halpern is mentioned in the article cited in the previous note; we also interviewed him, as well as Todd Broadie of Neruda.

162   The letter appeared in the March 1982 issue of *International Management*.

163   The sources for the companies that practice meditation are from unpublished master's degree theses by Steve Burka and provided with the assistance of the Transcendental Meditation program.

163   Roberts's quote appears in "States of Consciousness and Human Capacity," *Institute of Noetic Sciences*, Spring 1982.

163   Alvin Toffler, *The Third Wave* (New York: William Morrow, 1980).

164   "Science, Human Potential and Education," by Beverly-Colleene Galyean, appeared in *Institute of Noetic Sciences*, Spring 1982.

**164-
165**   The description of Dee Dickinson's approach is from personal discussions and interviews.

165   Stanford's course is described in "Business Students Taught to Rediscover Creativity," *San Jose Mercury*, May 16, 1983.

166   The quote on job-related courses is from "Adult Education: Newest Tool for Job Hunters," *U.S. News & World Report*, August 16, 1982.

166   The figures on declining college enrollments are from "How Academia Is Taking a Lesson from Business," *Business Week*, August 27, 1984

166   The increases in adult education are reported in *U.S. News & World Report*, "Adult Education," August 16, 1982.

166   The proportion of colleges accepting training programs for credit is cited in "Adult Education," *U.S. News & World Report*, August 16, 1982.

167   "Community Colleges Take Lead Role in Training for Real Life," *Chicago Tribune*, December 12, 1982.

167-   Programs at Illinois Institute of Technology and CIGNA
168   are from *Training by Contract*, published by the College Entrance Examination Board in 1983.

168   List of schools with Silicon Valley presence is from *San Jose Mercury*, August 16, 1982.

Chapter 5   Education and the Corporation

171   Ernest Boyer is quoted in "Business Must Form a Partnership with Schools," *U.S. News & World Report*, September 26, 1983.

172   Bank of America's contribution is cited in the *Economist*, April 17, 1982, while that of the Crocker National Bank appears in the *Los Angeles Times*, December 8, 1984.

172   *The Wall Street Journal*, March 22, 1984, reports that 400 companies match employees' contributions, and cites the example of St. Ignatius High School. Meredith's policies are from a personal interview.

172   The contributions of the Allegheny Conference are described in a story in *The Wall Street Journal*, October 5, 1981, by Fletcher Byrom, chairman of Koppers Co.

172   Information about the contribution of Travelers' Insurance Co. is from the company and from the *Hartford Courant*, January 30, 1983.

173   American Can Co. material is from "Corporations Are Discovering Fruitful Partnerships with High Schools," *The New York Times*, May 28, 1984.

173   Numbers of adopt-a-school programs are taken from the White House Private Sector Initiatives program.

173   Sources for schools adopted by Chase, Frito-Lay, and Federal Express are respectively *The New York Times*, May 28, 1984; the *San Antonio Express-News*, April 24, 1983; and the *Memphis Commercial Appeal*, April 26, 1983.

173- The figures on adopted schools in New York are from *The*
174   *New York Times*, May 28, 1984; adopted schools in Nashville from *Business Week*, April 16, 1984; and adopted schools in Dallas from *High Technology*, October 1984.

174   The description of the Dallas program and the quotes about it are from "Schools for Adoption," *San Antonio Express-News*, April 24, 1983.

174   The Chase program for principals is reported in *The New York Times*, May 28, 1983, while the actions of Fairchild Industries, Bechtel, Shell Oil, and IBM are reported in "Low-Tech Education Threatens the High-Tech Future," *Business Week*, March 28, 1983.

174- The material on Juarez High School's bilingual call squad
175   is from the *Chicago Tribune*, January 23, 1983.

175   Mose Walker is quoted in the *Memphis Commercial Appeal*, April 26, 1983.

175- We used the following sources for the story of Apple's
177   failure to give computers to the schools: "Political Clout," *California Business*, April 1984; "Polishing the Apple," *Inc.*, February 1983; and Jack Anderson's column on the subject in *The Washington Post*, December 13, 1982.

177   Tandy, IBM, and Xerox examples are from the White House Private Sector Initiatives program.

177   The 1.3-million figure on new illiterates annually is from "Business Is Joining the Fight against Functional Illiteracy,'' *Business Week*, April 16, 1984, as is the quote from Travelers' Robert Feagles.

178   Diane Vines is quoted in the April 16, 1984, *Business Week* story cited in the previous note.

178   Barbara Bush is quoted in ''A Nation of Illiterates?'' in *U.S. News & World Report*, May 17, 1982.

178   Examples of the corporate costs of illiteracy are from *Business Week*, April 16, 1984, cited above, as is the list of corporations taking action against illiteracy.

179   Sources for B. Dalton–led Coalition for Literacy are ''The End of Illiteracy Begins with Awareness,'' in the *Chicago Tribune*, April 19, 1983, and the April 16, 1984, *Business Week* story cited above—which is also the source for Gloria Lanza's quote.

180   The United States' eighth-place ranking in a standard math test is cited in ''More Brainpower Coming Down the Line from Japan,'' *International Management*, December 1982.

180   Requirements for Soviet students are from ''Are Soviet Schools as Good as They Look?'' in *U.S. News & World Report*, March 28, 1983.

180   National Science Teachers Association estimate is from ''Curriculums Fall Short of Business Needs,'' *Oregon Statesman*, December 12, 1982.

180   Sources for the other figures on the increasing math/science gap are ''Teacher Shortage Worsens,'' *USA Today*, July 26, 1983, and ''What's Wrong with Our Teachers,'' *U.S. News & World Report*, March 14, 1983.

181   The Chicago program is reported in the *Chicago Tribune*, April 17, 1983.

181   Examples of North Carolina's School for Science and

Math and Scientific-Atlanta, Inc., are from "Low-Tech Education Threatens the High-Tech Future," *Business Week*, March 28, 1983.

182   General Motors' $1-million annual contribution is cited in "Rebuilding Math and Science Education: Business Lends a Hand," *High Technology*, October 1984.

182-   Sources for Dallas's SEED program are "Math Exercises
183   Turn Calculating into Child's Play," *Dallas Morning News*, February 13, 1983, and the October 1984 story in *High Technology*, cited above.

183-   The examples of Kaiser, Arco, Honeywell, IBM, Digital,
184   and the Cleveland summer program are from the October 1984 story in *High Technology*, cited above.

184-   Our source for the information on Thomas Jefferson High
185   School was "Educators, Businessmen Creating High-Tech High School in Fairfax," *The Washington Post*, August 27, 1984.

185-   *The Boston Compact: An Operation Plan for Expanded*
188   *Partnerships with the Boston Public Schools*, September 1982.

186   Enrollment percentages are from a story about the Boston Compact in *Dun's Business Month*, May 1983, which also cites the percentage of high school dropouts. We used this article extensively in preparing this section.

187   List of companies subscribing to the Boston Compact is from the Greater Boston Chamber of Commerce.

188   The Shawmut Bank's John LaWare is quoted in the *Dun's Business Month* story, May 1983, cited above.

188   Updates on the Boston Compact come from the *Boston Globe*, November 11, 1984, and from the Boston Compact.

189   Milton Friedman wrote about vouchers in his *Capitalism &
          Freedom* in 1962, but his most definitive essay, "The
          Voucher Idea," appeared in *The New York Times Magazine*,
          September 23, 1973.

189   The 1983 Gallup poll on vouchers is from *Phi Delta
          Kappan*, September 1983.

190   Albert Shanker is quoted in "Libertarian vs. Egalitarian
          Vouchers," *School Product News*, May 1982.

190-   For a description of the Coons/Sugarman plan, see "Of
191   Family Choice and 'Public' Education," *Phi Delta Kappan*,
          September 1979.

191-   Information on voucher activities in other states comes
192   from the Educational Voucher Institute in Ann Arbor,
          Michigan.

192   Milton Friedman on the G. I. Bill and Catholic schools is
          from *The New York Times Magazine* essay cited above.

192   The information on Des Moines's energy curriculum is
          from *The Trend Report*, Volume 1, 1981.

192-   Ernest Boyer appears in *U.S. News & World Report*,
193   September 26, 1983.

194   The Robert Galvin quote is from Motorola.

194   *Corporate Classrooms: The Learning Business*, by Dr.
          Nell Eurich for the Carnegie Foundation for the Advance-
          ment of Teaching, 1985. It is to be published by Princeton
          University Press. Dr. Eurich is quoted in a January 28,
          1985, *New York Times* story about the Carnegie study.

194   The $100-billion estimate is from a story on the Carnegie
          study appearing in *The Chronicle of Higher Education*,
          January 30, 1985. We also used a story on the study from
          The Washington Post, January 28, 1985.

195   *Employee Training: Its Changing Role and an Analysis of New Data,* by Anthony Carnevale and Harold Goldstein, published by the American Society for Training and Development, 1983.

195-
196   Companies that must "deprogram" MBAs and the Robert Mills quote are from *Business Week,* April 25, 1983.

196   William Hamilton is quoted in *Business Week,* April 25, 1983.

196   The information on Kansas City Power and Light's program comes from the *Kansas City Star,* June 8, 1983.

196   Polaroid's program is described in the *National Report* of the American Society for Training and Development, December 17, 1982.

196   The Monsanto program is described in *Training by Contract: College-Employer Profiles,* published by the College Board in 1983.

197   Sources for the TVI program are the *Boston Globe,* October 3, 1982; the *Worcester Telegram,* October 3, 1982; and MIT's *Tech Talk,* September 28, 1983.

198   Information about courses offered by AIA, AMA, ASME, and NAHB is from the American Society for Training and Development.

198-
199   The three cooperative education projects described on this page are from the College Board's *Training by Contract,* 1983.

199   Information on the Henry Ford Community College program is from the college.

200   The ITA model was described to us by Linda Spencer of the House Northeast/Midwest Coalition. Legislation pending is known as the ITA Bill.

202-   We first read about the Motorola program in *Human
203   Capital Developments*, October 1983, published by the
        American Society for Training and Development, and we
        followed it up with extensive interviews with Ed Bales and
        Bill Wiggenhorn of Motorola.

203   Figures on declining college enrollments and Carnegie-
        Mellon's strategic approach are from "How Academia Is
        Taking a Lesson from Business," *Business Week*, August
        27, 1984.

203   George Keller is quoted in the August 27, 1984, *Business
        Week* article cited above, which is also the source for the
        example of the University of Miami.

204   "Colleges, Universities Hunting Leaders Experienced in
        Business," *Charlotte Observer*, January 24, 1983. David
        McLaughlin's previous position at Toro is cited by both the
        Charlotte paper and *Business Week*, December 20, 1982.

204-   The *Forbes* story on Trinity University and President
205   Ronald Calgaard appeared October 22, 1984.

205   The material on entrepreneurial incubators is from *The
        New York Times*, December 3, 1984.

206   The new policy at the *New England Journal of Medicine* is
        described in *Technology Review*, August/September 1984.

208   "Boston School Chief Picked for Fairfax County Post,"
        The Washington Post, February 22, 1985.

208   Dr. Boyer is quoted in *The New York Times* story cited
        above, January 28, 1985.

Chapter 6   Health and the Corporation

209   See "Paying Employees Not to Go to the Doctor," *Busi-
        ness Week*, March 21, 1983.

209   Smith is quoted in 1983 General Motors annual report.

209   Mercer quote and Goodyear tire estimate are in "The Corporate Rx for Medical Costs," *Business Week*, October 15, 1984.

210   The Hewlett-Packard health bill was provided by the company.

211   Health care as a percentage of GNP, and health care costs from 1960 to 1983, are from *Health Risk Management Program*, a booklet published by Methodist Hospital, Houston, July 1984.

211   The estimate of the health care bill in the year 2000 is from the Department of Health and Human Services' Health Care Finance Administration.

211   McDonnell Douglas and Boeing medical bills and Donald Melvine's quote are from "The Corporate Rx for Medical Costs," *Business Week*, October 15, 1984.

212   The 1984 Consumer Price Index from the Department of Commerce. Health care cost increase from Blue-Cross–Blue Shield.

212   The Volcker quote is from the Federal Reserve Board.

212   Appendectomy costs from the Department of Health and Human Services.

212   The quote from Paul Ellwood of InterStudy and the Employee Benefits Research Institute estimate are taken from the October 15, 1984, *Business Week*.

213   The Employee Benefits Research Institute estimates are from the October 15, 1984, *Business Week*.

213   Connecticut General Life Insurance's savings are reported
       in "Auditing Helps Cut Hospitalization Costs," *Business
       Insurance*, March 18, 1985.

213   The A. S. Hansen, Inc., estimates are from "Do Health
       Care Cost Containment Techniques Save Money?" a pub-
       lication of the Information, Reference and Statistical Ser-
       vices' Public Relations Division of the Health Insurance
       Association of America, Washington, D.C. Other reported
       savings and Lockheed's close scrutiny of bills are from
       same publication.

214   Equifax Services' estimate of errors in bills and the Hewitt
       Associates survey are from the March 18, 1985, *Business
       Insurance* article cited above.

214   Information on Motorola's review board is from the
       company.

214-   Savings of Pacific Mutual Life, Zenith, Chrysler, Uniroyal,
215   Pillsbury, Illinois Central Gulf Railroad, and Carson Pirie
       Scott are reported in "Do Health Care Cost Containment
       Techniques Save Money?" cited above.

215   Information on the United Technologies program is from
       the company.

215-   Savings of nine major Cleveland companies from October
216   15, 1984, *Business Week*.

216   The Omaha cost-cutting committee is cited in *The Trend
       Report*, Volume 1, 1981.

216   Maryland's cost-cutting consortium is cited in *The Trend
       Report*, Volume 3, 1982.

216   St. Louis firms' savings are reported in *The Trend Report*,
       Volume 3, 1981.

216   Information on Tampa price pressure is from *The Trend
       Report*, Volume 1, 1982.

217   Goodyear's medical facility is described in *Business Week*, October 15, 1984.

217   The Wyatt Co. and the Coopers & Lybrand estimates are from "Self Insurance: Surveys Find Most Employers Self-Funding Health Benefits," *Business Insurance*, January 28, 1985.

217-   Information on risk-free self-insurance and the survey on a
218   lower claims cost are from the Society of Professional Benefits Administrators, Washington, D.C.

218-   HMO rates are provided by the Group Health Association
219   of Washington, D.C.

219   Cost-effectiveness of HMOs and their memberships are cited in "HMOs Are Rushing Feverishly to Go National," *Business Week*, October 24, 1983.

218-   Blue Cross–Blue Shield statistics are from that institution.
219

219   Wisconsin, United Technologies, Ford, and FMC savings from the Department of Health and Human Services' Office of HMOs' "Fact Sheet," December 1984.

219   The quote from Bradley Arms of CIGNA Healthplans is from *Business Week*, October 15, 1984. TRW savings are from "Do Health Care Cost Containment Techniques Save Money?" cited above.

219-   The material on national HMO networks and Robert
220   Ditmore's quote are from "HMOs Are Rushing Feverishly to Go National," cited above.

220   Kaiser, Prudential, and Blue Cross–Blue Shield estimates are from the firms.

220-   North Carolina, Security Pacific Bank, and Dade County,
221   Florida, use of PPOs is reported in "The Corporate

Rx for Medical Costs," *Business Week*, October 15, 1984.

221   Numbers on emergicenters and visits to them are provided by the National Association for Ambulatory Care.

221-   Randy Brown's and Marilyn Shanahan's quotes are from
222   "Behind the Surge of Walk-In Medical Clinics," *U.S. News & World Report*, December 5, 1983. Material on St. Louis' MedStop is from "Medical McDonalds?" *The Economist*, June 5, 1982.

221-   Slang names for emergicenters and an Austin owner's
223   quote are from "Doc in the Box: Medical Care, Fast-Food Style," *Venture*, October 1982. The long office hours, the price of dressing a burn, and William DeLay's quote are reported in "Low-Cost Clinics—Patients Like Convenience; Some Doctors Skeptical," *The Washington Post*, March 21, 1983.

223   Cost of bronchitis treatment is provided by the National Association for Ambulatory Care.

223   Pensacola hospital's emergicenter is described in *The Florida Trend Report*, Volume 1, 1982.

223   New York doctors' shift rotations reported in "New Storefront Health Care," *The New York Times*, March 12, 1983.

224   The influence of the government and Blue Cross–Blue Shield from *The Trend Report*, Volume 3, 1982.

224   The material on hospital bills as a percentage of corporate health care costs is from "The Corporate Rx for Medical Costs," *Business Week*, October 15, 1984. Numbers of surgicenters and the size of the business are from *The Wall Street Journal*, February 20, 1985.

224   The Ehrenfried quote is from "Behind the Surge of Walk-In Medical Clinics," *U.S. News & World Report*, Decem-

ber 5, 1983, as is the quote on the next page about hospitals remodeling for surgery.

225   The savings of Uniroyal, General Medical Centers, and Pacific Mutual Life Insurance Co. are reported in "Do Health Care Cost Containment Techniques Save Money?" cited above.

225-
228   The Loring Wood quote, the Robert Beck quote, and smoking statistics on page 195 are from "Employers' Booklet on Workplace Smoking Policies," published by GASP of Summit, New Jersey, March 23, 1984. Mal Stampler quote is from Boeing.

227-
229   Nonsmoking fire fighters in Alexandria, Virginia, Shaker Heights, Ohio, and Wichita, Kansas, from "Employers Quietly Seek to Clear the Air on Smoking," *Los Angeles Times*, January 17, 1984. Unigard Insurance and the quotes from Dennis Burns of Pro-tec and Michael Eriksen of Bell are also from this story.

227-
230   Estimates on smokers' nonproductivity are from the GASP booklet noted above, which cites studies of Dr. William Weis, associate professor of business administration at Seattle University. Gallup poll also in GASP booklet.

228   The *Salina Journal* experience from "Salina Newspaper Bans Smoking," *Wichita Eagle*, December 29, 1983.

230   MSI and the Minnesota Coalition from "Minnesota Doctors Begin Effort to End Smoking in the State," *The New York Times*, November 18, 1984.

230-
232   The information on the money-saving programs at the New York Telephone Company and Toronto's Canada Life Assurance is from "Cashing In on Wellness," *Business*

Insurance, September 21, 1981, as is the material on the meditation program at NYTC and on the Hospital Corporation of America's pay-per-mile plan.

231   The quotes from Ann Kieshaver of the Washington Business Group on Health and from AT&T's Rebecca Parkinson are from the firms.

231-   The PepsiCo, Los Angeles Fire Department, Johnson &
232   Johnson, and IBM health programs are reported in ''Fitness, Corporate Style,'' *Newsweek,* November 5, 1984. The General Electric example is from a company spokesperson.

232   The information on the Rodale Press exercise breaks is from a company spokesperson.

232   The quote about Donald Kendall by PepsiCo's fitness director is from ''Companies Pour Millions into Programs Aimed at Keeping Workers Well,'' *The New York Times,* October 14, 1984.

232-   Aerobics Center, Overhead Door, and Texas Instruments
234   of Dallas and the Manufacturers Hanover race are from ''The New Competitive Edge,'' *Dallas Life Magazine,* September 30, 1984.

234   The Diet Workshop, Weight Watchers International, and the George Masteralexis quote are from ''Companies Sponsor Diet Programs to Help Workers Shed Pounds, Raise Productivity,'' *The Wall Street Journal,* August 9, 1984.

234   The survey is from ''Firms Help Workers Get Physical,'' *USA Today,* June 20, 1984. Hub Mail Advertising's seminars are reported in *The Wall Street Journal,* November 18, 1984.

234-   The Sentry Life Insurance material is from *Managing*
235   *Health Promotion in the Workplace,* Parkinson & Associates, Magfield Publishing Company, 1982.

235   The Control Data, Johnson & Johnson, Tenneco, and Lockheed health programs from "Fitness Corporate Style," *Newsweek*, November 5, 1984.

236   The Jeff Miller and Joe Zimmerman quotes are from "The New Competitive Edge," *Dallas Life Magazine*, September 30, 1984.

Chapter 7   Women and the Corporation
237   "Women at Work," *Business Week*, January 28, 1985.

239   The Conference Board study was reported in several places; the article we saw was in *Forbes*'s "Trends" section, November 5, 1984.

239   The figures on women's earnings compared with men's and the Rand Corp. study are from the *Business Week*, January 28, 1985, article cited above.

241   The Dartmouth study was reported in *Glamour* magazine, January 1985.

242   *The Androgynous Manager*, by Alice Sargent (AMACOM, 1983).

243   The percentage of college-educated working women is from a Conference Board study reported in "Women Push Families into Affluence," *USA Today*, October 4, 1984.

243   The percentage of working women with children under six is from "Families: Day Care Chains," *Working Woman*, August 1983.

243   Bureau of Labor Statistics estimate and percentage of working women are from the *Business Week* story, January 28, 1985, cited above.

244   The percentage of working mothers with preschool children is from *Encouraging Employer Support to Working Parents*, by Dana Friedman for Carnegie Corporation of New York, 1983.

244   The number of two-career couples is from Catalyst.

244-   Leon Bouvier is quoted in "The New Baby Boom," *The*
245   *Washington Post*, August 27, 1984.

245   The results of *The New York Times* poll appeared in the *Times* on December 4, 1983.

245-   The material on corporations and the relocation of two-
246   career families is from "Have Spouse, Will Travel (If You Find Us Both a Job)," *International Management*, March 1982, and "Employees on the Move," *Orlando Sentinel*, November 11, 1984.

246   The Conference Board study was reported in "Women Push Families into Affluence," *USA Today*, October 4, 1984.

247   Statistics on the increasing birthrate are from "Companies Start to Meet Executive Mothers Halfway," *Business Week*, October 17, 1983, and from interviews at the National Center for Health Statistics.

247   The maternity-leave section is based on "Conference Discusses Parental Job Leave," *The New York Times*, March 11, 1985.

249   Charlene Barshefsky and Janine Harris are quoted in "The New Baby Boom," and "Sometimes a Career Must Be Put Aside," *The Washington Post*. Both stories appeared August 27, 1984.

250   The number of women lawyers by 2000 was estimated by Donna Fossum, member of the District of Columbia Women's Bar and staff member of the House Committee on Government Operations. See also "Women in the Law,"

by Donna Fossum, *American Bar Association Journal,* October 1983.

250   The male executive is quoted in "Women on Fast Track Try to Keep Their Careers and Children Separate," *The Wall Street Journal,* September 19, 1984.

250   Dana Friedman is quoted in "The New Baby Boom," *The Washington Post,* August 27, 1984.

250-   "Companies Start to Meet Executive Mothers Halfway,"
251   *Business Week,* October 17, 1983.

251   The National Commission on Working Women study was published in 1980 and ran as a questionnaire in several major women's magazines.

251-   "New Businesses Helping to Bring up '80's Babies," *The*
252   *Washington Post,* August 27, 1984, reported the three new businesses for working women created by women entrepreneurs.

252   Bonnie Gillespie is quoted in "The New Baby Boom," *The Washington Post,* August 27, 1984.

253   The NANI material is from "School for Modern Nannies," *Newsweek,* May 21, 1984. Terri Eurich's quote and the information on other schools were taken from this article, too.

253-   The figures on the number of children who need day care
254   and on the available space in centers, and the projections for the next decade, are from "Families: Day-Care Chains," *Working Woman,* August 1983.

253   The increase in nursery school enrollments during the 1970s is from *The Trend Report,* Volume 3, 1981.

254   National Employee Supported Child Care Project's book is *Employer-Supported Day Care: Investing in Human*

Resources, by Sandra Burud, Pamela Aschbacher, and Jacquelyn McCroskey (Auburn House, 1984).

254   "What Price Day Care?," *Newsweek*, September 10, 1984.

254   The General Mills/Louis Harris study is called *Family at Work: Strengths and Strains*, Minneapolis, 1981.

254   Dana Friedman's statement, actually a summary of the study attributed to her, appears in "Corporate World Responds to Increasing Day-Care Needs," *The Christian Science Monitor*, May 23, 1983.

254-
255   *Encouraging Employer Support to Working Parents*, by Dana Friedman for Carnegie Corporation of New York, March 1983.

255   Centrally located day care in these three cities is reported in *The Trend Report*, Volume 1, 1981.

255   Child Care Service Center material is from "How to Find Child Care," *The New York Times*, July 24, 1983.

255   The information on Long Island businesses in day care is from *The Trend Report*, Volume 3, 1981.

255   Information and referral services are reported in *The New York Times*, July 24, 1983, and in the *Milwaukee Journal*, September 23, 1984.

255   Chemical Bank benefits program is reported in "Corporate Kids," *The New York Times*, March 6, 1983, as is the quote from Phyllis Silverman.

255-
256   Procter & Gamble's program is described in the *Cincinnati Enquirer*, August 22, 1984.

256   Grandkids Day Care Center reported in "Who'll Watch the Kids? Working Parents' Worry," in *U.S. News & World Report*, June 27, 1983.

256   Rent-A-Mom is described in "Raising Baby-Sitting to a High Art" in the *Seattle Times*, March 11, 1983.

256-257   St. Anthony's Hospital center, the study at Texas Women's University, and the Zale program are described in the June 27, 1983, *U.S. News & World Report* article, cited above.

257   The Intermedics, Inc., material is from "What Price Day Care?," *Newsweek*, September 10, 1984, and *The Trend Report*, Volume 1, 1981.

257   Valerie Riefenstahl is quoted in the *Dallas Morning News*, April 17, 1984.

257-258   The description of the Nyloncraft, Inc., program appears in "The Kids Are All Right," *Inc.*, January 1985.

259   The Sixth Annual Salary Survey in *Working Woman* magazine is reported in *USA Today*, December 19, 1984.

259   Average salaries are from "Women's Push for 'Comparable Worth' Aims at Balancing the Wage Scales," *The Christian Science Monitor*, January 19, 1984.

260   The Pendleton quote and the Chamber of Commerce estimate are from "Rights Chief Derides 'Comparable Worth,'" *The Washington Post*, November 17, 1984.

260   Bullets on state and GAO comparable worth actions from "Equity: The 'Comparable Worth' Debate Intensifies," *The Washington Post*, July 22, 1984, and "The 'Comparable Worth' Debate," *The Washington Post*, December 28, 1984.

261   Rep. Schroeder is quoted in the July 22, 1984, *The Washington Post* article cited above.

261   The description of the Washington state case is from "The 'Comparable Worth' Debate" in *The Washington Post*, December 28, 1984, and "Evening Pay Scales for Women," the *Los Angeles Times*, December 20, 1983.

261   The numbers on states and localities are from the November 17, 1984, *Washington Post* story cited above.

262   The material on AT&T, Westinghouse, and General Electric is from "New Push to Raise Women's Pay," *The New York Times*, January 1, 1984.

263   Hawaii and Pennsylvania actions are reported in *Fortune*, "Pay Equality Is a Bad Idea," May 14, 1984.

264   The information on women in state legislatures is from John Naisbitt's *Trend Notes*.

Chapter 8   Re-inventing the Corporation in Japan

267   Miyoshi speech is published in *Speaking of Japan*, Volume 5, Number 45, September 1984, Keizai Koho Center, Japan Institute for Social and Economic Affairs, Tokyo.

267   The twenty-six-part series was published in *The Japan Economic Journal* (hereafter *JEJ*) from April 17 to October 9, 1984.

268-
269   *JEJ*, May 15, 1984.

270   *JEJ*, April 17, 1984.

272   *JEJ*, August 21, 1984.

273   *JEJ*, August 21, 1984.

275-
276   *JEJ*, October 2, 1984.

277   *Speaking of Japan*, Volume 5, Number 46, October 1984.

278   *JEJ*, October 2, 1984.

278   (Nakamura) *Economic Eye*, September 1984, Japan Federation of Economic Organizations, Tokyo.

278   *JEJ*, August 7, 1984.

282   *JEJ*, February 5, 1985.

288   *JEJ*, August 14, 1984.

288-   *JEJ*, August 17, 1984.
289

293   *JEJ*, June 26, 1984.

293   (Kumou) *Speaking of Japan*, Volume 5, Number 46,
       October 1984.

Conclusion
294   "The Airline That Shook the Industry," by Sara Runer,
       The New York Times Magazine, December 23, 1984.

294-   "Every Employee an Entrepreneur," interview with Allan
295   Kennedy, *Inc.*, April 1984.

300   "The Fortunate 500" is the formulation of independent
       consultant Wilfred Lewis, Weston, Connecticut.